Brothers Under the Skin

By Carey McWilliams

BROTHERS
UNDER THE SKIN

BY CAREY McWILLIAMS, 1905-

> The mystic chords of memory, stretching from
> every battle-field and patriot grave to every
> living heart and hearth-stone all over this broad
> land, will yet swell to the chorus of the Union,
> when again touched, as surely they will be, by
> the better angels of our nature.
>
> — LINCOLN

BOSTON

LITTLE, BROWN AND COMPANY · 1943

DEDICATED TO THREE FRIENDS

LOUIS ADAMIC
ROSS WILLS
JOHN FANTE

Contents

Brothers Under the Skin

Introduction

THE realization that this is not merely a war for survival but that it is a people's revolution grows slowly but steadily — hour by hour, day by day, month by month — in the consciousness of the American people. "This is a fight," as Vice-President Wallace has so eloquently said, "between a slave world and a free world. Just as the United States in 1862 could not remain half slave and half free, so in 1942 the world must make its decision for a complete victory one way or the other." With all the cards down, the stakes are so high that calculation is beyond our immediate comprehension. This is, indeed, the Great Showdown which will determine not only what nations will survive and in what form but the direction of social evolution for decades and perhaps centuries to come. Not only is the struggle world-wide in scope, but it cuts across national lines and also across social groupings. "The people's revolution," as Mr. Wallace has said, "is on the march."

Because of the nature of the war, half measures cannot be successfully employed in its prosecution. It is a war that is being fought on the world stage with every conceivable weapon, by every known means, and by every segment of the population. We have been repeatedly reminded that it is a global war and a total war. Our imaginations, however, seem unequal to the task of appreciating either the significance of the war or its nature. We say that it is a global war and yet act as though it were localized in character; we admit that it is total war but shrink from the implications. The most unimaginative minds in America nowadays admit that we cannot return to a prewar *status quo*, and yet we continue to prosecute the war as though its prime purpose were to preserve business as usual.

Not only have we been slow to grasp the character of the war, but we have failed to realize that we occupy a unique position in relation to it, since we are a unique people. "Our nation," as

Mr. Wendell Willkie has said, "is composed of no one race, faith or cultural heritage." Traditionally America has always been "a nation of nations." It is pre-eminently our assignment, therefore, to demonstrate to the world that peoples of diverse racial and national origins, of different backgrounds and of many cultures, can live and work together in a modern democracy. As a nation of nations we alone are in a position to exercise real political leadership. At the same time, however, the divisive forces that have brought disaster to the world also threaten our national unity. Our unique position constitutes both our strength and our weakness. If we fail in the world, we fail at home; if we fail at home, we are not likely to succeed in the world.

The Nazis have long recognized our uniqueness among the nations of the earth. According to Hermann Rauschning, Dr. Goebbels once remarked that "nothing will be easier than to produce a bloody revolution in America. No other country has so many social and racial tensions. We shall be able to play on many strings there. North America is a medley of races." One of the great questions, therefore, which we must face is whether the Nazi doctrine of racism is likely to make progress in the United States. No other question so seriously threatens American unity; at no other point are we so vulnerable to Axis propaganda. These same observations can be projected further, for the same issue threatens the solidarity of the United Nations and similarly exposes them to Axis propaganda. Nor can we afford to be complacent on either score. "At first glance," writes Dr. Louis Wirth, "one would think that in a country so diverse in its ethnic and racial composition as ours the prospect of infection by the virus of racism is negligible. But we should not underestimate the latent feelings of racial prejudice and the racial and ethnic conflicts which, given adverse economic circumstances, war, and propaganda, can be aroused to white heat." What Dr. Wirth has said about the possibilities of internal disunity has been said, in slightly different terms, by Pearl Buck on the possibilities for disunity within the United Nations front.

The two risks are, in fact, essentially the same, for this is becoming a very small world. "The Negro's fate in the U. S.," writes *Fortune*, "affects the fate of white American soldiers in the Philippines, in the Caribbean, in Africa; bears on the solidity of our alliance with 800 million colored peoples in China and India; influences the feelings of countless neighbors in South America. In this shrunken world of ours, a fracas in Detroit has an echo in Aden, and what a southern Congressman considers to be a small home-town affair can actually interfere with grand strategy."

The ideological character of the war dictates much the same conclusion. For this is a war, to quote *Fortune* again, "in which ideas weaken, enforce, and sometimes are even substitutes for armies." In the consciousness of peoples everywhere this war represents a clash between the idea of racial superiority (central to the Nazi doctrine) and the idea of racial equality (central to the concept of democracy). It is for this reason that we cannot ignore the consequences which arise by reason of our being a nation of nations. Just as in peacetime we could afford waste and inefficiency in our industrial system — "the margin of error," in Max Lerner's phrase — so we could afford a margin of inefficiency in our social system. But the balance of forces in this war is such that no tolerances of this kind can be risked; there are, in fact, no "margins." Given the ideological character of the war, we are forced by an ineluctable necessity to square practice with preachment, theory with reality. "America's constitution, like Christianity," argues *Fortune*, "is based on the principle that every man is born with the inalienable right to equality of opportunity. Whether or not this assumption is 'realistic' — we must either stick to it or change sides. Anything else would be not only immoral, it would be a military mistake. For men do not die for causes they are cynical about; and they cannot conquer on behalf of a principle they discount." The necessity is real enough, although *Fortune*'s statement of it is somewhat wide of the mark since men *are* dying, unfortunately, every day for causes about which they are cynical. The point is that we can no longer permit this state of affairs to continue.

It is generally recognized in America that Great Britain has made a tragic error in its effort to keep this gigantic struggle, as Albert Viton has said, "another white man's squabble." We deplore the British policy which has resulted in the overwhelming majority of its colonial peoples maintaining a passive attitude to the war. The shortsightedness of such a policy on the part of Great Britain is so obvious that few people in this country condone it. For, out of 525,000,000 inhabitants in the British Empire, 70,000,000 are white and the rest are colored.[1] But, on a restricted scale, we face precisely the same problem. To the extent that our minorities remain unconvinced that their interests are identified with those of the nation as a whole, "to that extent the Nation will fall short of achieving its maximum effectiveness in the War." [2] As Albert Deutsch has said: "The morale factor in race discrimination transcends national boundaries and reaches around the globe. Let's not forget that the overwhelming majority of our anti-Axis allies belong to the colored races. We can't hope to win the war without them. . . . Race prejudice is Hitler's weapon; it is our danger."

The war has thus forced hard upon us the necessity of taking stock of our American tradition. We are in the process, in fact, of revaluing almost every element in American life. Total war implies that plant capacity must be comprehensively surveyed; that physical resources must be carefully guarded; that manpower requirements must be closely analyzed. Some activities must be arbitrarily curtailed, others artificially expanded, as planning becomes a national imperative. By the same token, institutions must also be reappraised and traditions re-examined, for social engineering and social planning have become as essential as industrial planning. It becomes necessary, therefore, to examine the structure of the nation's population and to study the relationships between different groups. In the process of making such an over-all reappraisal, for purposes of war, we find that many of these relationships have been profoundly altered by the fact of war itself.

[1] "Britain's Jim Crow War" by Albert Viton, *New Republic*, September 15, 1941.
[2] "Minorities Peoples in a Nation at War," *Annals of the American Academy*, September 1942.

To use Mr. Wallace's metaphysics: if this war is a continuance of a people's revolution begun one hundred and fifty years ago, then it also means that the progressive tradition must go forward in this country. If we fail to extend democracy, in the revolutionary situation which has arisen throughout the world, then a counter-revolution from the right is a foregone conclusion. "War is an instrument of politics," said General von Metsch, " – an instrument that cannot any longer be applied without revolutionary incidents resulting." We are a part of this world-wide revolution just as we are a part of this war. When we say that imperialism must be banished from the postwar world, we forget that it must also be eliminated at home. "The attitude of the white citizens of this country toward the Negroes," as Mr. Wendell Willkie has said, "has undeniably had some of the unlovely characteristics of an alien imperialism, a smug racial superiority, a willingness to exploit an unprotected people. . . . When we talk of freedom of opportunity for all nations, the mocking paradoxes in our own society become so clear that they can no longer be ignored. . . . Our world is breaking to pieces. And with the break-up arises the opportunity to fashion a newer and a better life." [3] All the more reason, therefore, to take stock of our colored minority problem *now*.

1. Vanishing Majorities

In the past when we have thought of our minority problem, in moments of occasional reflection, it has usually been in relation to immigrant groups. When in the early twenties a spate of books and magazine articles began to appear on the "racial question," it was the "new immigrant" from Southeastern Europe, the fellow with the brachycephalic skull, who was the chief concern of our race-purists. Behind most of this writing was an immediate political objective: revision of the immigration laws. To be sure, Madison Grant was incidentally concerned with the Negro. He thought that Negroes should be established in large colonies and allowed outside the pale only as laborers. [4] But, generally speaking, Dr. Ruth Benedict is un-

[3] *PM*, July 21, 1942. [4] *The Passing of the Great Race*, 1916.

doubtedly accurate in saying that "the racist literature of the United States deals hardly at all with our great national racial problem, the Negro. Our treatment of the Negro," she observes, "conforms so closely to the predilections of these authors [Madison Grant, Lothrop Stoddard, Henry Fairfield Osborn] that they doubtless had little to suggest." The rush of European immigration between the Civil War and the first World War was such that it completely overshadowed the problem of racial minorities. When we thought of a minority problem, therefore, it was generally in terms of national minorities.

Actually immigrant groups from Europe have never presented a serious long-range minority problem in this country, though they did constitute a temporary problem. They disturbed the labor market, they tended to cluster for a time in immigrant slum settlements in urban areas, and there was much work to be done in the field of cultural adjustment and individual social case-work. But prior to the first World War even these problems seldom reached serious proportions. The Melting Pot was obviously functioning, perhaps imperfectly, perhaps too slowly, but nevertheless it was working. As Dr. Ralph Linton has said: "The phenomena of contact between groups of different culture has been with us since the first Whites landed, but in the rich new land they did not cause much trouble to the dominant group. Prior to the World War it was assumed that the absorption of minority groups into the American population required nothing more than time and not a great deal of that." Common observation and experience point to the fact that the absorption of European immigrants up to the first World War did proceed, particularly in view of the magnitude of the immigration itself, with remarkable rapidity. While there was some prejudice against immigrants which, in times of depression, stimulated the growth of nativist movements, still no firmly entrenched caste system developed. Recent immigrants may have had special difficulties and handicaps to surmount, but that they were able (in most cases) to surmount them is an obvious fact. So thoroughly were these groups assimilated that, with the second and third generation, they became almost completely absorbed in the larger dominant group. Joe, Vince, and Dominic DiMaggio, sons of an immigrant couple from the South of Europe, are, I should say, pretty typical Americans in every sense of the word.

Today immigrant problems have ceased to be of major importance. The Immigration Act of 1924 virtually stopped further immigration. Under this act, a total of 150,000 immigrants annually may enter the United States from all quota countries. But in point of fact, as the National Resources Planning Board pointed out in May 1938, "the number of immigrants entering this country during the past few years has been less than the number of emigrants." Since 1938, the refugee problem has become, of course, most acute. But this is distinctly a special problem and has not materially changed the situation. Many refugees unquestionably intend to return to their respective homelands after the war. In general it can also be said that the policy defined by the Immigration Act of 1924 probably represents a permanent shift in national policy. Even if the act is modified or relaxed or amended in the future (as I personally hope it will be), still it is not likely that, in the immediate future, we shall re-establish a policy of unrestricted immigration.

This change in national policy has been reflected in the make-up of our population. The drastic restrictions on immigration in effect since 1924 have resulted in consistent declines, in both absolute numbers and relative proportions, of foreign "whites" in our population. In 1930, for example, there were 13,983,405 foreign-born whites in the United States; but by 1940 there were only 11,419,138. Thus there has been a decline of 18.3 per cent in the number of foreign-born whites during the decade 1930–1940. At the present time, they form 8.7 per cent of the total population as compared with 11.4 per cent in 1930. This trend is likely to continue indefinitely, with the percentage of foreign-born whites steadily declining. Foreign-born immigrant groups do not, therefore, constitute the real minority problem in this country. The problems to which their presence gave rise have been largely temporary in character and have usually passed with the second, and certainly with the third, generation. That is not to say, of course, that all foreign-born immigrants have been completely or satisfactorily absorbed into the main current of American life. "Although many of the European immigrant groups have been completely assimilated," writes Dr. Linton, "others show a strong tendency to survive and encyst themselves in the body politic." It is not part of my intention to account for this phenomenon or to inquire into the status of these remaining nonassimilated foreign-born groups. Suffice it to say that they will most probably be absorbed, as their predecessor groups were absorbed, although the process may proceed, due to changed economic and social conditions, at a somewhat slower pace than in former years.

When we turn from the foreign-born "white" immigrants to the resident "colored" groups, an entirely different situation is immediately apparent. By "colored" I do not necessarily mean yellow, brown, black, or red, but any degree of color-visibility or physical differentiation sufficient to constitute a recognizable difference. For example, Mexicans are generally listed in the census as "white persons," and there is no doubt that the classification is ethnically correct. But in most areas of the United States, a Mexican is a Mexican — that is, the general population recognizes a degree of visibility. What creates the difference here is not so much visibility of skin color as, according to Dr. Benedict, "the fact that racial characteristics are transmitted over so many generations." That these physical differences do affect the pace of assimilation is generally recognized. Speaking of assimilation in general, Mr. Herbert J. Seligmann has said: "The problem becomes an entirely different one for those who are 'racially' set off from the mass of Americans. This is especially true of Chinese, Japanese, Filipinos, and other Oriental people. Here the merging with the American population, so that all distinctive marks are lost from view, is immeasurably slower. In a sense, the initial problem is never entirely transcended. It takes new forms, often more difficult even than the first adjustments with which all immigrants are confronted. Regardless of the inner, spiritual, cultural adaptation, there is always the physical difference to raise questions." A man, as Dr. Benedict points out, can stop going to Mass, but too dark a Negro cannot "pass" and not even his children's children may be born light enough to do so.

By contrast with white immigrants and the melting-pot doctrine, to quote Dr. Everett V. Stonequist, "the position of the colored and mixed blood groups of the United States is quite another problem." This is particularly true insofar as the Indian and the Negro are concerned. The Indian was not an immigrant, yet he remains today outside the pale of American life. Negroes were originally "immigrants" but out of 12,865,518 Negroes (1940 census), 99.4 per cent are American-born and about 97 per cent are of purely native parentage. Of the general population in the United States, nearly 10 per cent were born abroad and less than 70 per cent are of native parentage on both sides. "If nativity were really the measure of citizenship," observes *Fortune*, "the Negroes would excel any other national or racial stock in this country."

Numerically, just how important are these colored minority peoples in the United States? In presenting the following totals, I do so with no pretense of statistical accuracy. Some small groups must be omitted; and the size of other groups can only be approximated. Complete accuracy is not important, however, for the purpose of demonstrating the numerical significance of these groups. Here, then, are a few totals based on estimates for the year 1940: —

Negroes	12,865,518
Mexicans	3,500,000
American Indians	361,816
Japanese	126,947
Chinese	77,504
Filipinos	45,563
Hindus	2,405
Koreans	1,711
Total	16,981,464

It can be seen from this table that these groups constitute a sizable proportion of our total population of 131,669,275. They are numerically of greater importance than the foreign-born groups (11,419,138), although large numbers of the colored minority groups would also be included in the foreign-born category.

The figures quoted in the foregoing paragraph are based upon totals for the continental United States. When the totals for the outlying territories and possessions are included, important adjustments must be made. Consider, first, the totals for Hawaii: —

Japanese	157,905
Part-Hawaiians	50,470
Chinese	28,834
Filipinos	52,607
Hawaiians	14,359
Puerto Ricans	8,322
Koreans	6,854
Total	319,351

When these totals are added to the respective groups in the United States, the actual number of Japanese and Filipinos is more than doubled and the Chinese and Korean totals are considerably increased. If we turn to Alaska and include the totals there, then we must increase the number of American Indians by 32,464 (and add negligible totals to a few other groups). There should also be included in these totals sizable portions of the population of American Samoa (12,908); of Guam (22,290); of the Panama Canal Zone (51,827); of the Virgin Islands (24,889); of Puerto Rico (1,869,255); and of the Philippine Islands (16,355,678). Here, of course, we are dealing with uncertain totals. For example, the census lists 23.5 per cent or 438,511 "colored" people in Puerto Rico, when, as all experts agree, the percentage having some degree of color would be much higher than the census figures indicate. The status of the Philippine Islands hardly warrants its inclusion since it is neither a territory nor a possession; nevertheless, until the war is over, the totals should be noted, for the American flag was still flying in Manila on December 7, 1941.

The importance of these groups can be gauged in still another way. I am not a population expert and, after examining many of the reports on the subject, I am moved to wonder if there are, in fact, any experts in the field. If what is said in this paragraph is wavering and uncertain, it is because the sources indicate a similar uncertainty. Generally speaking, however, it can be said that colored groups in the United States have an expanding future. In other words, it would seem that these groups are increasing relatively faster than the "white" portion of our population. For example, Indians are increasing at a more rapid rate than any other group in this country: 1 per cent a year compared with 0.7 per cent for the whole population. Dr. S. J. Holmes, after making elaborate adjustments of the census data to allow for possible inaccuracies, states that "a slight increase of Negroes relative to whites is a distinct possibility at no very distant date." Dr. Frank Lorimer is more emphatic: "On median assumption," he writes, "with regard to trends of mortality and fertility, and on the assumption of no immigration, the expected increases in population during the fifty-year period 1930–1980, as estimated by Thompson and Whelpton for the National Resources Committee, run as follows: whites, 19 per cent; Negroes, 50 per cent; Indian, Mexican, and Oriental, combined, 139 per cent." Certain of these groups have, to be sure, declined as a percentage of total population: Negroes constituted 19.3 per cent of the population in 1790 and 9.7 per cent in 1940. The long-range rate of increase for the Negro population depends, also, on many variable factors: the extent to which death rates can be reduced; the extent of rural-to-urban migration; and variations in fertility rates on a regional basis. These and many other variable factors make it impossible, apparently, to summarize trends with much greater precision. All that can be said is that there is good reason to believe that the Negro population is growing more rapidly than the white population; that Indians show the same tendency; and that there are about twice as many children under 5 years of age per 1000 women aged 20–44 years, in the minor racial groups, as in either the white or the Negro population.

2. In the World

By its very nature the war has made for an increasing hemispheric unity. To an extent which we cannot fully realize, the lines of trade, cultural exchange, and possibly of future migration, are destined to run north and south rather than along the transatlantic route. Whereas formerly we were, in many respects, an extension of Western Europe in the New World, now we are in the process of being orientated toward Central and South America. In the light of this new orientation, which is most certainly not a temporary phase of historical development, it is interesting to note how our resident colored groups take on new significance. It is not necessary to examine population totals for the Western Hemisphere in detail (in many cases the figures are not available or are admittedly incomplete); general estimates will be sufficient.

While there are 12,000,000 Negroes in the United States, there are 37,000,000 persons of African origin in the Western Hemisphere (including those in the United States), with large concentrations in the West Indies, Brazil, and other areas. While there are 390,000 Indians in the United States and Alaska, there are 30,000,000 Indians in Central and South America. The totals for even the minor groups are increased by this type of computation. For example, there are 162,537 Japanese in Brazil and a great many in Canada. There are also many Chinese in Canada, Mexico, and Central and South America. To the estimated total of 3,500,000 Mexicans in the United States should be added the totals throughout Central and South America and Mexico. In thinking of Western Hemisphere totals, we should also have to consider literally millions of mixed breeds — part Indian and part Spanish, part Indian and part Negro. In short, if we were to divide the population of the Western Hemisphere into two general classifications, "white" and "colored" (including in the latter group all those who, in the United States, would be distinguishable by a different coloration), we should probably find that the balance tipped in favor of the colored and mixed-breed groups. Such a method of computation would be scientifically inexact and many groups would deny most vehemently that they belonged in the "colored" category; but from the point of view of the prevailing race *mores* in the United States the grouping would be most significant. Nor is this point of view merely of academic interest. For, as Mr. Seligmann has pointed out, "the United States and Brazil have the largest contingents of mixed-blood peoples — as the term is ordinarily construed — of any countries in the world. The test of their continued existence as nations lies partly in the "perfectly natural absorption and mutual accommodation of the various ethnic groups within their borders. In a sense, these are the chief crucibles in the world-laboratory which will try whether men of various colors and creeds, of diverse traditions and nationalities, can still come together and live in peace."

The achievement of unity in the Western Hemisphere, as we are being constantly reminded, involves many far-reaching changes and adjustments. These changes and adjustments are implicit in any serious attempt to accommodate such diverse economies, with such diverse political and social forms, as are to be found in this hemisphere. Just as important as these types of accommodation (which imply mutual adjustments) are those which must be made in the matter of ethnic policy and race attitudes, for in this field the disparity is as sharply marked as in the economic field. In most Central and South American nations the color line is nonexistent. The treatment accorded Negroes in Brazil is at sharp variance with the treatment accorded them in the United States. "Brazil," wrote Lord Bryce, "is the one country in the world, besides the Portuguese colonies on the east and west coasts of Africa, in which a fusion of the European and African races is proceeding unchecked by law or custom. The doctrines of human equality and human solidarity have here their perfect work. The work is so far satisfactory that there is little or no class friction. The white man does not lynch or maltreat the Negro." "In South America," writes Dr. Oliviera Lima, "our experience of centuries has taught us that there is no real understanding except the one that comes through the fusion of races." This is hardly the prevailing sentiment in the United States, not to mention the rather turgid views that prevail south of the Mason-Dixon line.

If hemispheric solidarity is to exist in fact, if it is to become a social reality rather than a wistful sentiment, it would seem to be obvious that these sharply conflicting attitudes must be reconciled in some manner. Can Brazilians ever be wholly *simpatico* with us so long as we suppress a large Negro minority in the United States? In this field, it is we, the people of the United States, who must make the accommodation possible. We could hardly expect Brazil, as part of the program of hemisphere solidarity, to adopt an elaborate system of Jim Crow legislation. The fusion process has gone much too far in Brazil for it to be reversed overnight. Even in our own family, so to speak, the same conflict of views is noted. The color line is not drawn in Hawaii or in Puerto Rico. There is, also, a reverse aspect to the matter. American Negroes are quite conscious of the sharp difference in treatment accorded members of their race in the Western Hemisphere outside the United States. As we become increasingly conscious of South America, this discrepancy in treatment and attitudes will become more pronounced.

So swiftly has the world shrunk in size, in our minds, during the last few decades, that today it is a commonplace that we must now think in global terms: economically, politically, strategically. In 1914 Frederick Jackson Turner said that "the age of the Pacific Ocean begins, mysterious and unfathomable in its meaning for our own future." Within a matter of months, the whole Pacific area has been injected into the consciousness of every thinking American. Overnight Burma, New Guinea, the Solomon Islands, Borneo, and the Dutch East Indies have become topical subjects in this country. Whether we relish the idea or not, a new world society, a new world economy, and possibly even a new world political organization are likely to emerge from the war. To think in hemispheric terms is not enough; we must think in world terms. Just as the "race question" was with us, first, a sectional matter, then a matter of national concern, so now it has become a world problem, and must be thought of as such.

The necessity of taking such a view of the problem indicates that our colored minorities are no longer a subject matter of purely domestic concern. In terms of world-wide totals, their importance has been suddenly magnified a thousandfold. Here, again, exact totals are unimportant; gross estimates tell a sufficiently impressive story. Dr. Hans Kohn has made the following estimates, as of 1930, of world populations: —

Continents Predominantly White (totals stated in millions):

Europe	505
North America	168.75
South America	82.75
Australia	9.88

Continents Predominantly Non-White:

Asia	992.5
Africa	142.4

This computation leaves out of consideration, of course, some 37,000,000 Negroes in the Western Hemisphere as well as 30,000,000 Indians. It also entirely ignores the important mixed-breed groups. Even so the totals should be sufficiently impressive, for they indicate that the continents predominantly white are outnumbered by 1134.9 millions to 766.38 millions. It should also be remembered that war itself has made devastating inroads upon the white totals for Europe. Not only are vast numbers being killed, but thousands more are dying of famine and starvation, and, as someone has remarked, "prisoners do not breed well." There is no doubt whatever that the white peoples are a minority in the new world that is emerging from the war.

As long as America and Europe could think of Western civilization as being, somehow, identical with universal history, this racial division of the world did not present an acute problem, although its significance was often recognized. But for several centuries now we have been victimized by a kind of myopia and have come to think of Western Europe and America as the world. Prior to the first World War, it seemed altogether plausible to think of a single world order based on the expansion of European civilization. "Western civilization," as Karl Korsch has written, "came near fulfilling the conditions which had been fictitiously assumed for so long by its historians. It cast the net of its economic system around the world and brought under its sway the whole of mankind and all the inhabitable lands and navigable seas on the face of the earth. Western technics and industries, Western sciences and Western institutions, were eagerly imitated in the four quarters of the globe. The whole contemporary world seemed converted into a single world market, the fifty to sixty existing states united in a single comity of nations." Along with this unprecedented political and economic expansion, Europe also aimed at cultural dominance based upon an attitude of cultural superiority which, over a long period, tended to become chronic. Thus, as Messrs. Locke and Stern have said, "European culture contacts for this whole period have been typically characterized by unequal rather than reciprocal cultural influence upon the countries and races which were contacted." [5]

Now, with China and India in the throes of profoundly revolutionary developments, we are forced to recognize a whole new set of realities. Science and technology can no longer be limited to any one group of nations. This is a world where, as it has been said, "no one general form of culture has a clear or permanent majority." The conviction of racial superiority, the doctrine of cultural incompatibility, have been pretty thoroughly debunked, not only by modern science but by the tangible achievements of so-called backward peoples. As a consequence, the period of Western tutelage and control is just about over. Spengler's pessimistic conclusion that the nations of Western Europe did not dare permit the subject peoples of the world to acquire a working knowledge of technics has been scotched by the war itself. Given the present state of organized knowledge, no nation or groups of nations on earth can hope to monopolize science and technics. The mere thought of the

[5] *When Peoples Meet*, p. 88.

nations of Western Europe and America trying vainly to maintain such a monopoly by force conjures up, as Dr. Kohn has said, "the danger of a coming racial struggle of unprecedented dimensions, the fear of which will necessarily strengthen everywhere the illiberal and bellicose forces which will plunge humanity into a real Armageddon." The possibility of such a world-wide war of races takes on added significance when considered in light of the present (or rather prewar) distribution of resources. Ignoring the Polar regions, Griffith Taylor has estimated that the white races, so-called, control 47,000,000 square miles of the earth's surface, or eight ninths of the land area, while the so-called colored peoples control 6,000,000 square miles or the remaining one ninth. "The so-called backward races," writes Mr. Seligmann, "are appropriating the essential elements of contemporary civilization, and the more than nineteen hundred millions who now live are 'thrown together on a shrinking earth and rubbing shoulders in every field of human activity'!"

Prior to the outbreak of war between Japan and the United States, speculations of the type indicated seemed to be the special prerogative of "world historians" and population students. But today these same considerations have taken on very real and practical significance. "The Japanese weapon of racial propaganda in Asia," writes Pearl Buck, "is beginning to show signs of effectiveness. . . . Tokyo radio programs daily send their broadcasts over Asia in their campaign to drive out the white man. . . . Germany is helping Japan to stir up race hatred in Malaya, India, and the Philippines by insisting that the interests of Asia lie with Japan and not with England and the United States." Today, as Miss Buck states, the peoples of Asia are still waiting, still watchful. Not only are the subject peoples of Asia waiting and watchful, but our allies in the Far East share the same concern; and inside the United States the same forces are at work. "The growing identification of the American Negro with non-white people all over the world," writes Mr. Horace R. Cayton, "is no figment of Nazi propaganda. A recent issue of a Negro weekly contained five articles and an editorial on colored peoples outside of America. One article was on the African trade-unions in South Africa; two were on the Indian situation; one was on the Churchill statement that the Atlantic Charter was not to be applied to colonies held by the United Nations; and one was on Negroes in South America. . . . The feeling throughout the colored world is that there is going to be a change in the status of non-white people, and there is little fear that the change could be for the worse. Whereas for years Negroes have felt that their position was isolated and unalterable, some of them are now beginning to feel that dark people throughout the world will soon be on the march." American Negroes have come to feel that they must accept a measure of responsibility for the welfare of the members of the Negro race throughout the world;[6] and there are many evidences of a growing sense of solidarity between American Negroes and the peoples of India.[7] This consciousness has grown among American Negroes in direct relation to the expanding opportunities that they have won for themselves in the United States. Similarly, the more rights Negroes have won here, the more progressive they become and the more existing tensions are aggravated. "At no time in American history," notes *PM*,[8] "has the Negro enjoyed so much liberty as he does today. At no time has the Negro been so conscious and so resentful of the injustices and indignities still imposed upon him. Unless Americans understand this paradox and *act upon it quickly* the all-out war drive may be gravely handicapped." This feeling of unrest is manifest all over the country. In the primaries in Arkansas, in July 1942, Negroes employed at a defense plant at Pine Bluff put up a militant fight to be allowed to vote. They contended, amusingly enough, that they were not Negroes but were of Mohammedan descent and petitioned to have the suffix "Bey" added to their names. Similar considerations are also disturbing many white groups in this country. For, as Mr. Cayton says, "just as there is a feeling in the non-white world that things are changing,

[6] See *The Negro Around the World* by Willard Price, 1925; and *The Negro in the Americas*, 1940, edited by Charles H. Wesley.

[7] See *PM*, December 7, 1941.

[8] May 9, 1942.

that this is the time to press for gains, so there is a feeling among whites that their position of dominance is being challenged and that they must resist any encroachment on their prerogatives." The acuteness of the general situation, in fact, becomes even more apparent when the specific application of Axis propaganda is examined.

3. Propaganda Front

In considering how the Nazis attempt to make capital out of our colored minority problem, it is interesting to take an example which, on the face of it, would appear to be utterly fantastic — namely, the Nazi concern over the American Indian. In February 1942, Senator Dennis Chavez of New Mexico delivered a radio address in Spanish to the peoples of Latin America. Naturally, he emphasized the blood and cultural ties which unite the Spanish-speaking people of this hemisphere against the Axis powers. Nine days later, a Goebbels stooge, calling himself "Antonio Sorel," broadcast in Spanish over the Berlin short-wave radio to South America. This correlation of broadcasts from Berlin, timed to counteract Good Neighbor programs from the United States, has become, in fact, most pronounced. In these broadcasts aimed at South America, the Nazis consistently harp upon the treatment accorded the Indian in this country.

Some years ago a high court in the Nazi Reich pronounced the American Indian to be a member of the Aryan family. Not long after this decision was announced, Mr. William Dudley Pelley, of Silver Shirt notoriety, published a series of pamphlets attacking the present administration of Indian affairs in this country for attempting to "communize" the Indians. These pamphlets found their principal outlet, interestingly enough, through the bookstores then maintained by the German-American Bund. Later the same charges were picked up and repeated in numerous articles in Latin-American publications. In this propaganda, Dr. Goebbels has an interesting habit of referring to past episodes in Indian history as though they were current happenings. For example, the Battle of Wounded Knee, which took place at the end of the last century, has been described in short-wave broadcasts from Berlin to Latin America as a bloody battle in World War II. Throughout all of this Nazi propaganda, an attempt is made to picture the American Indians as an Irredentist element in American society which has been forcefully suppressed.

To most Americans, propaganda of this type must seem slightly cockeyed, but it is well to remember that it has several different orientations. Dr. Goebbels is too well informed to believe for one moment that such propaganda could possibly be successful in fomenting actual unrest on American Indian reservations. But in Europe such talk serves an important purpose, for it is skillfully utilized to smear the government of the United States and to counteract the indignation which Hitler's treatment of the Jewish minority in the Reich has aroused. Even more important, however, is the manner in which this propaganda is aimed at the Indian element of the republics of Central and South America. For when due regard is given to the present distribution of Indian population in the Western Hemisphere, the real orientation of the Berlin propaganda becomes painfully clear.

In Canada only 1 per cent of the Dominion population is Indian and Eskimo; and in the United States, of course, Indians constitute only a fraction of the total population. But in Mexico, 53 per cent of the total population is Indian: 4,620,886 full-blood and 4,040,590 predominantly Indian. In five Central American countries (Panama, Honduras, San Salvador, Nicaragua, and Guatemala) 61 per cent of the combined population is Indian: 1,945,000 full-blood and 1,478,080 predominantly Indian. In eight South American countries (Brazil, Venezuela, Chile, Colombia, Paraguay, Ecuador, Bolivia, and Peru) 25 per cent of the combined population is Indian: 6,879,784 full-blood and 11,115,416 predominantly Indian. Thus there are upwards of 30,000,000 Indians in the Americas and, once this fact is recognized, it becomes apparent that Dr. Goebbels has a real audience for his Indian propaganda.

"Daily, weekly, and monthly," states Mr. John Collier, "this sort of propaganda is addressed exclusively or partly to the Indians. Many of these activities are financed from sources entirely obscure. And they are working by telling the Indians exactly what the fifth-column people up here have tried to tell our Indians — that the Indian is being done to death by Uncle Sam, exploited, poisoned, starved, whipped around. There is nothing that they do not allege." Most of the radio propaganda emanates from sources in South America.

In considering the effect of such propaganda, one or two facts must be kept in mind. In the first place, there are numerous highly organized German, Japanese, and Italian colonies in South America. In the southern part of Chile, for example, the population is almost exclusively Indian and German. In Brazil the Japanese colony has grown enormously: 110,000 Japanese migrated to Brazil between 1924 and 1933.

"We cannot possibly send down enough individuals," said Waldo Frank, on returning from South America, "to compete with the 50,000 Japs who work with the Indians on the farms of Peru and tell them, in the sweat of the day's work, that the Japs and the American Indians are one people and that the chief enemy of all dark peoples is Uncle Sam or John Bull." [9] In the second place, Indians are concentrated in those areas in South America which we hope to tap for such strategic raw materials as rubber, tin, copper, zinc, quinine, sisal, and other materials (generally speaking those materials which we formerly got from the Dutch East Indies and the Philippines). According to Mr. Collier, substantially the entire rubber resources of the countries to the south are in an area where the population is more than 75 per cent Indian. If these resources are to be developed, it will largely be through the use of native Indian labor. That Axis propaganda aimed at these native Indians can seriously affect production is a demonstrated fact. For as a result of German propaganda and sabotage, according to the Associated Press, the output of Bolivian tin was cut in half for a time.

In approaching this problem, it is apparent that our American Indians and our resident Spanish-speaking population constitute

[9] *Christian Science Monitor*, October 24, 1942.

our living alliance with the peoples of the Western Hemisphere. Long before World War II, many scholars and statesmen in the Americas sought to create an international body which would serve as a clearinghouse for the exchange of data, information, and experience on the Indian problem. This movement received recognition in 1938 at the Eighth International Conference of the American Nations at Lima, Peru. As a result of this recognition, there took place at Patzcuaro, Mexico, in April 1940, the First Inter-American Indian Congress. At this congress most of the American Republics were represented, not merely by diplomats and Indian experts, but also by delegations of Indians from as far south as Peru. Conspicuous at this conference was a delegation of Pueblo Indians from the Rio Grande Valley of New Mexico. These Pueblo Indians, observers noted, were the best representatives that this country could have selected as its ambassadors of good will. They took a leading part in the deliberations of the conference and made a deep impression on the other delegates. Today, ratification of an international treaty has brought formally into existence the Inter-American Indian Institute (*Instituto Indigenista Inter-americano*), which is likely to become one of the main props of the Good Neighbor program.

If England is haunted by the problem of India, so are we haunted by the problem of our resident 12,000,000 Negroes. In many respects, ours is the more serious problem. India is thousands of miles removed from Great Britain and can be dealt with as a nation; but our Negro problem has ramifications which reach throughout the whole complex of American life. It has affected our entire attitude toward other colored minorities and toward colored people in general. It lies at the heart of the series of tasks that go by the name of the unfinished business of democracy. Like a cancer it has fibers which reach out in all directions and the removal of this cancer is, indeed, a major operation. Just as England is embarrassed by India, so are we embarrassed by the Negro problem. Our embarrassment is not merely ethical: it has the most serious practical connotations, not the least significant of which is the way it lends itself to Axis propaganda.

On January 25, 1942, the Japanese broadcast throughout the Far East the story of how, a few hours previously, Cleo Wright, a Negro, had been seized by a mob and burned to death in Sikeston, Missouri. For months Japanese radio propaganda, aimed at South America, has capitalized upon the Negro situation in the United States. On March 15, 1942, a Japanese radio spokesman said: "Democracy, as preached by the Anglo-Americans, may be an ideal and a noble system of life, but democracy as practised by Anglo-Americans is stained with the bloody guilt of racial persecution and exploitation." On August 17, 1942, *Newsweek* reported that "the latest Jap propaganda theme charges that the United States is manipulating the draft so as to take a disproportionate number of Negroes." Falsely charging that mobs had attacked the Japanese who were evacuated from the West Coast, Japanese radio spokesman denounced the evacuation program as "the most dastardly act ever carried out by a so-called Christian nation" and said that it had "deeply shocked Christian circles in Japan." [10] Seeking to arouse dissension in the United Nations front, Nazi propagandists have broadcast throughout South Africa a statement that America is sending thousands of Negroes to fight in Africa, thereby agitating the notoriously troubled race problem around the Cape.[11]

The fact that we have large colored minority groups in this country constitutes a fulcrum on which the Axis propaganda levers can be placed to exert pressures in multiple directions. "Axis agents," says Mr. Ernesto Felix Diaz, "directly or indirectly, have had a hand in promoting the recent wave of juvenile gang outbreaks which have resulted in the murder of two men in Los Angeles County and other acts of violence." [12] Axis-paid saboteurs and agitators, Negro and white, according to Mr. Clark Foreman, are now hard at work trying to inflame

[10] *PM*, October 11, 1942.
[11] *Christian Science Monitor*, article by Selden Menefee, October 15, 1942.
[12] *Los Angeles Times*, October 15, 1942.

disunity. "Although these agents are numerically few," writes Mr. Foreman, "in both races, their influence is magnified by the tendency of many Southerners to embrace Fascism unconsciously, however much they may hate Hitler. The enemy agents have so far apparently made more headway among white people than among Negroes. Curiously enough, one of their most effective weapons among white people is to tell of their alleged success among Negroes, although of course attributing it to others than themselves. Aside from the wildly exaggerated rumors that are now afloat in Southern white circles, there is evidence of Axis attempts to cause trouble among Negroes. Negro union members have been approached by white men and asked why they support the war since it is a white man's war against colored people. It has also been reported that public toilets for Negroes now have their walls inscribed with inflammatory statements against white people and against the war." One young Negro, on being inducted into the service, is supposed to have said: "Just carve on my tombstone, 'Here lies a black man killed fighting a yellow man for the protection of a white man.'" In Negro communities across the nation the story is current about the Negro who wanted to get a pair of slant eyes "so he could kick a white man in the ass and get away with it." In August 1942 there was a revival of the Universal Negro Improvement Association, the old Garvey movement. Some four hundred delegates attended a conference in Cleveland at which considerable attention was given to the application of the Atlantic Charter to Africa. In a speech at the annual convention of the NAACP in Los Angeles, on July 16, 1942, Mr. E. Frederick Morrow pointed out that, while Negroes realize that "America is ours by right of birth, events find us growing bitter-green around the edges of our souls as we experience the invidious distinctions of color in American life." At this moment, he said, "when most Americans have been shocked into some kind of thinking, is it not pertinent to remind them that the Negro is the acid test of democracy in America? If it does not work with him and for him, it cannot work for others, and it is not becoming to American intelligence to hold our ideology before the world as a palliative for the ills of downtrodden and enslaved men, if we find thirteen millions of our citizens denied its benefits and responsibilities."

The point to observe about Axis racial propaganda is the almost infinite possibilities or orientations which it can serve in this kind of war. It can be used to frighten the white population of this country; to arouse unrest among the Negro population; to embitter colored and mixed-breeds in Central and South America; to arouse distrust and suspicion among our colored allies; to mislead the subject colored peoples of French Indo-China and the Dutch East Indies; to cause trouble between the United States and Great Britain; to stimulate Indian nationalistic ambitions and, at the same time, to make the fulfillment of these ambitions more difficult; to get the American people fighting among themselves over the Negro question; to undermine the British in Burma and Malaya; and, lastly, to call in question the entire Allied war ideology. Nor have I even begun to exhaust the propaganda possibilities of this theme which, indeed, lends itself to literally hundreds of variations. *Fortune* has noted what, so far as we are concerned, is the most crucial consideration of all: "That one tenth of our population may lack enthusiasm is bad enough, but not crucial. What counts in a war like this is whether the nine tenths feel at peace with themselves." Thus Axis race propaganda is calculated not merely to undermine the Negro's morale, but to destroy our confidence in the cause for which we fight. A more effective propaganda theme could not, in fact, have been devised. It is insidious, plausible, powerful, many-faceted, and inherently adaptable to multiple motivations.

It is impossible, of course, to measure the effectiveness of such propaganda, but one incident alone will suffice to indicate that it can be effective. On September 14, 1942, Robert Jordan, a West Indian Negro, and four leaders of what was termed "an Ethiopian-Pacific movement envisaging a coalition of Africa and Japan in an Axis-dominated world," were indicted in a sedition conspiracy indictment filed in New York. Here the connection between inspired propaganda and a series of planned overt acts has been clearly established. "Jordan and his colleagues," according to the Associated Press, "spoke approvingly of Japan and Germany and counseled members of their audiences to resist service in the United States armed forces." They also spoke, at various meetings, about an Africa ruled by 20,000,000 American Negroes. This has about it more than an echo of Marcus Garvey's doctrines. "If sixty million Japs," Garvey once said, "have been able to establish a government in sixty years so powerful as to make every nation fear it, surely four hundred millions of black people ought to be able to accomplish the same thing in ten years."

When twenty-eight Nazis were recently indicted in New York, one of the presentments of the Grand Jury was that they had organized a conspiracy to set afoot the rumor of a campaign to "pollute" Aryan Christian soldiers by injecting into their veins the blood of "Negroes, Japs, and Jews." [13] Indeed, it must be remembered that Axis propaganda aimed at American Negroes takes place at a time when Negroes, as such, have become extremely — one could say militantly — race-conscious. It takes place against the entire background of the development of Pan-Africanism,[14] and the spread of the Asia for Asiatics doctrine. That Pan-Africanism and Pan-Asianism have some interconnections is obvious. B. Schreike observed that "the modern evolution of Japan is viewed [by American Negroes] with undisguised sympathy: educated Negroes as a rule are decidedly pro-Japanese." [15]

4. On the Home Front

No sooner was America involved in the war than the quasi-dormant Negro problem began to plague the nation. As soon as we began seriously to prepare for war, it was immediately discovered that the problem had taken on entirely new dimensions and that it had entered an entirely new phase. We began to realize that the Negro problem was a national, not a sec-

[13] PM, July 31, 1942.
[14] See Race: A History of Modern Ethnic Theories, by Dr. Louis L. Snyder, 1939, Chapter 18.
[15] Alien Americans, New York, 1936.

tional, problem; and that it was definitely involved in larger world issues. That the problem had qualitatively changed was indicated by the type of leadership that Northern Negro communities provided. Negroes had constituted a problem in World War I, but in the years intervening thousands of Negroes had moved into Northern areas so that they were in a position to protest discrimination effectively and to afford an energetic leadership. Gradually we have awakened to the fact that this is, indeed, a revolutionary war and that half-measures will no longer suffice, even in dealing with such an old and familiar problem. For not only are the Negroes asserting their rights effectively through an energetic leadership, but the ferment of the times has affected the entire population, powerful segments of which are pressing militantly for "concessions" to the Negroes. In order to realize how completely the problem has changed, it is only necessary to ponder the timetable of events since 1940.

The Negro question immediately intruded itself upon every phase of the war effort: in the armed services; in defense industries; in civilian organizations; in the general morale problem. It was no longer possible to isolate the problem geographically, functionally, or otherwise. The problem came to the surface not only because the dynamics of the war forced it there, but because the ideological character of the war had affected the entire population and, as this process developed, thousands of Americans began to be acutely conscious of Negro discrimination and increasingly determined to do something about it.

Negroes have an old and honorable record of excellent service in our armed forces. They have served with distinction in every war in which this nation has been involved: the Revolutionary War, the War of 1812, the Indian Wars, the Mexican War, the Civil War, the Spanish-American War, and the World War. In World War I, however, they learned a lesson — namely, that they could not rely upon wartime promises of postwar adjustments. Their hopes had been raised high by the democratic slogans of 1918; but they had been cruelly disillusioned by the aftermath. In the years from 1918 to 1940, moreover, they had become increasingly race-conscious and the depres-

sion years had made for accumulated resentment. As the drift
toward war became unmistakable, Negroes determined that
this time they would demand equality of treatment as a
condition for their unstinted support of the war effort. This
determination quickly crystallized into firm resolve as it became apparent that the dominant white groups were attempting
to repeat the 1918 pattern of wartime discrimination. Naturally
the issue first became acute in the armed forces themselves.

By January 1942, the draft had brought some 100,000 Negroes
into the army. The Army, of course, takes the position that,
since it did not create the Negro problem, it cannot undertake to
change the views of the citizens who fill its ranks. It aims, therefore, at repeating the pattern of segregation and discrimination
that prevails in civilian life. Generally speaking, it aims at keeping Negro personnel in the Army down to about 10 per cent,
thus approximating the ratio of Negroes to whites in the population. With the exception of white officers who are serving with
Negro troops, segregation in the Army is total — that is, Negroes are assigned to Negro units, and trained and drilled in
these units. One concession was made at the outset, in reference
to the training of Negro officers. Today Negro officer candidates are interspersed in almost all the officer training schools:
they train, eat, and are housed in the same camps with white
candidates. By and large, there have been no difficulties as both
Negro and white candidates seem to get along well enough
together, even in Camp Benning, Georgia. Outside the camp,
however, discrimination prevails. Negro officers have to travel,
in some cases, as far as nine miles from the camp to get a haircut; and they are discriminated against, and segregated, insofar
as social and recreational facilities are concerned. The Army,
moreover, has not seen fit to open all of its services to Negroes.
At first Negroes were not accepted in the Army Air Corps.
But on January 17, 1941, Yancey Williams, a Negro with two
years college training and a graduate of two aeronautic courses,
filed a suit in the federal courts, demanding that his application
for admission to the Air Corps be considered on its merits. Almost two hours after the suit was filed, Undersecretary of War

Patterson announced that a Negro pursuit squadron would be formed. Thereafter the 99th Pursuit Squadron, the first all-Negro tactical air unit, started training at Tuskegee Institute. A few months later, Frank Lambert, instructor at the school, announced that "national or racial characteristics have little or no bearing on skills and abilities." The Army now has hundreds of applications from Negroes for admission to the Air Corps, but has not, to date, expanded its facilities at Tuskegee, which are so limited that only a few candidates can be trained. Repeatedly reports have appeared in the press [16] in which the Army has praised the excellent work of its all-Negro units, such as the 93rd Division in training in Arizona. [17]

Unlike the Army, the Navy has attempted to maintain its tradition of a "white navy." This tradition, however, is only about twenty years old; a much older tradition indicates that Negroes were acceptable to the Navy for every kind of naval service. They served, for example, with great distinction during the War of 1812. On April 3, 1942, Dorie Miller, a Negro messboy in the Navy, was cited for gallantry at Pearl Harbor. Apparently embarrassed by this incident, the Navy announced, on April 9, that it would start to enlist Negro volunteers for service in the reserves of the Navy, Marine Corps, and Coast Guard. Prior to this announcement, Negroes had only been accepted in the Navy as messmen, waiters, and busboys. The Navy has frankly stated that its new policy is purely "experimental" and that Negro reservists will be accepted only for service in "district craft of various kinds, in maritime activities around shore establishments, in navy yards, and in the Navy's construction crews and companies." Later, it was announced that Negroes may be recruited as crews on a single all-Negro-unit destroyer. Generally, the Navy has adhered to its policy of not mixing whites and Negroes as part of the same crew. The theory is, of course, that racial integration on naval units "implies much more than in any other service"; and that, therefore, the Navy "cannot take a chance on a social experiment." After recently

[16] See PM for July 7, 1942.
[17] On army policy generally, see PM, October 10, 1940.

surveying the entire situation, *PM* has stated that "the color line still exists." It seems to be in the process, however, of disintegration, since on June 7, 1942, two Negroes were named to Annapolis (a number of Negroes have, over a period of years, been appointed to West Point), thus breaking another so-called Navy "tradition."

What has served to arouse public concern over Negroes in the armed services, however, has been, not the policy of adhering to civilian patterns of segregation, but the apparent failure of the Army to enforce respect for its uniform outside of Army centers. For the facts indicate very clearly indeed that the Army respects Jim Crowism. On August 7, 1941, Negro and white soldiers clashed at Fort Bragg, North Carolina (but outside the post), with two dead and a score or more wounded. The same day similar riots were reported in Wilmington, North Carolina, when Negro soldiers on leave refused to respect Jim Crow regulations. Inspecting the situation at Fort Bragg on August 10, Tom O'Connor of *PM* reported that "the color line stands out everywhere." As a result of these incidents, Undersecretary of War Patterson felt prompted to point out, in an NBC broadcast on August 13, that "there is nothing exclusive about the war that is flaming on three continents. Let me remind you that an aerial bomb draws no color line." On October 1, 1941, the 94th Battalion of Engineers, comprised of Negroes (most of them from Detroit and Chicago), was encamped near Gurdon, Arkansas. While on leave, a Negro soldier attempted to order a meal in a local hotel, only to be promptly arrested. Tension swiftly mounted in the community as state patrolmen impudently ordered Negro sentries off the highways. In an effort to keep the situation in hand, the Army ordered the camp of the battalion moved five miles away from the highway "into the woods and swamps." Even this order failed to appease the ignorant and bigoted whites, who, visiting the Negro camp, stated: "If we catch you niggers here in town after sundown, you are going to hang." On January 13, 1942, 700 Negroes, including 500 Negro soldiers, engaged in a pitched battle with 300 police in Alexandria, Louisiana. Investigating the incident, Penn Kimball

of *PM* reported that "the shooting and beating of 28 northern
Negro soldiers here two weeks ago was ordained long ago when
the Army took on the job of enforcing discrimination against the
men who wear its uniform." In the same story, it was reported
that "Negro soldiers are prohibited from loitering in any part
of the main business and entertainment section of white Alexandria. . . . White MP's stationed at every corner shoo them
along into the city's Little Harlem, a shoddy, poverty-ridden
area." This incident aroused a storm of protest, including a
blistering statement from Dr. Frank Kingdon of the Union for
Democratic Action. "At a time when we are engaged in an all-
out effort to overthrow the totalitarian forces bent on destroying
liberty," he said, "it is a mockery to treat Negroes with the same
means employed by the Fascist powers." On April 5, 1942, a
somewhat similar riot occurred at Fort Dix, which resulted in
the death of three soldiers. This latter incident climaxed a whole
sequence of disturbances which occurred after white troops,
formerly stationed at Camp Claiborne, Louisiana, were imported
and started "kicking the Negroes around." Prompted by this
series of incidents, Senator John H. Bankhead of Alabama had
the colossal effrontery to write General Marshall protesting
against the assignment of Negro soldiers to Southern areas. "Military requirements," replied General Marshall, "make it necessary to send Negro soldiers to the South."

Segregation, discrimination, and the failure to enforce respect
for the Army's uniform have profoundly disturbed many Americans, including soldiers and prospective draftees. On January 3,
1941, Mr. Ernest Calloway, educational director for the United
Transport Service Employees of America, demanded exemption
from military service until the Jim Crow policy was terminated
in the Army. For many months, Jimmy Davis, a New York
Negro composer, refused to be inducted into the service as a
protest against Jim Crowism. "I want to fight Hitlerism," he
said, "and its racial superiority myth, but I can't see how I can
fight it in an army that practises racial discrimination." [18] On
October 6, 1942, Lewis Jones, a conscientious objector against

[18] *PM*, July 18, 1942.

Jim Crowism in the Army, pleaded guilty in New York to a charge of refusing to answer a draft call. A native of Texas and a graduate of Morehouse College in Atlanta, Georgia, Jones felt that he could not conscientiously serve in an army which upheld nonsensical notions of racial superiority. On August 6, 1941, a white private at Camp Croft, South Carolina, wrote to *PM* complaining of the treatment accorded Negro draftees. White soldiers, he said, were admonished by their commanding officers not "to drink with niggers and don't shake hands. Of course the Negro draftees here are segregated from the minute they come to the camp, sleep in separate barracks and eat in separate mess halls, but most of the white boys show very little Jim Crow sentiment. But it is bound to increase, with these official incitements to national disunity — especially since the U. S. Army throws its whole weight behind such incitement. The whole picture is a very raw and ugly one. It looks, smells, and tastes like Fascism." Noting these series of incidents, President Roosevelt announced on May 13, 1942, that "the day of the white man's burden is over. Henceforth we must treat all races with respect as equals." Not only have these incidents affected the morale of prospective inductees, and both Negro and white soldiers, but they have also disturbed relatives of inductees, thus reacting upon general civilian morale. Dr. Arthur B. Lee, a Negro graduate of Howard University, enlisted in the Army and was stationed at Fort Bragg. On April 16, 1942, his wife, Dr. Eulalie Mitchell-Lee, was traveling south to visit her husband. On crossing the Mason-Dixon line she was told to transfer into the Jim Crow section and, with excellent firmness, she refused to comply. "If I were a Jap or a Siamese," she said, "you wouldn't think of disturbing me." Passengers on the train rallied to her side of the controversy, and she was not forced to move.

Similar issues arose almost immediately in connection with the various women's auxiliary units. The Army policy dictates that 10 per cent of the WAAC's must be Negro women, but various Negro organizations have protested to President Roosevelt over the appointment of Mrs. Hobby, from Texas, to head the or-

ganization. "She is known," these protests stated, "to share
the lily-white traditions of Jim Crow." Consistent with its general policy in such matters, the Navy announced as late as
August 25, 1942, that the WAVES would not accept Negro
women. The same question has arisen in some civilian defense
organizations, and also in relation to various local rationing
boards. On May 27, 1942, *PM* reported that, in many areas
throughout the nation, Negroes were demanding representation
on rationing boards. The Army, according to *PM*, has turned
away hundreds of available Negro graduate nurses. "The army
ought to limit its race prejudice," observed the *New Republic*,[19]
"at least when it comes to care of the sick and wounded. Yet
it is reported on good authority that the Surgeon General will
not permit the recruiting of enough Negro nurses and doctors
even to care for the Negro soldiers, nor will he allow corps commanders to use their own judgment in permitting Negro and
white physicians to work together, even where they are in the
habit of doing so."

An even more serious situation rapidly developed in defense
employment. Sidney Hillman reported on April 11, 1941, that
"in many localities, qualified and available Negro workers are
either being entirely restricted to unskilled jobs, or barred from
defense employment entirely." This situation was by no means
restricted to Negroes; Mexicans and other colored minority
groups experienced the same difficulties in obtaining defense
employment. The aircraft industry had virtually no Negroes
in 1940. In May 1941, Consolidated Aircraft Company in San
Diego still adhered to its policy of hiring no Negroes; Boeing
Aircraft Company in Seattle had three Negroes on its payrolls;
Vultee Aircraft Company, of Los Angeles, had announced that
"only members of the Caucasian race will be employed in our
plant" (out of 6500 employees at the time, none were Negroes);
none of Lockheed Aircraft's 42,000 employees were Negroes;
and, at the same time, J. H. Kindelberger, of North American
Aviation, Inc., had stated that "no matter what their qualifications are, they will only be used as janitors." In a survey made

[19] April 13, 1942.

by the Bureau of Employment Security in September 1941 (two months after President Roosevelt's Executive Order No. 8802, of June 25, 1941, against discrimination in defense employment, had been issued) it was found that out of 282,245 prospective openings in defense employment, 144,583 (51 per cent) were barred to Negroes as a matter of policy. This situation, indeed, became of increasing urgency since, in terms of their respective numbers, there were more Negroes in the labor market than whites. Instead of being utilized in defense employment, Negroes tended to remain unemployed. The Negro category on WPA rolls actually *rose* from 14.2 per cent in February 1939 to 17.6 per cent in February 1942. Of New York's Negro population of 400,000, some 160,000 were being supported in 1941 by public-assistance agencies. "Thus to be without a job during the defense boom was no longer an American fate, as it had been during the depression; it began to be a Negro fate." [20] Mexicans were similarly affected.[21] Although the Social Security Board could report on November 5, 1941, that the color restrictions had been relaxed, nevertheless its current report indicated that only 14 Negroes had been selected among 11,000 newly hired skilled and unskilled workers in aircraft; that of nearly 60,000 placements in the metal trades, less than 500 were Negroes; and that out of 115,000 trainees under the defense training program, only 1900 or 1.6 per cent were Negroes. And all of this despite the fact that Negroes constituted nearly one half of the unemployed labor reserve in the South and nearly one third in Northern urban areas. "The continued refusal to hire or train them," reported the Board, "is likely to generate increasingly serious labor market problems. Failure to use locally available Negroes has not only delayed production, but it is compelling employers to recruit labor from distant areas, with two serious consequences: it is intensifying existing housing shortages and it is increasing the amount of labor turnover." The *Evening Sun* reported that Baltimore, with its sewer, water, highway, transportation, police, fire, and school

[20] *Fortune,* June 1942.
[21] See the *Employment Security Review,* July 1942, p. 7.

facilities already overstrained by migration, was faced in 1942 with an influx of an additional 35,000 defense workers, primarily because local defense plants were refusing to utilize the services of some 167,000 resident Negroes. In many other areas, exactly the same situation developed. Slight wonder, therefore, that Mr. Donald Nelson should have characterized the willful refusal to employ Negroes as tantamount to "treason" or that Mr. Ralph Ingersoll should have observed that "this country is not strong enough to go on persecuting — discriminating against — 10 per cent of its population and win the war, too." Even after the issuance of the President's Executive Order No. 8802 (of which I shall have much to say later), discrimination persisted and Negroes and Mexicans were generally handicapped. Many Negroes, for example, found that they had no way of obtaining certified copies of birth certificates, since, as one of them pointed out, "we come from areas where the authorities thought our births too insignificant to register." An estimated 80,000 Negroes in New York alone were up against this barrier.[22]

This persistent discrimination was all the more remarkable because of recent studies which had thoroughly demolished the theory that Negroes were not adaptable to industrial employment. In December 1941, the National Industrial Conference Board issued a report which demonstrated that, with respect to ability and skill, regularity of attendance, and many other tests, Negroes compared very favorably with whites. *Modern Industry*, in its issue for May 1942, reported that "out on the production lines, Negroes are proving that there is no color line in skill and efficiency." Part of the difficulty, of course, was due to the attitude of trade-unions, both A. F. of L. and C.I.O. It was also traceable to long-standing industrial practices which, over a period of time, had become sanctified as "company policy."[23]

Once Negroes began to obtain defense employment, the struggle still continued: over recreational facilities, over housing,

[22] *PM*, September 20, 1942.
[23] See, in particular, *Racial Factors in American Industry*, by Herman Feldman, 1931.

over transportation. On August 13, 1942, *PM* reported that Negroes were barred from a government housing project in New London, Connecticut, on the ground that "our southern white tenants would object to the presence of Negroes on the project and it would lead to trouble." On February 28, 1942, a savage riot occurred at the Sojourner Truth Housing Project in Detroit, in which prospective Negro tenants were attacked with clubs, knives, rifles, and shotguns, resulting in many injuries and over 104 arrests. When 14 Negro families moved into the project in May, some 2000 guardsmen were on duty to give them protection. The Axis powers naturally got busy on the short-wave radio broadcasts and made the most of this sorry episode. As a matter of fact, subsequent investigation revealed that the entire incident had been inspired. Two of the men arrested were, according to the *New Republic*, revealed to have been officers of an organization disseminating pro-Axis propaganda. The Sojourner Truth riot followed almost immediately after the lynching in Sikeston, Missouri, on January 25, 1942. These episodes, plus the execution of Odell Waller on July 2, 1942, the lynching of A. C. Williams, a Negro, in Quincy, Florida, on May 14, 1941, the stupid and shameless attack on Roland Hayes in Rome, Georgia, on July 11, 1942, and the lynching of *three* Negroes in Mississippi *in a single week*,[24] served to fan the flames of race hatred. Referring to the Sojourner Truth riots, Mr. Francis Biddle stated that there are points "beyond which compromise becomes intolerable" and warned that "such bigotry must be stamped out to make democracy work." The housing riot was particularly uncalled for, since, in many areas, it has been clearly established that Negroes and whites get along well enough in government housing projects. "Race prejudice," observed *PM*, "festering in the wounds of social degradation, is fostered by landlords to exact higher rents from the inhabitants of all-white houses." Transportation difficulties arose in many communities, as public vehicles became more crowded and the difficulty of enforcing Jim Crow ordinances multiplied. In Arlington, Virginia, the Army was

[24] See *PM*, October 28, 1942.

forced to take action in order to make sure that Negro employees gained access to government buildings. Negro commuters were formerly stopped as busses crossed over to Arlington, and made to move into the Jim Crow section. But Negroes now ride across the bridge under protection of Army orders. This action, however, was rather exceptional. On August 16, 1942, Private Charles J. Reco, a Negro, was taken off a bus in Beaumont, Texas, and beaten with nightsticks and clubs, because he had taken a seat in a section reserved for white passengers. As Negroes moved westward in response to the demand for defense jobs, similar disturbances, over housing, recreational, and transportation facilities, occurred in Portland, San Francisco, Los Angeles, and Las Vegas, Nevada. In the first World War, Negroes moved north by the tens of thousands. Today they are moving in all directions and a noticeable westward migration has occurred.[25]

Perhaps the most revealing incident of all had to do with the Red Cross's campaign for blood donations. Shortly after the initial appeal for donors was made, it was discovered that the Red Cross, acting on its own initiative, was keeping Negro blood separate from white. It would be difficult to imagine a more insulting procedure. Protests were loud and vehement. Mr. William Hodson, Welfare Commissioner in New York, promptly announced that "the Department will establish a blood bank station only if the blood of all healthy persons is received, regardless of race, religion, or color." Despite the fact that the OCD manual said nothing about segregating blood, the Red Cross doggedly adhered to its policy. Finally a statement was bullied out of S. Sloan Colt on behalf of the Red Cross: "It is recognized," he said, "that there are many persons in this country who object to having Negro blood used for the transfusion of white persons. This is a matter of tradition and sentiment rather than of science, as there is no difference in the physical properties of white and Negro blood. When this situation is accepted, it seems that the feelings and perhaps even the

[25] For tensions engendered in Portland, Oregon, as a result of this migration, see *PM*, October 4, 1942.

prejudices of individuals to whom transfusions are given should be respected as a symbol of democracy." [26] Mr. Colt also explained that, in establishing this policy, the Red Cross was not relying upon Army or Navy orders. That such a policy should be defended as a "symbol of democracy" by the official of a humanitarian organization is almost incredible. Actually the reason Southern Congressmen and Senators have been so vocal on the subject is because a mixture of Negro and white blood *would be* a symbol of democracy, which is precisely what they are determined to avoid. The policy is all the more stupid by reason of the fact that many blood donations are used in effecting a single transfusion. In Massachusetts, 372 physicians petitioned the Red Cross to change this despicable policy; in its issue of May 16, 1942, the *Journal of the American Medical Association* thoroughly demonstrated that there is no scientific warrant for the belief that the physical properties of Negro blood are any different than those of white blood; and, on June 24, 1942, the American Association of Physical Anthropologists added their protest against the policy of blood segregation. Yet the Red Cross still adheres to its policy.

This controversy gave rise to a remarkable speech in Congress on September 29, 1942, by Representative Rankin of Mississippi. "Mr. Speaker," he said, "one of the most vicious movements that has yet been instituted by the crackpots, the Communists, and the parlor pinks of this country, is that of trying to browbeat the American Red Cross into taking the labels off the blood bank they are building up for our wounded boys in the service so that it will not show whether it is Negro blood or white blood. That seems to be one of the schemes of these fellow travelers to try to mongrelize this nation. Thank God, the Red Cross has stood its ground and refused to permit this outfit to have Negro blood pumped into the veins of wounded white men on the various fronts. That is no discrimination against the Negroes. I am not sure that it would not be as detrimental to a Negro to pump blood of some other race into his veins as it would be to pump Negro blood or Japanese blood into the veins of a white man."

[26] *PM*, January 22, 1942.

Commented Kenneth Crawford: "Even Rankin's blood is acceptable; Rankin's degree of civilization, his ignorance and ill will are not, physiologically speaking, in his blood."

Early in the war, our embarrassment over the Negro problem began to assume international proportions. On October 16, 1941, the NAACP felt called upon to lodge a protest with Winston Churchill because of the manner in which British missions, in this country, were discriminating against Negroes in employment. The Civil Service Commission in Washington was told that the British government had requested that no Negroes, regardless of qualifications, be referred to jobs in Trinidad. While respecting Jim Crowism here, the British disclaimed it in Great Britain. Queries have recently been raised in the House of Lords as to why the U. S. Army continues to discriminate against Negroes in England where the color line does not, in theory at least, exist. "A handful of unreconstructed British imperialists," observed the *Nation*,[27] "share the Southern American attitude toward the Negro, but the vast majority of our allies regard Jim Crow practices as hateful and undemocratic. The British have welcomed black American soldiers as warmly as they have white. They are impressed by their smartness and discipline, by their good manners and their cheerfulness, and they see no reason why they should not welcome them into their homes, drink with them in their pubs, and carry on normal social relations with them. When, therefore, a Southern white soldier, seeing a Negro dancing or walking with an English girl, feels called upon to 'protect' her by socking his fellow citizen, the British are outraged. There have, unfortunately, been numerous incidents of this nature. . . ." "Liverpool," writes Richard Lee Strout, "likes the Negroes, but there are racial problems, raised by adjacent white American outfits, which I hope will be adjusted."

At the outset, the Negroes were apathetic to the war effort. "As our country dashes about shouting millions for defense and death to traitors," editorialized the *Crisis*, "about the sweetness of Democracy and the terror and degradation of dictator-

[27] October 24, 1942.

ship, Negro citizens are being insulted and humiliated." "We don't want to fight Hitler or anyone else," said the *Afro-American;* "we seem to have too many battles to settle right now." Early in May, 1941, 160 American Negroes, including Richard Wright, Paul Robeson, W. C. Handy, Countee Cullen, Dr. Max Yergan, and others, issued a statement saying that "as the United States prepares presumably for the defense of democracy at home, it discriminates against Jim Crows and segregates the Negro. The Negro people want nothing of Hitler; they detest him and all his practices. On the other hand, the British war makers hold Africa, India, the West Indies, and other colonial areas in a cruel bondage often infinitely worse than the oppression known by Negroes in America." Gradually, however, they began to realize that this war had its revolutionary aspects and that it presented an opportunity for Negro advancement. The war began to take on, for them, a dual aspect: a fight against Hitlerism on a double front, here and abroad. Many Negro organizations are now fighting the propaganda which tells the black man that this is a white man's war. As Charles Collins, of the Negro Labor Victory Committee, has said, "Negroes know what living in a ghetto is; they know the pain of the lash and the degrading poverty that comes from job discrimination. The Negroes will gain equality through a United Nations victory only if we open a double second front — against Hitler and against America's worst domestic foe, race discrimination. Unless we have both these things we may lose the war; or we may lick Hitler and lose the aims for which we fight — the Four Freedoms."

But while the Negro leadership in general has swung in behind the war effort, the masses of Negroes have become restive and disturbed. "Negro leaders in Charlotte," says a story in *PM*, "are frankly worried today about the growing unrest and discontent among their people. The 40,000 Negroes in this city of 120,000 are not represented politically; they are denied municipal jobs; they are unable to obtain desperately needed better housing and skilled jobs." The same story quotes Dr. J. S. Nathaniel, a local Negro: "I am afraid for my people. They have grown restless. They are not happy. They no longer laugh. There is a new feeling among them — something strange, perhaps terrible." Negroes in the city recently rioted and attacked a café owner who had killed a woman customer. "Axis propaganda among the illiterate has been so effective that the FBI is checking up. Negroes — denied proper education in this Jim Crow community — are swallowing the lie that the Nazis don't discriminate against their race." Eighteen murders were committed in Charlotte in 1942; juvenile delinquency spreads; and assaults with deadly weapons have tripled in the Negro sections. From New York to Los Angeles, similar stories of unrest have been reported, usually emphasizing a serious increase in juvenile delinquency. As evidence of discrimination has accumulated, as stories have appeared of the mistreatment of Negro soldiers in the South, Negro communities all over the nation have held protest meetings. Meeting after meeting has been called in Harlem in the last two years protesting every imaginable type of discrimination. Just as the race issue in this country has played into the hands of Axis propagandists, so it has given the "race men" of the Negro community their chance to wax demagogic.

Naturally, as unrest has swept the Negro communities of the nation, the inveterate Negro haters have themselves been aroused to action. Generally unnoticed in the news has been the undercover revitalization of the K.K.K. which began in 1939 with the election of a new Wizard, Mr. James E. Colescott, of Terre Haute, Indiana. In May 1941, Colescott, speaking in Detroit, announced the opening of a million-dollar "Americanization Drive," as part of the Klan's determination to keep this country "white, Protestant, and gentile." On October 14, 1941, a sound truck preceded a parade in Miami of 200 cars filled with sheet-draped Klansmen; some of the slogans displayed were: "When the Law Fails You, Call on Us" and "Don't worry about the Niggers moving in on you" (apropos of the opening of a new housing project). Many Southern communities, in the face of mounting Negro unrest, have begun to tighten their Jim Crow regulations. Beaumont, Texas, recently enacted an ordinance providing a fine of $100 for a Negro caught riding in a public vehicle in the section reserved for whites. The enactment of such an ordinance in an important war-industry town, with transportation being in its present snarled condition, constitutes a serious interference with the war effort. There are ample indications of an organized revolt in the South against President Roosevelt's Executive Order No. 8802. On July 23, 1942, Governor Dixon of Alabama refused to sign a contract to furnish war material to the government (by prison labor), solely because the contract carried a nondiscrimination clause in accordance with federal policy. This, again, is tantamount to an actual interference with the war effort. In recent elections in South Carolina and Georgia, the "white supremacy" doctrine was raised in a most provocative manner. Negroes are quite aware of this mounting wave of white hysteria in the South. On August 14, 1942, the National Negro Congress urged President Roosevelt to halt further Negro discrimination in the South. "A small but powerful band of political hooligans," to quote from their statement, "wrapped in the bloodstained robes of the K.K.K., and fed by a group of anti-administration, anti-labor, pro-Hitler industrialists, have taken the first treasonable step in their effort to undermine national unity and scuttle the government's victory program. Utilizing Hitler's false theory of white supremacy, they are spreading their campaign of racial hate, labor-baiting and defeatism, through the medium of newspaper columnists, inspired press stories, speech and word-of-mouth rumors. They would use the Fair Employment Practice Committee as the very instrument to drive a wedge between Negro and White people in the South." [28] A League to Maintain White Supremacy, designed to supplant the K.K.K., has already been organized in the South.[29] Recently a delegation of union officials, civic leaders, and liberals from the South visited Washington "to get federal agencies to do something about white-Negro tension." Race feeling was noticeably intensified after the Fair Employment Practice Committee held its open

[28] See also "Race Tension in the South" by Clark Foreman, *New Republic*, September 21, 1942.

[29] See *PM*, September 9, 1942.

hearing in Birmingham, in July 1942. The delegation charged, in fact, that

Negroes and whites in the iron ore mines and in the Mobile shipyards were going armed to their jobs.

Scores of Negroes had been beaten and arrested in Memphis, Beaumont, and Columbus (Georgia) in trying to get transportation on public buses.

A number of wildcat strikes had been called because white workers had refused to work alongside Negroes.

Negro and white union officials of the C.I.O. had received anonymous letters threatening their lives.

On June 27, Walter Gunn of Macon County, Alabama, a Negro, had been shot in the leg and beaten to death by a deputy sheriff in the presence of his wife and children. Previously, Gunn had been stripped in public and beaten.[30]

Equally significant is the way in which the general white population has tended, in many communities, to support the Negro drive against discrimination. "Whenever historic groups are threatened from the outside," observe Messrs. Locke and Stern, "they immediately minimize all internal distinctions, and minority discriminations are held in abeyance. This crisis-patriotism is recognizably different from the normal variety. Such hectic courting and inclusion of minority groups is in marked and often ironic contrast to the more normal 'divide and rule' policy and tradition of dominant groups, to which they are apt to revert under conditions of assured dominance and control." Early in the development of the defense program, a group of leading non-Negro Americans, including William Allen White, Governor Herbert Lehman, and Mayor La Guardia, issued a statement demanding that Negroes be given a larger share of defense employment.[31] Later the trade-unions began to adopt the same position and to eliminate Jim Crow provisions in their constitutions. In New York, the legislature, following recommendations by Governor Lehman, adopted an admirable anti-discrimination program. In many communities,

[30] See *PM*, August 8, 1942.
[31] See *PM*, May 7, 1941.

anti-discrimination committees have been formed which have
been moderately successful.[32] Following a series of incidents at
Steamboat Road, Long Island, a mixed committee was established, on a voluntary community basis, to combat discrimination. A Negress, speaking at the initial meeting of this committee, said: "We can tell you what Hitlerism is because we know
it. We face it every day. Our task is to tell America: you don't
want a dictatorship — it's hell. I don't want the meanest Southern white planter to go through what the American Negro
goes through in one day. The cancer is here in Great Neck,
in Nassau, and it's in India and in China, too." [33]

A number of local defense councils have also taken up the
problem of discrimination as part of their activities. Newspapers, magazines, and periodicals, in some cases, have adopted
a strong anti-discrimination policy; and the number of conferences dealing with discrimination has multiplied. Communities, groups, organizations, and individuals that were never before conscious of discrimination have been forced since the
war to consider race issues. Overnight many institutions have
become conscious of the fact that they practised Jim Crowism.
Protests have flooded the press over discrimination in private
employment agencies; in newspaper advertisements; in athletic
programs; in professional baseball; in private welfare agencies;
in radio programs; in Northern colleges and universities,[34] and
in the preparation of textbooks. While much of this activity
may be characterized as crisis-patriotism, the ferment is so widespread, has touched so many groups and interests, and is so
definitely related to the character of the war itself, that it cannot be lightly dismissed in this fashion. "In the daily press and
on the air," as Mr. Cayton observes, "the Negro is getting more
attention than he has enjoyed since the old Abolitionist days.
And there is a growing awareness on the part of labor that the
Negro problem requires action. In normal conditions all these

[32] See the admirable report of the San Francisco Bay-Area Council Against
Discrimination, August 1942.
[33] PM, July 19, 1942.
[34] See the Nation, January 10, 1942.

things would be considered gains for the Negro. But they are *sporadic and unintegrated* and are insufficient to counteract the apparent inability of the government to set up a comprehensive plan." This ferment, however, has created the necessary climate of opinion in which it becomes possible to execute such a plan.

What we have attempted thus far, however, has been a program of limited concessions, of appeasement, of rhetorical exhortations. And such methods are too limited to cope with the problem itself. "Any real change in the morale of Negroes," writes Mr. Cayton, "will come only with a real change in the position of the Negro in the social structure of the country. Such a change will involve, especially in the South, a complete revamping of the social relations between the races." Today there is little evidence that the nation as such thoroughly appreciates the extent of any such program. "There is no evidence," as Charles S. Johnson has said, "that the fundamental occupational and racial patterns have been permanently changed; and in many cases they are not changed at all."

At the present time, in fact, we have reached a partial stalemate. There is a strong segment of opinion which feels that "now is not the time to engage in social experimentation" — "these matters will have to wait until the war is over," and which feels that any serious attempt to cope with such questions now would only interfere with the war effort itself. Actually such a position is amazingly shortsighted. Given the character of this war, it is ridiculous to think that Negroes (and I use them merely because they are the most powerful minority group) are going to wait until the peace for an adjustment of many of their more immediate problems. Time is short and our continued failure to act aggressively is prejudicing our position in the eyes of the world. We can never assume a position of world leadership following this war unless we have demonstrated a willingness to treat fairly and democratically the colored minority peoples in this country. Furthermore, a really constructive program would do much to further the war effort itself; it would aid, not interfere, with the prosecution of the war. Lastly, we should recognize that the war provides the dynamics by which such a program can or might be put into effect now; whereas if we wait until after the war, the present momentum will be lost. Mr. Willkie recognizes this fact most clearly. He wants to develop, as he says, "by a forewarning of the consequences, a sober public judgment that will prevent any tendency toward a repetition of such national ignominies as the Ku Klux Klan and such calamities as the series of race riots in our cities which grew out of the emotionalism of the first World War." In the aftermath of war, ugly currents of opinion are likely to arise. Minorities are apt to be charged with responsibility for the war itself. Age-old racial and religious distrusts are likely, also, to be stimulated. Certainly the immediate postwar period will not be the time in which to carry forward such a program.

We have been slow to recognize that, given full expression, our revolutionary tradition is unquestionably the greatest psychological asset which we possess in this war. If this tradition is frustrated or perverted, however, it can become our most embarrassing liability. War has exaggerated and intensified every tension dormant in the Negro communities of this country. Negroes and other colored minorities are on the march; they are not going to be satisfied with a program of limited concessions and piecemeal adjustments and tardy appeasement. If this is the kind of war which Mr. Wallace has stated it to be, then Jim Crowism must be eliminated, now, in America. Most Americans would agree on this proposition, for, outside the South, the Negro question has become an annoyance and an embarrassment to most thinking Americans. But the crucial question is *how?* And on this point our theorists have been more rhetorical than useful. They exhort, plead, persuade, and harangue; but they have not been conspicuously successful in suggesting practical expedients. They take, moreover, too limited a view of the problem. For as Mr. Cayton says, "the shape of things to come — the new pattern of race relations — will be worked out on a global basis and will necessitate tremendous internal changes in many countries," including our own. We have also overemphasized the Negro and failed to correlate the Negro problem, for example, with the Chinese problem, the Mexican problem, the Filipino problem. When such a correlation is made, it poses the issues in a more understandable fashion. What Americans must realize — what they can no longer afford to ignore — is the simple and obvious fact that the color of America has changed. Nothing that we may say or do can possibly alter this fact.

In the chapters that follow, I propose to show just how the color of America has changed. I should like to emphasize, however, that I am not a sociologist or an anthropologist. No attempt whatever has been made to treat each of the colored minority groups exhaustively. Such an undertaking would be obviously impossible in a single volume. I have tried to emphasize, in each case, the correlations between these groups and to bring out facts that will throw some light on the problem of devising an immediate, practical, wartime program for dealing with race problems in the United States. Essentially, therefore, the following chapters are designed as a description of a general problem and as an argument for a point of view and a program outlined in the concluding chapter.

CHAPTER I

The Non-Vanishing Indian

ANY consideration of colored minorities in the United States must, perforce, start with the American Indian. Apart from historical or chronological considerations, the Indian problem is central to the whole question. It represents not only the point of departure, but the point to which any discussion of the larger problem must ultimately return. For it was with the Indian that our patterns of "color-reaction" and "color-behavior" were first conditioned. So deep-seated and ingrained have these patterns become that it seldom occurs to the average American that a large part of his race psychology might be traced to the experiences of his ancestors with Indians on an ever-shifting American frontier. Today the recognition of such a relationship is essentially difficult, since the Indian has come to be a favorite figure in our mythology. There is no triteness involved, therefore, in saying that, with race attitudes in America, one must begin at the beginning.

1. Satanic Consolation

At the time of the discovery of the American continent, there were probably not more than 850,000 Indians in what is now the United States. These Indians, moreover, were widely scattered and their tribal organizations were largely unrelated. The geographical distribution of this sparse population was such that North America, unlike tropical lands, offered a unique opportunity for the transfer of a large European population without the necessity of having to mix its blood or its culture. "It was a case," writes Dr. Everett V. Stonequist, "where the existing racial and cultural slate could be wiped relatively clean." Not 1 per cent of the immense area of agriculturally valuable topsoil, the virgin timber, and the mineral resources of the land was used intensively by the indigenous Indian population.[1] While the phenomena of contact with groups of a different culture have existed since the first whites landed, in this rich new land these phenomena did not cause much concern to the dominant group. Had there been a large compact native population (such groups did exist in the Rio Grande Valley), then some type of adjustment might have been effected. From the Indian's point of view, however, the native population was making full use of its environment. Within the limitations of native technology, there was literally no room for additional people on the continent. The European settler could never understand this fact, but it was an agonizing reality to the Indian. Out of this cultural conflict came war; then race hatred; then more wars in which race hatred served as a cause. "War and hate," writes William Christie Macleod, "made a vicious circle which all too frequently broke out into the most brutal massacres." [2] These Indian Wars, in colonial times, "ended once and for all any receptivity on the part of European settlers to the idea of race amalgamation. Instead came the desire for extermination." There was, however, *no prejudice at the outset*. "Race prejudice," writes Mr. Macleod, "is a social, not a racial — that is, not a biological — phenomenon." Despite the sense of strangeness on both sides, there was no initial aversion. Intermarriage did take place and might have taken place on an extensive scale had it not been for the cultural fact that, while an Indian wife was an asset to a fur trader, she was not an asset to a farmer. Later, after the patterns of reaction had been formed, Francis Walker, a Commissioner of Indian Affairs, stated that he would prefer to see the Indians exterminated than to see an amalgamation of the two races.

Since they did not have to adjust their culture to that of the Indian, the colonists never bothered to understand him. In fact, the growth of a considerable body of sound information about Indian life dates from comparatively recent times. To the colonists, Indians were "savages," "heathens," and "barbarians."

[1] Report of the Land Planning Committee, 1938.
[2] *The American Indian Frontier*, 1928.

Having had only a limited experience with native peoples, the colonists came to this country with pretty firmly held views on what later came to be termed "white supremacy." As John Moffatt Mecklin has said: "The framers of our democracy were excusable in ignoring entirely the factors of race difference because their political ideals were for the most part inherited from a people which had attained ethnic homogeneity in the insular atmosphere of England." The Americans and the British, notes Dr. Romanzo Adams, are known the world over as being more race-conscious than other peoples. It was, indeed, a great tragedy that our first contact with peoples of a different race should have been with Indians on the frontier (along which warfare was more or less continuous), and later with Negro slaves. The result of these contacts has been the creation of a definite system of race mores "highly adverse to marriage with non-whites." Formed in relation to Indians and Negro slaves, these attitudes have strongly conditioned our whole feeling toward colored people.

Not only were we extremely ignorant of Indian life and culture, but we were determined to convert the heathen to our way of thinking, and, failing this, to kill him. An early Pilgrim, thanking God for a pestilence that practically wiped out an entire Massachusetts tribe, wrote in his journal: "By this means Christ, whose great and glorious works throughout the earth are all for the benefit of his churches and his chosen, not only made room for his people to plant, but also tamed the hearts of the barbarous Indians." Beeson, an early emigrant to Oregon, wrote in his journal that "it was customary [for the settlers] to speak of the Indian man as a buck; of the woman as a squaw; until, at length, in the general acceptance of the terms, they ceased to recognize the rights of humanity in those to whom they were so applied. By a very natural and easy transition, from being spoken of as brutes, they came to be thought of as game to be shot, or as vermin to be destroyed. . . . The domineering spirit," he wrote, "grew by what it fed on, until, excited to madness by these recurring scenes of blood, men became utterly regardless of justice, even towards those of their own race." Methodist clergy, in early-day Oregon, felt no compunction when they saw Indian women being clubbed to death and Indian babies being dashed against trees. An early-day California emigrant said: "I had often argued with Good regarding disposition of the Indians. He believed in killing every-man or well grown boy, but in leaving the women unmolested. . . . It was plain to me that we must also get rid of the women." Children — "the seeds of increase" — must also be killed.[8] Early in the history of the state, the Colorado legislature considered offering bounties for "the destruction of Indians and Skunks." Every American is familiar with the classic dictum that "the only good Indian is a dead one."

Fear and anxiety were unquestionably factors in the formation of this fixation — fear of the unknown perils of the wilderness and of its equally unknown inhabitants. D. H. Lawrence once pointed out that, in a purely subconscious way, the symbol of "whiteness" had become almost an obsession with Herman Melville (and F. O. Matthiessen has noted the same point). So ingrained has all this early conditioning become that, as Dr. Stonequist notes, most Americans do not even have Indians or Negroes in mind when they think of America. In our popular mythology, no American ever thinks of Indians or Negroes when the symbol of "the melting pot" is mentioned. Somehow this symbol has been reserved for white immigrants from Europe. Thus hostility to race mixture has become, as Dr. Stonequist says, "a ground pattern of American social organization"; and, by contrast with white immigrants, "the position of the colored and mixed blood groups of the United States has become quite another problem."

Warfare along the frontier was almost continuous. "Every river valley and Indian trail," wrote Frederick Jackson Turner, "became a fissure in Indian society." Each of the successive frontiers which punctuated the history of national expansion was, as he wrote, "won by a series of Indian wars." Open hostility between whites and Indians was almost continuous from the beginnings of settlement until the so-called Battle of

[8] See Macleod, p. 487.

Wounded Knee in 1890, which was not so much a battle as a premeditated massacre of several hundred defenseless Indians.[4] As long as this warfare lasted, the Indian never had a chance to know white society. "The constant jostling from pillar to post," writes Mr. Macleod, "and repeated pushing back from contact with the sources of civilization, was one of the facts which prevented the rapid acculturation of the natives. Peace and security are necessary for the absorption by one people of the more advanced culture of another." Such a prolonged record of active conflict could not but have profoundly influenced American behavior in ways of which today we are wholly unaware.

These deep-seated sources of prejudice have not only been obscured by lapse of time, but they have been inextricably confused by habitual rationalization so that we no longer recognize their existence. For just as greed and piety were hopelessly confused at the outset, so, at a later date, our attitude toward Indians came to be a fusion of personal greed and public spirit. After a time, as Mr. Macleod states, "the avowed feeling that the function of Indian policy was after all merely to keep the Indian at peace pending his gradual dying off from more insidious causes than the sword or the bullet" became a national dogma. Senators got into the habit of quoting Spencer and Buckle to prove that Indians were incapable of advancement. General Sanborn, expressing a majority sentiment, once said that "little can be hoped for them as a distinct people. The sun of their day is fast sinking in the western sky. It will soon go down in a night of oblivion that shall know no morning. No spring time shall renew their fading glory, and no future know their fame." Getting rid of the Indians was rationalized as "opening up the country for settlement"; and the dispersal of the Indian tribes was justified as "assimilation." Since the Indians seemed to be dying off, we concluded "that it was inevitable, and the popular mind was in harmony with this feeling and its resulting attitude of watchful waiting." During the heyday of our attempt to assimilate the Indian, we sternly refused to

[4] See Report of the Acting Secretary of the Interior on HR 2535, dated April 28, 1937.

accept him, as an Indian, into our society. Such an inconsistent attitude cannot be dismissed as hypocrisy. (One Mallery, in 1888, referred to the "satanic consolation of the convenient extinction doctrine.") It represents today as yesterday a type of social blindness induced by confused motivation and concealed by habitual rationalization.

The significance of the Indian, in relation to other colored minorities, consists in more than the role which he was destined to play in the creation of a national psychosis. For when we begin to consider ways and means of eliminating this psychosis, the Indian becomes, once again, the central, and in a sense the key, figure. Only in connection with the Indian have we adopted the principle of federal responsibility for the protection and assimilation of a colored minority. In this one instance the federal government has long acknowledged its responsibility, not only for the welfare of a particular colored minority, but for its eventual assimilation into the main currents of American life.

It is, indeed, strange that we should have failed so completely to correlate our experience with the Indian to somewhat similar experiences with other colored minorities. With the exception of one or two individuals, the Northern abolitionists never showed the slightest interest in the Indian. The historical relation between Indians and Negroes has been noted by such persons as William Christie Macleod and Loring Benson Priest; but no one has attempted to correlate the achievements of both races. To so much as suggest, today, that the experience of the Indian Bureau might have *some* relevance to other minorities is to invite a reaction of mingled incredulity and derision. To most Americans, the Indian Bureau has come to be synonymous with the notion that *any* governmental intervention for the purpose of protecting minorities or assisting in their acculturation is not only iniquitous *per se*, but doomed to failure. Actually the recent experience of the Indian Bureau indicates just the opposite; and points to the conclusion that this experience constitutes an invaluable aid in dealing with the problem of colored minorities in general. "The federal government's treatment of its American

Indian minority," writes John Collier, "while perhaps not applicable in precise detail to all other racial groups, reveals basic democratic principles for the protection of their rights and the administration of their affairs." Historically the experience of the Indian Bureau also indicates how *not* to handle minority problems. The negative aspect of this experience may be more valuable than the affirmative; but in any case it is worth analysis for whatever light it may throw upon the minority problem.

2. *Beans and Blankets*

We started dealing with the Indian tribes as nation to nation. This general policy we had, in effect, inherited from Spain, France, and Great Britain. The eagerness of these nations to draw the Indians into alliances, during the time when they were rivals on the American continent, made eventually for extreme delicacy in dealing with them. The policy was premised upon strategic, not ethical, considerations. Also underlying the policy was the assumption that Indians had a possessory right to the lands which they occupied (this assumption was only indulged in when it became necessary for one power to claim title to Indian lands already claimed by a rival power). We pursued this inherited policy as long as it suited our purposes. But once we had staked out the continent for ourselves and eliminated our foreign rivals, we rapidly dispensed with it.

There developed an increasing tendency to deny the sovereignty of Indian tribes and to deal with them by force of arms. Instead of being regarded as sovereign nations, the Indian tribes became, in Chief Justice Marshall's phrase, "domestic dependent nations." An Indian Office was established in the War Department in 1824 to deal with the Indians; and later, in 1871, Congress prohibited the making of further treaties with the tribes. During the purely military phase of the development of our domestic imperialism which followed, the Indian was in effect isolated from the rest of the world. Had the ensuing exploitation taken place on the world stage, it might have aroused widespread condemnation. But since we had previously eliminated our rivals on the continent (they were themselves bent on plunder in other parts of the world at the time), no one gave heed to the eloquent protests of the Indian. Indian exploitation had become a purely domestic concern.

Our military conquest of the Indian, interrupted by the Civil War, was largely completed by 1880. It had been a costly and time-consuming, but on the whole a profitable, undertaking. We had succeeded in driving most of the Indians west of the Mississippi and had acquired a vast domain for exploitation. In carrying out the military conquest, we had refrained from interfering with the internal affairs of the tribes (the technique of boring from within was not practised at the time). During the course of the military conquest large numbers of Indians had been concentrated, for convenience in surveillance, upon so-called reservations. These represented all that was left of the once vast Indian Territory. In a belief that it was cheaper "to feed than to fight them," most of the Indians had been placed on reservations by 1880. A reservation, someone said, was "a government almshouse where an inconsiderable number of Indians are insufficiently fed and scantily clothed at an expense wholly disproportionate to the benefits conferred." The military phase of the conquest being completed, the Indian Bureau was, in 1849, transferred from the War Department to the Department of the Interior. Having acquired most of the Indian Territory, we rationalized the ensuing change of policy by saying that it was no longer dignified for us to make war against the Indian. But since we had dispensed with the policy of making agreements with the tribes, an impasse had been reached in the further exploitation of the remaining Indian lands. Here, then, was the situation: the frontiersman was impatient to possess the Indian lands and to get rid of the Indian; but the Indian, disarmed and in custody, refused to bestow his tribally owned reservation lands upon his oppressors.

By 1880 there had developed a strong public opinion in favor of some measure of reform in Indian affairs. The reservation policy of providing beans and a blanket for the Indian was obviously robbing him of initiative and self-confidence. Since Indians constituted "a vanishing race," and since they were doomed to ultimate extinction as collective entities, then the quicker this end was achieved the better for all concerned. To many of these Indian reformers it seemed that the continued isolation of the Indian on the reservation and the maintenance of tribal organization and custom were his chief barriers to immediate assimilation. The assimilation would be greatly accelerated, so the argument ran, if the Indian's tribal governments were disbanded; if his culture and religion were destroyed; and if his iniquitous system of communal land ownership were outlawed. These factors were supposedly all that was standing in the way of the complete absorption of the Indian into the main current of American life. Furthermore, these same reformers believed that unless some swift method could be devised to distribute the remaining Indian lands, frontier aggressiveness might force a resumption of military conquest. They also feared — and with good reason — that unless the remaining lands were quietly distributed, the frontier population might take possession of reservation lands and the Indians would receive nothing. This theory of individual assimilation by contrast with group adjustment is sympathetically and plausibly outlined by Elaine Goodale Eastman in a life of Richard Henry Pratt,[5] one of its leading exponents. It was by adopting the concepts of this school of thought that Congress was able to break the deadlock on Indian affairs that existed in 1880.

3. Cultural Attack

In general, the policy that Congress gradually put into effect after 1880 consisted in a wholesale cultural attack upon Indian life with the objective of "freeing" the Indian from the fetters of tribal organization, custom, and religion, so that he might rapidly become assimilated. "To smother, to exterminate the entirety of the Indian heritage," writes Mr. Collier, "became the central purpose in Indian affairs. Extermination was applied beyond the tribe and its government to the local community governments out of which the tribes were compounded, and

[5] Pratt: *The Red Man's Moses*, 1935.

beyond the local governments to the family. . . . As tribe and local community crumbled under the pressures, remote authority had of necessity to be extended past the group to the individual, and this authority was applied horizontally and exhaustively. . . . Invidious absolutism and yet benevolent: invidious toward all that constituted Indianhood, toward every instrument for moulding or implementing personality, while yet benevolent toward the *individual* Indian. And through its benevolence, the far more subtly destroying. Always, through so many mediums, the Indian was told that as a race he was doomed by social inferiority or impracticability. Always he was challenged to build a new personality out of no cultural heritage at all."

Naturally the cultural attack was directed primarily against the system of tribal land ownership which was the basis of Indian life and culture. The principal instrumentality used, in this phase of the campaign, was the General Allotment Act of 1887. The passage of this act — known as the Dawes Act — was celebrated as "franchise day" by the Indian reformers and the act itself was hailed by such a distinguished Indianist as Francis E. Leupp as "the Emancipation Proclamation of the red man." Given the philosophy of the reformers who sponsored the bill, it seemed ideally suited to accomplish a twofold purpose: first, to permit the land-hungry white population to burst the barriers of the Indian reservations; and second, to destroy the basis of Indian culture. In general the act provided that every Indian, regardless of his wishes, should eventually be given a piece of reservation land to hold in fee simple. The sponsors of the act rightly reasoned that, once the communal ownership was destroyed, the backbone of Indian cultural resistance would be broken. At the same time the Indian would be given the same property rights and responsibilities as the white man. This would make for the creation, among Indians, of that spirit of selfishness which, according to Senator Dawes, was the main motivation of white civilization. It would make the Indian a go-getter and a rugged individualist, who would no longer need the protection of the government. It would also scatter the Indians among their white neighbors so that, in time, they might acquire our folkways.

To give the Indian some protection against the sharp practices which were eulogized as "thrift" and "prudence" he was not to be permitted to alienate his allotment for a period of twenty-five years. But it was not long after the act was passed until, by amendments in 1891, 1902, and 1907, the provision against alienation was almost completely nullified. Since the Indians were a dying race, there was no need to provide for their descendants: therefore the remaining reservation lands, after the general allotment, were to be purchased by the government at $1.25 an acre and thrown open to settlement. In the course of this distribution, as Mr. Collier observes, "by a process of natural selection, the whites saw to it that they got the best and richest of the Indians' lands." The motivation behind this seemingly Machiavellian maneuver was, as Mr. Ward Shepard has said, "partly greed, but it was also partly sentimental reliance on one of those easy formulas for salvation. The formula was that by giving each Indian a homestead you could automatically do a number of desirable things: you could give him certain means of self-support, you could make him civilized and respectable by the magic of making him a property owner, and then also you could quite properly, having done these things, take away the surplus land that he didn't really need."

The economic consequences of the allotment policy were, to put it mildly, disastrous. At the time the act was passed, the Indians had around 138,000,000 acres of land. In 1933 they had 52,000,000 acres, fully half of which was desert or semi-desert in character. In other words, under the act the Indians lost upwards of 86,000,000 acres. Over 60,000,000 acres of the so-called surplus land — the ceded surplus and the surplus open to settlement after allotment — were largely disposed of after 1887. The Indians were induced to sell their individual allotments almost as rapidly as the limitations on alienation expired or were removed. As applied to timber and grazing lands, which must be managed in large blocks, the policy was economically suicidal.

Even in the sale of their individual allotments, the Indians were swindled, defrauded, and grossly imposed upon. Because of the restrictions on alienation (which also applied to alienation by will), the allotted lands became hopelessly ensnarled in legal complications (some 6,000,000 acres are still in heirship status). So complicated did the titles become that Congress authorized the Indian Bureau to sell or lease these lands. In the process of leasing them, gross mismanagement occurred. Out of some 37,000,000 acres of grazing land, it is estimated that 50 per cent of the carrying capacity has been lost through overgrazing and consequent erosion. Since the management policy was premised upon the necessity of getting an immediate cash income (which was doled out to the Indians), virtually none of the income was spent on capital improvements. The folly of the allotment measure must be considered in light of the fact that the Indian was placed in possession of a tract of land without adequate capital, or even the means of raising capital, with which he might develop it. Nor were adequate means taken to provide him with the necessary machinery and equipment or the technical guidance essential to successful competition with white farmers. So badly had the Indians' education been neglected that in 1880, according to Mr. Priest, very few spoke English despite a century of contact with English-speaking people. Inevitably, therefore, the allotted Indian was converted into a petty landlord living off a rental check which, as time went on, got smaller and smaller. At the same time, the Office of Indian Affairs developed into an enormous real-estate agency "with the income from operations constantly decreasing while the cost of real-estate transactions multiplied." Needless to say, the cultural inadequacy of the Indian was constantly exploited, not only by the notorious "grafters" of the Indian territories but, in some instances, by officials of the Indian Bureau.

The cultural consequences of the allotment policy were, however, more disastrous than the economic. The policy undermined the economic, tribal, and social solidarity of the Indian tribes. In weakening tribal organization, the allotment theorists assailed the only foundation upon which a transformed Indian society might have been built. The policy of individual assimilation tended to shatter family organization, since the allotments were made to individuals and not to family units. Far from making a go-getter of the Indian, it destroyed his initiative and self-confidence. By shattering the foundation of his culture, it robbed the Indian, as Mr. La Farge has said, of the drive that comes from believing in the future of one's race and nation. It came, moreover, after a century of defeat and humiliation. And, as Mr. Macleod has pointed out, "it is not easy to comprehend or to measure the spiritual bitterness of continuous moral and physical defeat."

The allotment program was merely one prong of the cultural attack upon the Indian. Not only must he be assimilated overnight, but his children must be liberated from the baneful influence of family, tribe, and culture. Children between the ages of six and eighteen were "snatched" from their parents and kept in boarding schools which, in many cases, were hundreds of miles removed from the reservations. Here they were kept from four to eight years consecutively, including vacations. The objective of their education consisted in the destruction of family life and the liquidation of the Indian heritage. Captured or kidnaped for enrollment, these teen-age youngsters were deloused, their hair was clipped, they were dressed in uniforms and arbitrarily assigned to one or another of the Christian sects represented at the particular institution. Overcrowded and ridden with disease, these schools were truly nightmarish institutions. As part of an ill-considered vocational program, youngsters were forced to work long hours in laundries, boiler rooms, and workshops. Told to be Christians and good citizens, they were subjected to a discipline without parallel, in its harshness, in American pedagogy. Superintendents sponsored "the grotesque development of military bands which could parade in the nearest towns, and of football teams." In one instance, $25,000 was spent on a gymnasium in an institution where the youngsters were crowded into filthy dormitories. As late as 1931, only a few Indian schools carried instruction into the junior grades; and until 1929 the use of the Indian languages, as well as Indian dress and hair styles, was forbidden. In spite of the qualified emphasis placed on vocational training, most of the students returned to the reservations after graduation. Since they were not absorbed into the larger community, the trend "back to the blanket" prevailed. For years this hodgepodge educational policy was defended, as Oliver La Farge has said, "on the score of the beastliness of the culture from which the children were being rescued."

The cultural attack had still other fronts. "The rooting-out process," writes Mr. Collier, "penetrated likewise into the deeper spiritual strata of Indian culture. The Indian languages were systematically suppressed in the Indian schools; the religious ceremonies, the poetry, music, and traditions were discouraged or suppressed; the precious and beautiful ancient arts and crafts were allowed to decline and in many cases to completely disappear. Proselytizing, through compulsion, in violation of the constitutional guarantees of freedom of religious conscience, in alliance with missionaries," was the established practice as "Indian schools were illegally used for the practically forced proselytism of Indian children, regardless of the consent of their parents."

4. Rum and Rags

Such a prolonged cultural attack took a frightful toll of Indian life, health, and well-being. By 1923 Indians had declined in numbers from the pre-Columbian estimate of 850,000 to around 220,000. They had lost at least two thirds of all their land in area and about four fifths in value. "Outside the boundaries of Russia, India, or China," wrote Dr. Haven Emerson, "I know of no nation, race or tribe of human beings which exhibit such tragic neglect of the most elementary protection against sickness and death as is to be found among the American Indians." It was not until 1924 that a Division of Health was created at the Indian Bureau. Tuberculosis, trachoma, infant mortality, syphilis, had taken a frightful toll of Indian lives. One observer characterized the reservations in 1931 as "germ-ridden cess-pools of sickness and disease." Changes in the Indian's environment and mode of life had resulted in dietary deficiencies which robbed him of energy and made him an easy victim of disease. By 1923 his estate had been largely destroyed; his health had been seriously undermined; his cultural heritage had been under ceaseless attack for decades; and his personal, family, and social life showed every indication of being profoundly disorganized. It is largely upon the basis of this ghastly record that the average American has concluded that our whole policy of Indian supervision has been a mistake and that it would, perhaps, have been better never to have recognized the wardship principle. It was also upon the basis of this record that the Indian problem came to be generally recognized as "unique and seemingly hopeless," just as the Negro problem came to be regarded, after 1876, as quite insoluble.

The policies used in carrying into effect the cultural attack upon the Indian were pursued for decades after their folly had been demonstrated. Even such relatively enlightened administrators as Carl Schurz and Francis Leupp, while effecting some reforms in the service, adhered to these same policies. They remained, in fact, the chief tenets of Indian administration until as late as 1929.[6] To understand how it was possible for such shortsighted policies to become imbedded in institutional practice, it is necessary to keep one or two extraneous considerations in mind. Since the field of government action was small, our federal bureaucracy in the seventies and eighties offered only limited opportunities for political patronage. But there were hordes of hacks and political camp followers who had, somehow, to be provided with jobs. The developing Indian Service became a major dumping ground for these "deserving" politicos. Personnel standards were nonexistent; and later many of these people were "blanketed into" the service without competitive examination. "There is a tradition on the border," said Bishop Whipple, "that an Indian agent on $1500 a year can retire in four years upon an ample fortune." In fairness, however, it should be said that the real corruption existed not so much in

[6] See "The Indian Bureau's Record" by John Collier, *Nation*, October 5, 1932.

the service itself as in policy and the dishonest legislation. "The outstanding evil," as Allen Harper has said, "was neither corruption nor incompetence; it was the lack of integrity in administering a national trust, a failure to stand up for the Indian interest, and a willingness to apply laws and policies which were detrimental to the Indian without any compunction." It was the failure to adhere to the principle of wardship, not the principle itself, which was at the bottom of the difficulty.

It is also necessary to remember that little attempt was made, say between 1880 and 1929, to apply scientific information in the administration of Indian affairs. "It was a startling thing in the early 1920s," writes Oliver La Farge, "to see how utterly the Indian Bureau remained insulated against all this, to see how it continued to exist and work not even in the nineteenth but in the eighteenth century." Founded in 1875, the Bureau of American Ethnology was never given an opportunity to participate in the formation of Indian policy. The same policies pursued by the Indian Bureau were, unofficially and indirectly, applied to non-Indian minorities. "It may be argued," writes Dr. Carl J. Friedrich, "that we in America have never gone far enough in maintaining the native culture of our immigrants. The spirit of the nineteenth century was against it. All over the world cultural values were squandered and often recklessly destroyed." The whole climate of opinion, so to speak, predisposed the Indian Bureau to take the line that it did. There was more than a trace of Darwinism in the suggestion that "you can't prevent the Indian from finding his own level." The prevalence of this type of thinking tended to rob the Indian Service personnel of a strong conviction of the worth of what they were doing. Cynicism was rife throughout the service and many key positions were occupied by men and women, thoroughly addicted to the ideology of racial superiority, who actually hated the American Indian and never lost an opportunity to sneer at any manifestation of assumed Indian incompetence. By forming powerful political alliances with the missionary foundations (which were in part supported by Indian Bureau funds) and with the Western land sharks (who were living off the Indian) these functionaries made themselves and their policies almost invulnerable to attack.

For years we have failed (*a*) to appreciate the importance of the contributions which colored minorities have made to American culture; and (*b*) to recognize how our treatment of them has warped American institutions and influenced American character. On the score of the Indian's contributions to American culture, a passage from Allen Harper's monograph on American Indians will indicate the extent of the debt: —

As determined as they were to transplant intact the civilization of their homelands, the European settlers were, on their part, not slow in introducing modifications that gave a distinctly different *quality* to the life which they constructed in the New World. The Indian's contribution to their civilization in foodstuffs and drugs alone was phenomenal. It has been estimated that four-sevenths of the total agricultural production of the United States consists of economic plants domesticated by the Indian and adopted by the white man. A writer has observed that "the extent of the debt to the Indian for his work of domestication is emphasized when we recall that the white man has not yet reduced to cultivation a single important staple during the four hundred years that he has dominated the New World." The white man appropriated the Indian's canoe, snowshoe, and toboggan; built his roads and canals over the Indian's trails; emulated the Indian's methods of warfare, fishing, and recreation; copied and adapted the Indian's clothes for life in the forest. The Indian passed immediately into the literature created in the New World; and, indeed, in far-off Europe, reports of him and his life inspired a number of writers to grow nostalgic in their enthusiasm for the primitive man. The Indian quickened and revitalized the imagination of the white man, caused him to reawaken an old instinct for the outdoors, and taught him how to live with the outdoors — one of the greatest arts.

Our treatment of the Indian adversely affected the development of American institutions in many ways. The immense loot obtained in the spoliation of the Indian estate, as Angie Debo has shown, "exerted a powerful influence upon contemporary opinion and standards of conduct. The reaction of this process upon the ideals and standards of successive frontier communities is a factor in the formation of American character that should no longer be disregarded by the students of social institutions." Our handling of Indian lands had not a little to do with the creation of the sharecropper and the dust bowl. In *Ill Fares the Land*, I have shown how the allotment policy was in part responsible for the creation of rural communities of marked instability. When all of these influences are finally traced out and correlated then I think that the strange dualism in our American tradition can be largely explained.

For we have not one, but two, American traditions: the generous, liberal, and democratic tradition; and the narrow, bigoted, and authoritarian tradition. The existence of the latter can be largely explained in terms of our long-standing neglect of colored minorities, particularly the Indian and the Negro. For these are the skeletons in the closet so far as American democracy is concerned. Just as our initial contacts with Indians on the frontier created psychoses which we have not yet outgrown, so our treatment of the Negro has fostered a spirit of intolerance and bigotry. Just as slavery created the plantation system and the sharecropper, so the early dissipation of the promise of the American frontier may be traced to the manner in which Indian lands were plundered. In fact the phenomenon of land monopolies in supposedly frontier communities cannot be understood or explained apart from an examination of Indian land policies. After a fashion, therefore, both the Indian and the Negro have had their revenge.

5. New Phase

Fortunately a new trend is apparent in the administration of Indian affairs. While phases of this reversal in policy date from the middle twenties, the real turning point came with the appointment of Commissioners Rhoades and Scattergood in 1929 and the subsequent appointment, in 1933, of Mr. Harold Ickes as Secretary of the Interior, of Mr. Nathan Margold as Solicitor, and of Mr. John Collier as Commissioner of Indian Affairs. For years prior to 1933, Mr. Collier had been exclusively concerned with the Indian problem.[7] As executive secretary of the American Indian Defense Association, Inc., he had worked out a comprehensive philosophy of Indian administration. While it has not been possible for him to realize in practice every item of this program, nevertheless the progress that has been made is certainly encouraging.

Just what are the tenets of this new philosophy of Indian administration? In Mr. Collier's own analysis, there are three main objectives involved: —

Economic rehabilitation of the Indians, principally but not exclusively upon the land;

Organization of the Indian tribes for managing their own affairs; and,

Civic and cultural freedom and opportunity for the Indian.

The philosophy underlying these objectives "goes back to the simple principle of treating the Indians as normal human beings capable of working out a normal adjustment to and a satisfying life within the framework of American civilization, yet maintaining the best of their own culture and racial idiosyncrasies." It goes back even further, in Mr. Collier's thinking, to that reverence for the personality of the other person which, to him, is the heart of our civilization. "The central value," he writes, "is just that universal value: that the personality of the other, the different personality, group, or race, is dearer to the civilized man than anything else." This hypothesis of action derived not so much, in the opinion of one close to Mr. Collier, from an evaluation of pre-existing research data as from simple direct insight into living situations. It is just possible that Mr. Collier got something of this philosophy from the Indians themselves. Pleasant Porter, Chief of the Creek Nation, told a senatorial committee in 1906 that "the Indians haven't had time to grow up to that individuality which is necessary to merge them with the American citizen. The change came too soon for

[7] See page 15 of his speech of May 21, 1942, before the Santa Fe Indian School for an interesting statement of how he happened to become interested in Indians.

them . . . there is no life in the people that have lost their institutions. Evolving a thing out of itself is natural, transplanting it is a matter of dissolution, not growth. There may be a few that will grow . . . but the growth will not be natural." [8]

Since land use is the essential problem of Indian economy (90 per cent of the Indians are rural), reform of land policies was the first concern of the new administration. By secretarial order, all further sale of Indian lands was prohibited. Then, under the Indian Reorganization Act of June 18, 1934 (approved by 74 per cent of the Indians by referenda provided for in the act itself), the further allotment of lands was terminated. Most of the remaining unentered ceded land has been restored to the Indians in perpetuity. The act also provides a mechanism by which the involved heirship lands may also be restored to tribal ownership. Not only has the existing land base been protected, but about 4,250,000 acres have been added by purchase, recapture of unentered surplus land, and transfer of public domain. Indian lands can no longer be frittered away and means have been provided by which much of the remaining lands, and those to be purchased, may be vested in tribal ownership. Excellent progress has been made in preventing soil erosion, overgrazing, and the deterioration of the lands. Much of this work, moreover, has been performed by the Indians themselves. By the use of proper transitional devices, the Service now believes that the Indian can become adapted to an agricultural economy in which he figures not as a landlord, but as a farmer. A revolving fund has been established so that he may acquire the necessary capital to become a competitively successful farmer. Sound farm management and educational programs have been created in order to get the Indian into the productive use of his land through the application of his own labor. Through the Indian Arts and Crafts Act of 1935, the government is now assisting the Indians to develop their crafts and expand the market for craft projects. Co-operative marketing associations of all types have been established. Throughout, the emphasis is now placed on the rehabilitation of the Indian

[8] *And Still the Waters Run* by Angie Debo, 1940, p. 132.

society and the Indian economy and not upon the assimilation of individual Indians.

Critics have charged that the new policy is retrogressive and that Mr. Collier, influenced by the spectacle of the government providing doles and rations to the general population during the depression, is attempting to turn the clock back. The present policy, however, is based upon two realistic considerations: first, that *for most Indians* a planned existence on the land, or in a non-land-use vocation within the context of rural society, is reasonable and dictated by the facts since the land is the Indians' one, outstanding, substantial economic asset. Secondly, all the emphasis of the educational system upon going to the city, all the deliberate disintegration of tribalism, and all the laws calculated to break up the reservations and force Indians into urban society have not succeeded in transferring any appreciable portion of Indian population from rural to urban society.[9]

As important as the measures aimed at economic rehabilitation have been those aimed at stimulating local self-government among the tribes. Indians are now made equal partners in the administration of their affairs. Tribal constitutions, when approved by the Secretary of the Interior and ratified by the tribe, cannot be arbitrarily revoked. Indians may now form corporations not merely to carry on economic activities but to enter into contracts with counties and states for local welfare services. They now enjoy the protection of old-age pensions, aid to the blind, and aid to dependent children. A marked effort has been made to have the states take over such functions as education and public health protection. The main function of the Service has shifted from that of despotic management to that of co-operative advice and technical assistance; from direct to indirect administration. While technical wardship still obtains, its substance is being gradually liquidated.

The cultural attack upon the Indian has ceased. The Service now insists upon "the fullest constitutional liberty in all matters pertaining to religion, conscience, and culture." In ac-

[9] See monograph by Allen Harper, pp. 60–61.

knowledgment of their services in the first World War, all Indians were made citizens of the United States in 1924 (although there are at least three states in which they are refused the right to vote). The number of boarding schools has been drastically reduced and over seventy-five new day schools established. Important steps have been taken in the development of a bilingual educational program. Every effort is now made to insure the fullest freedom of cultural choice and to encourage the development of all types of Indian cultural expression. "Through generations," writes Mr. Collier, "the government did deliberately seek to destroy the Indian cultural heritage; and only because the roots of it lay so deep in the Indian soul, and only because age-old, instinctive modes of thought and expression are so much less destructible than individual life itself, has the Indian culture stubbornly persisted." While protecting Indian culture from a violent uprooting, the new policy seeks to give "the Indians the full advantage of science, and thus fit them for modern life."

Important reforms have also been effected in the personnel of the Service. A preference is now given to Indian candidates and promising Indian students may obtain loans so that they may acquire technical training. The employment of Indians in the Service has increased from 30 per cent in 1933 to 59 per cent in 1935. Indian labor is now used in building schools, roads, and hospitals on the reservations. With the construction of new hospitals and the development of medical personnel, a vast improvement has been effected in the Indian's health. New medical techniques have been worked out (witness Dr. Michel Pijoan's work in the study of nutritional deficiencies in the Indian's diet) that give every promise of success. At the same time, the Service is now making full use of the available scientific research into Indian life and culture. It has called in for consultation such distinguished social anthropologists as Dr. W. Lloyd Warner, Dr. Laura Thompson, and Mr. Fred Eggan. It is seeking to devise methods whereby all that has been discovered about the adaptation of so-called primitive cultural groups may be applied in its programs.

"The essence of the New Indian policy," writes Mr. Collier, "is to restore the Indian to mental, physical, social, and economic health; and to guide them, in friendly fashion, toward liberating their rich and abundant energies for their own salvation and for their own unique contributions to the civilization of America." Or, restated by the National Resources Planning Board, "the present official policy toward the Indians is to accept the permanence of divergent cultures, accompanied by the interaction of these cultures within the American system. . . . For the Indian, this policy means the preservation of cherished traditions, and an increased sense of personal dignity; for the Nation as a whole it means an enlargement of interests and perspectives."

One thing is certain: the trend toward extinction has been definitely arrested. Indians now constitute our most rapidly growing minority. On January 1, 1940, there were 394,280 Indians in the United States and Alaska (of the total of 361,816 for the United States, approximately 241,000 live on reservations). While most of the Indians are concentrated west of the Mississippi, they reside, in small numbers, in most of the other major regions. In some states, such as Arizona, New Mexico, and Oklahoma, they are destined to play important roles. As to their rate of increase, the National Resources Planning Board states: "In 1935 the full-blooded Indian population increased nearly twice as fast as the general population of the United States. No group in the country has a higher rate of natural increase." Based on this rate of increase and the sharp decline in death rates, interesting theoretical projections of the Indian population have been made. These estimates indicate that it might total around 700,000 or 800,000 by 1980. At any rate, the expected rate of increase for the period 1930–1980, for the various ethnic groups, is as follows: whites, 19 per cent; Negroes, 50 per cent; Indians, Mexicans, and Orientals combined, 139 per cent.

All of the foregoing is not to imply that the Indian problem has been "solved." Thirty per cent of the Indian population are still illiterate; infant mortality rates, among them, are still more than twice as high as the national average; tuberculosis still takes a heavy annual toll of Indian lives. Taking the group as a whole, probably two thirds of its members are either completely landless or own insufficient land on which to make a living even on a subsistence level. A survey of 131 Indian jurisdictions made in 1937 shows that, excluding four well-to-do jurisdictions, the average per capita income (including subsistence) was $161 a year. Housing conditions are still deplorable, despite some progress since 1933. "The all-pervading fact of Indian life is dire poverty," writes Mr. Collier; "a poverty which, expressing itself in squalid housing, malnutrition, and apathy, is largely accountable for a death rate among the Indians nearly twice that of the rest of our population, including Negroes." In the future, moreover, it is going to be extremely difficult to expand the land base sufficiently to provide for the existing population without even making provision for the expected increase. The war, moreover, is bringing a host of new problems to the Indians. As thousands of them have gone into the armed services or entered defense industries, the process of assimilation into the general stream of American life has been greatly accelerated.[10] With the multiplication of contacts between Indians and other groups in our society which the war has brought about, the whole problem of providing for a gradual and orderly adjustment of Indian culture to the demands of a modern industrialized society has become increasingly acute. Today one can still repeat, despite the progress that has been made, the famous opening statement of the Meriam report of 1928: "An overwhelming majority of the Indians are poor, even extremely poor, and they are not adjusted to the economic and social system of the dominant white civilization."

6. The Future

Just what are the implications of this new policy? There are many people who, with the utmost good will toward the Indian, regard the Collier-inspired policy as exotic, mystical, and ata-

[10] See "The Indian in a Wartime Nation" by John Collier, *Annals of the American Academy*, September 1942.

vistic. One still hears the statement, "The sooner they are assimilated the better." But just what is meant by assimilation? In the political sense, assimilation might imply merely the full and equal exercise of political rights and privileges. In this sense, the Indians have been largely assimilated. But assimilation does not necessarily imply cultural uniformity; nor does it imply that, for certain purposes, ethnic groups cannot be regarded as separate or distinct entities. "America," as Louis Adamic has said, "has always welcomed diversity, variety, differences."

While conceding that there is room for permanent cultural divergence within the framework of American democracy, nevertheless it must be admitted that there is an element of ambiguity in the present Indian policy. Mr. Collier has said that "the Indian property must not pass to whites; that Indian organization must be encouraged and assisted; that Indian family life must be respected and reinforced; that Indian culture must be appreciated, used, and brought into the stream of American culture as a whole; and that the Indian as a race must not die, but must grow and live." With all this one may readily agree, but the issue remains: does this imply that islands of Indian life and culture must forever remain within the framework of, but not fused with, American culture? Occasionally one comes across the phrase "economic self-sufficiency" in the writings of Mr. Collier, which gives rise to an uneasy conviction, expressed by Edwin R. Embree, that "in a social order such as ours, based on private property and personal gain, it is hard to protect communal ownership and sharing. The modern competitive world is scarcely safe for the old easy-going native democracy." But our economic order is not static; it is constantly changing; and there may be more room for such adjustments in the future than there have been in the past.

Paradoxically it has been by reviving the best, the enduring, the indestructible elements of Indian life and culture that progress toward assimiliation has been most rapidly effected. It seems impossible, in fact, to destroy an indigenous culture; to revive it, therefore, creates the most favorable prospect for acculturation. As Mr. Embree has said: —

These fresh growths of old stems are just the things that mark a vigorous and growing culture. Opportunity for the Indian does not mean merely freedom to revive the old ways or to stand still. . . . The Indian must find his place not in an ancient culture but in a modern world. But he has a right to expect that he be given religious and cultural freedom so that, like other groups in our very mixed population, he may continue to follow the beliefs and ceremonies that mean so much to him. And he has a right to ask that he be allowed to move over into the new economic order without too great haste and without any racial discrimination against him.

Indians recognize that change is inescapable; that self-support implies successful competition. Their aspiration, as voiced by Oliver La Farge, is this: "We shall learn all these devices the white man has, we shall handle his tools ourselves, we shall master his machinery, his inventions, his skills, his medicine, his planning, and still be Indians." Right at this point it becomes extremely important, therefore, to relate the Indian to other racial minorities, by insisting that all discriminations based on race or color be removed from our society. For, as Mr. Embree adds, although "sentimental regard for the Indian is now the fashion in America, we do not think of admitting him as an equal. . . . The great American middle classes are so full of color prejudice that Indians, no matter how fully they adopt white ways, will not for many years be accepted into the white world." Merely to create, therefore, an atmosphere in which Indians may develop a new personality type — a type that will be capable of acquiring the essentials of our culture in an extremely rapid manner — is not enough. The remaining race barriers must be removed.

* * *

The new Indian policy represents, in the words of a report of the National Resources Planning Board, "the *first conscious official* attempt to preserve and creatively develop cultural traditions fundamentally divergent from those of the majority." The new respect for the integrity of Indian tribal life may be influenced by the possibility that anxiety concerning Indian raids on white settlements has been supplanted by anxiety concerning the economic costs of supporting a population that older methods have been forcing into chronic dependency. Such an interpretation of official policy would, however, be inadequate, if not wholly unjust. It is much more accurate to conceive of the policy as symbolizing the newer approach to the whole question of cultural diversity." Here, for the first time, an *affirmative* effort has been made to assist in the adjustment of a non-European culture to the prevailing American pattern. For it should be remembered, as the National Resources Planning Board also points out, that cultural considerations in general have as yet played a very minor role in shaping the nation's destiny; and that where such considerations have been invoked it has usually been on a rather meager scientific or theoretical basis.

Just how much of this new Indian policy is applicable to other minorities? Obviously "a policy adapted to a group already largely isolated from other cultural groups is *not directly applicable* to groups in the main channels of national enterprise." The mere fact that there are 300 different Indian tribes speaking 250 different dialects should be enough to remind us that the Indian problem is highly specialized. While the problem has its own background, its own peculiarities, its own complications, still I believe that there are *certain* conclusions of a general nature that can be drawn from the new policy: —

1. I believe that this experience has demonstrated that science has an extremely important contribution to make to the solution of minority problems, if this knowledge can be related to action programs.

2. I believe that the Indian Service experience indicates that before science can make an effective contribution to such problems, scientific research must be purposively directed toward the problems themselves; that to utilize such scientific knowledge, it must, somehow, somewhere, find a focus in government through agencies directly concerned with the problems. To accumulate research without devising means for its application merely creates a cultural lag between research and policy.

3. I believe that the Indian Service has demonstrated that there is great merit, as Mr. Ward Shepard has said, in "the principle of the over-all, the integral, the simultaneous, the all-out attack on the complex of problems (of the Indian) in its entirety. This method is at the opposite pole from the dispersive and discrete, the haphazard and unarticulated application of science to human welfare which has distinguished this age of much knowledge and little wisdom. And this principle of action has a surprising human result: it unlocks unsuspected depths of spirit and will and creative purpose in common men, whether their skins are white, black, or red." In other words, scientific knowledge should be applied to such problems as part of an over-all integrated plan for their rehabilitation as groups. This is the point that Mr. Collier has in mind when he says that the Indian Service aims "to incorporate the group into the national system" and that it seeks to "reach the individual through his re-enfranchised group."

4. I believe that any administrative agency concerned with minority problems should not attempt to monopolize the whole sphere of administrative activity; but that it should seek to bring to bear upon the problems within its field all of the rapidly expanding resources of government: local, state, and federal.

5. I believe that the best method to be pursued, in working out an administrative approach to the problem of minorities, is that of indirect administration — that is, working through the organized group, helping the group to help itself.

6. I believe that it is sheer obscurantism to contend, in the face of the achievements of the Indian Service, that the resources of government cannot be effectively used to bring about a better adjustment of minority groups. If the Indian Service can reduce Indian death rates, then the same death rates among Negroes can be reduced by the same or similar methods. The special problems of other colored minority groups are no more "insoluble" than the Indian problem.

7. I believe that the Indian Service experience indicates that the preservation, enrichment, and stimulation of native cultures holds great promise of enriching our entire cultural heritage;

and that there is nothing undemocratic or invidious about regarding minorities, for administrative purposes, as special groups. As Dr. Max Ascoli recently said: "We cannot rely too blindly on the automatic melting of all the immigrant groups in our melting pot. Possibly the system of the wholesale melting is wasteful and hazardous. I think we can acknowledge the existence of racial and national groups in the United States without falling into racialism or nationalism. The tendency to say that there is not an Italian, or a German, or a Polish, or a Jewish problem is exactly the same as that of those American conservatives who used to deny the existence of a class conflict in America and were alarmed at the Wagner Act. But the Wagner Act has not exactly sharpened the class conflict. The same may be the case with future acts and measures that may be inspired by a frank and open acknowledgment of racial and national problems in the United States."

Finally I believe that colored minorities face a problem which, as Mr. Collier has stated (with reference to the Indian), "is in essence a problem of the whole world and one which must be solved if we are to achieve an ordered stability in the international and internal relations of states. It is the problem of reconciling the rights of small groups of people to cultural independence with the necessity for larger economic units demanded by modern methods of production and distribution. This is the problem of small states and small cultural groups everywhere." If a solution of this problem can be effected in the United States, then there is at least reason to believe that a similar solution might be made of similar world problems.

CHAPTER II

The Long-Suffering Chinese

THE fable reads that mysterious and inscrutable China, determined to live in isolation from the world, built an enormous wall to protect its empire from outside penetration. It may have been this legend which induced the Occidental world to build its vast hemispheric wall — comprised of legal statutes rather than bricks and stone — against the Chinese. The creation of this hemispheric wall dates from the period when America, in its feverish push westward across the continent, reached the Pacific. For it was not until we had reached the Pacific that we enacted our first restrictive immigration measure. With the enactment of this measure we broke with our tradition of free migration. It was at this point that the westward movement of European peoples reached a new frontier: Europe looked at Asia across the Pacific. As Dr. Robert E. Park has said: "It is as if we had said: Europe, of which after all America is a mere western projection, ends here. The Pacific Coast is our racial frontier."

The first section of this great wall against the Orient was established in 1882, with the passage of the Chinese Exclusion Act. Today there is no land, under either the British or the American flag, where Chinese labor is admitted. Following the pattern established here, Australia, Canada, and New Zealand likewise legislated, at an early date, against Oriental immigration. A great wall, as Ching Chao Wu has said, has also been built from Tia Juana to Cape Horn, as Mexico, Guatemala, El Salvador, Nicaragua, Colombia, Ecuador, and Peru legislated against Chinese immigration. "European peoples around the Pacific," wrote Mr. Chester Rowell in 1926, "regard their borders as a racial frontier, which they are determined to maintain inviolate." Throughout the whole Pacific area, these dykes have been built, sometimes only against the Chinese, but in other instances against all Oriental people. The United States, for example, has barred immigration from China, Japan, the Philippine Islands; and, by the enactment of the Barred Zone provision of the Immigration Act of 1917, the same prohibition has been extended to peoples from India, Siam, Indo-China, Java, Sumatra, Ceylon, Borneo, New Guinea, and the Celebes. In most instances, legislation against Oriental immigration throughout the Pacific area has taken the form of a rigid legal prohibition which has had the effect of setting the peoples of Asia apart from those of Europe and America. In each instance, also, the prohibition has been based directly on so-called racial considerations, thereby creating a situation certain to have resulted, sooner or later, in open conflict. In the Atlantic, the Open Door; in the Pacific, the European Wall.

For years there has been a marked tendency on the part of students of immigration to dissociate the movement of immigrants across the Pacific from the movement of immigrants across the Atlantic. Our "immigration problem," as such, was associated almost exclusively with the movement across the Atlantic. It became associated, in our minds, with Ellis Island, the Statue of Liberty, and the doctrine of the Melting Pot. Conversely, the movement across the Pacific became associated with an entirely different set of symbols. We came to associate it with the Yellow Peril, the Chinese Must Go!, and Japanese Picture Brides. It was, in the words of so distinguished a student as Dr. Edith Abbott, "an entirely different problem." In time this difference in attitude crystallized into a dogmatic assumption of the absolute unassimilability of the yellow and brown races. Friends of the immigrant in the East did not want to embarrass their cause by discussing the highly controversial problem of Oriental immigration; and consequently, over a period of years, the two problems became sharply separated in our thinking and the same divergence of attitude crystallized in our immigration policies.

Interestingly enough, the whole movement around the rim of

the Pacific to set the European peoples apart from those of Asia had its origin in the state of California. For here, in the words of Chiang Chao Wu, "for the first time in the history of mankind, large numbers of Orientals and Occidentals, who had developed different racial characteristics and cultural traits during the long period of isolation, were thrown together to work out their destiny in the new land." Even today it is impossible to appraise the consequences of this initial meeting of the East and the West. To review some aspects of the matter is not, therefore, a merely academic exercise. In these cataclysmic times, as Dr. Oscar Jaszi has said, "past history becomes living history." For the consequences set in motion by the passage of the Chinese Exclusion Act of 1882 are still with us and have assumed, once again, major proportions. Half-solutions of problems have an inconvenient habit of bobbing up, in the most unpleasant manner, to haunt the future. Some years ago, for example, we thought that the Japanese problem in this country had been settled; today we have nearly 100,000 Japanese in protective custody and, as a consequence, have been forced to admit that the "solution" was, indeed, imperfect.

It would be impossible to trace the history of the Chinese in this country without, at the same time, writing the history of California from 1850 to 1900. Consequently I do not propose even to outline the sequence of events; but rather to touch upon one or two neglected aspects of the matter which, today, have particular significance, especially in view of certain proposals to be advanced in later sections. Throughout the Pacific area and beginning in California, the exclusion movement has followed, as Dr. R. D. McKenzie pointed out, a definite course: from local agitation against a particular class or race of Asiatics to national movements directed against all Asiatics of every race and class; from economic arguments to cultural and biological arguments for restriction and exclusion. The pattern of the entire exclusion movement throughout the Pacific area is implicit in the agitation against the Chinese in California. Just how did this breach with our tradition of free migration occur? How was it possible for a particular state to force its views upon the nation and thereby to set in motion a chain of events of world-wide significance?

1. The Politics of Exclusion

The year 1876 marked a definite turning point in the history of anti-Chinese agitation in California. Prior to 1876, most of the barbarous and obnoxious anti-Chinese legislation passed in California had been declared unconstitutional in the courts, as violative either of treaty provisions, of the Fourteenth Amendment to the Constitution, or of the Civil Rights Statute. As a matter of fact, California kept the federal courts busy during the period from 1860 to 1876 declaring its outrageous "Hottentot," or race, legislation unconstitutional. In later years Japanese publicists, in an effort to dissociate the Japanese from the anti-Oriental tradition in California, charged that the Chinese were themselves largely responsible for the treatment accorded them. Mr. K. K. Kawakami, for example, in 1921, said that the early Chinese immigrants were "slavish, utterly callous to Occidental environment, and content with the inhuman treatment meted out to them." A grosser libel was never printed. It would be difficult to imagine a more dignified, forceful, and statesman-like defense than the Chinese in California conducted during these years. Their conduct, in fact, was in marked contrast to the simian behavior of their opponents. And, in the course of their defense, the Chinese made constitutional history in the United States. It should not be forgotten that such celebrated cases as *United States* v. *Wong Kim Ark* and *Yick Wo* v. *Hopkins* involved California Chinese. I know of no other single precedent, in the field of civil liberties, of greater practical value than the doctrine enunciated in the latter case. By conducting their fight on strictly legal and constitutional lines, the Chinese won victories which have redounded to the advantage of every minority group in the United States.

By 1876, however, the attack against the Chinese had suddenly shifted from a state to a national basis. Not having been successful in its efforts to drive the Chinese out, California determined to force and, if necessary, to blackmail the national government into adopting its theory of the Chinese question. It is significant, in retrospect, that the year 1876 also marked a turning point in the history of the Negro problem. For it was in 1876 (and surely with the inauguration of President Hayes) that a bargain was made in Congress whereby the Negro problem, as such, was relegated to the states — that is, to the Deep South — and ceased to be, as it had been from 1865 to 1876, a matter of national concern. With the narrow construction placed on the Fourteenth Amendment in the famous Slaughter House decision in 1873 and the decision in 1875 which held the Civil Rights Statute unconstitutional, the Supreme Court had, so to speak, let the bars down so far as the Negro problem was concerned. Prior to this time, the South had shown a lively interest in the possibility of substituting Chinese coolie labor for Negro slave labor. It had been suggested in Memphis, in 1869, that such a substitution might be in order; and on several occasions about this time Southern planters had visited California with this purpose in mind. Once they realized, however, that they had again regained control of the Negro, their interest in Chinese labor swiftly abated.

"No small part of the persecution of the Chinaman," wrote Mary Roberts Coolidge in 1909, "was due to the fact that it was his misfortune to arrive in the United States at a period when the attention of the whole country was focused upon the question of slavery." This correlation between the Negro problem and the Chinese question is clearly indicated in the vote in Congress on the important measures introduced after 1876 affecting the Chinese. Without exception, these measures were passed by the vote of representatives from the Pacific Coast and the Deep South. Again and again, Southern Senators and Congressmen lined up with representatives of the Pacific Coast to railroad through Congress measures aimed at driving out the Chinese. No longer interested in Chinese labor, the South was quite willing to join with the Pacific Coast in fitting the Chinese into a caste system which, in many respects, closely resembled that which prevailed throughout the former slave belt. Just as the national government capitulated to the South on the Negro question, as the price of the peaceful inauguration of President Hayes, so the national government capitulated to California on the Chinese question. The two sellouts were, so to speak, part and parcel of the same deal. They mark the successful culmination of the movement to denationalize civil-rights legislation in the United States. Not only was California successful in capitalizing on the sharp national cleavage over the Negro question, but it consistently blackmailed the national government and both major political parties by constantly bringing up controversial measures affecting the Chinese on the eve of Presidential elections (most of the important anti-Chinese measures passed by Congress were enacted on the eve of national elections). With the Pacific Coast vote becoming of greater national significance as population continued to move westward, the two major political parties vied with each other in seeking to appease California on the Chinese question. Had it not been for the sharp national cleavage over the Negro question, it is highly questionable that this initial anti-Chinese legislation would have been passed by Congress.

As a matter of fact, the Chinese and Negro problems had been intimately related in California long before 1876. "The antiforeign feeling in California," writes B. Schreike, "was unquestionably intensified by the presence of Southerners, who comprised nearly one-third of the population in the first decade of American rule." Southern Democrats dominated California politics prior to the Civil War. Many of them had brought their slaves with them to the Coast. The first evidence of color prejudice there arose not in connection with the Chinese at all, but against the Indian and the Mexican, and later against the Chilean and the Hawaiian. With Southern opinion dominant in the state prior to the Civil War, it was relatively easy to build up a general pattern of color prejudice which, at a later date, was directed almost exclusively against the Chinese.

On still another plane, the Chinese were directly related to the slave question. In 1833 Great Britain had abolished slavery; and in 1838 it was outlawed in the West Indies. The great outward movement of coolie labor which followed in the years from

1845 to 1877 was a direct consequence of the discontinuance of slavery in the British Empire. During these years a traffic developed in Chinese coolie labor which rivaled "the palmiest days of the Middle Passage." These were the days of "pig dealing," as Chinese "pigs" were rounded up in the notorious barracoons of the Far East for shipment to the West Indies, where the contracts for their employment were sold to the highest bidder just as slaves themselves, at an earlier period, had been sold at the auction block. Over 40,000 Chinese coolies were imported to Cuba alone, of whom it has been said that at least 80 per cent had been decoyed or kidnaped. The report of the Chinese Commission on the traffic in coolie labor in Cuba has been pronounced "the most serious indictment ever made by responsible officials against a labor system." By 1862 the West Indies traffic in coolies had reached such proportions that the American government was forced to prohibit American ships from participating. Similar action soon followed on the part of Great Britain, and in 1876 China herself outlawed the traffic. By the time the coolie traffic had been brought under control, however, Chinese were scattered throughout Central and South America and the West Indies. Wherever they were imported, they were used as substitutes for slave labor in plantation areas. Few, if any, of the Chinese who came to California were contract employees; virtually all of them were free immigrants. Nevertheless, Chinese immigration to California smacked, to some degree, of slavery; and the "Civil War was altogether too recent to make these earmarks attractive."

The famous Congressional debate on the Naturalization Act of 1870 clearly indicates how the Chinese question came to be inextricably related to the Negro problem. This act extended the privilege of naturalization to "aliens of African nativity and persons of African descent." The extension was, in fact, an inescapable corollary of the Emancipation Proclamation. If Negroes were no longer slaves, it followed that they were eligible to citizenship. During this same debate, however, the question arose as to whether or not the same privilege should be extended to Chinese. "The very men," said Senator Carpenter of Wisconsin, "who settled the question of Negro suffrage upon principle now hesitate to apply the principle . . . and now interpose the very objections to the enfranchisement of the Chinaman that the Democrats urged against the enfranchisement of the Freedmen." The arguments against extending the privilege to Chinese were, in fact, absolutely identical with those urged against Negroes. The outcome of the Civil War, however, left no alternative but to extend the privilege to Negroes; but the opponents of the measure did succeed in denying it to the Chinese. Here, for the first time, a definite racial basis, utterly at variance with the American tradition, crept into our naturalization law. Undeniably the bias against the Negro jeopardized the case for the Chinese. And once the exception had been allowed, it was easy to apply it at a later date against Japanese, Filipinos, and Hindus. The Negro or slave question was, however, at the bottom of the whole difficulty from the beginning.

From the time of the 1870 debate on naturalization until 1924, California never ceased to urge that the "ineligible-to-citizenship" test in naturalization matters should be made the basis of our immigration policy; and the California view ultimately prevailed. It was in this manner that a fundamental breach occurred in our whole policy toward immigration. The progression here is unmistakable. As Miss Lucile Eaves has written: "The regulations made in the miners' meetings are repeated in the state laws and even in the federal statutes; the demands of the labor unions are reflected in city ordinances, and these in turn suggested measures passed by the state legislature; while the futile attempts at state exclusion furnished the models for Federal laws regulating immigration." For the first time in our history the nation decided (a) to deny naturalization on racial grounds; and (b) subsequently to exclude certain races altogether. At no time was this grave departure from an established tradition debated on the merits; from the very beginning it was at all times obscured by the shadow of the Negro. Once the policy was established, however, it was quickly adopted throughout the Pacific area, with the gravest implications. For once America was committed to a policy of discrimination based on race, national self-consciousness was stimulated throughout the Far East.

2. *The Technique of Exclusion*

Whatever may be said in behalf of our policy of Oriental exclusion and the denial of the privilege of citizenship on the score of race alone, little can be said in mitigation of the crude manner by which both measures were effected. Viewing this political manipulation in retrospect, it is, indeed, almost incredible that we have a single friend in China today. Since certain of these measures will, of necessity, have to be re-examined in light of the postwar situation, it is not amiss to summarize the major steps by which they were promulgated.

In the early treaties with China (1844 and 1858) nothing whatever was said about the rights of the Chinese residing in this country; presumably, therefore, they had the same status as other aliens. The words "free white persons" in the Naturalization Law of 1870 did serve to exclude them from citizenship; but as a matter of fact any number were naturalized, since the courts had not adopted a fixed definition of "free white persons." At this time — the middle of the nineteenth century — China was an unknown country: a mysterious kingdom, walled in by tradition, without contact with the Western world. Along with other Western nations, however, the United States was exceedingly anxious to end this isolation. We wanted to open up the Far East to trade and commerce. The Pacific Mail Steamship Company had, in 1867, established the first direct steamship service to the Orient; and in 1869 the Central Pacific had completed its line across the continent. These two great systems of transportation opened up a new route for trade and travel between Europe and Asia. Our interest in Chinese trade and the completion of these two communication systems were largely responsible for the execution of the Burlingame Treaty in 1868, which was hailed in this country as the opening of a new era in the Pacific. In the negotiation of the treaty, *we* were the active party. As Dr. Richmond Mayo-Smith has said in *Emigration and Immigration:* —

This treaty of 1868 marks the dividing line between two distinct and contradictory policies on the part of the United States toward the Chinese. Up to that time our efforts had been directed toward *compelling* the Chinese to admit Americans to China for the pursuit of trade and commerce. In this contention we placed ourselves on the broad platform of the right of free migration and the duty of international intercourse.

The Burlingame Treaty was intended to be reciprocal. Article VII conferred on American citizens in China the "same privileges, immunities and exemptions" enjoyed by the citizens of the "most favored nation"; and, conversely, Chinese subjects in the United States were afforded similar protection. The only exception noted was that "nothing herein contained shall be held to confer naturalization upon citizens of the United States in China, nor upon the subjects of China in the United States." The reason for the inclusion of this proviso was obvious: Negro suffrage was being hotly debated in Congress and it was deemed expedient, in order to secure ratification of the treaty, to insert the clause.[1] The purpose of the clause was to make it clear that the treaty did not, *per se*, confer the privilege of naturalization. But it was not construed, at the time, as forbidding the naturalization of Chinese. The essential point about the treaty, in the light of subsequent developments, is simply this: the United States was knocking at the walls of China for admission — China was not seeking rights in the United States.

In 1880 the federal government, in response to California political pressure, sought a modification of the treaty. The amendment negotiated provided that the United States might *regulate, limit,* or *suspend* Chinese immigration; but "may not absolutely prohibit it." It was also provided that the limitation or suspension must be "reasonable." No sooner was the ink dry on the new treaty than Congress began to pass bills suspending Chinese immigration. Both President Hayes and President Arthur vetoed as unreasonable, and contrary to the spirit of the treaty, bills that suspended immigration for twenty years. In 1882, however, Congress passed the Chinese Exclusion

---

[1] *Chinese Immigration*, by Mary Roberts Coolidge, 1909, p. 149.

Act which suspended all immigration for ten years. This bill represented the first restriction ever placed by Congress on immigration. In the debate on the bill, Senator Hawley of Connecticut pointed out that we, as a nation, had bombarded China for precisely the same privilege — namely, free migration — which we now sought to deny her. "Make the conditions what you please for immigration and for attaining citizenship," he pleaded; "but make them such that a man may overcome them; do not base them on the accidents of humanity." As finally passed by a coalition of Southern and Western votes, the bill not only suspended immigration but contained an express prohibition against the right of naturalization. Thus, writes Mrs. Coolidge, the clamor of a single state "was sufficient to change the policy of a nation and to commit the United States to a race discrimination at variance with our professed theories of government, and this so irrevocably that it has become an established tradition."

Shortly after the first Exclusion Act of 1882 was passed agitation against the Chinese reached unbounded proportions throughout the Far West. Rioting took place in California, Oregon, and Washington; and at Rock Springs, Wyoming, 28 Chinese were murdered and property valued at $148,000 destroyed. At the same time Chinese merchants, exempt from the exclusionary features of the bill, were being heckled and harassed and humiliated in this country, while American merchants in China were reaping a rich harvest. These facts served to induce the Chinese government to seek a further modification of the treaty. Accordingly the Senate authorized a new treaty, suspending all immigration for twenty years and providing an indemnity for the loss of Chinese life and property in this country. While this treaty was in the process of being ratified by China, Congress abruptly passed the Scott Bill of 1888. This outrageous bill trapped some 20,000 Chinese who had temporarily left the United States, but who, at the time, had a perfect right of re-entry. In other words, it was tantamount to deporting 20,000 Chinese who had established lawful residence here. As one Senator said: "It is a game of politics and not a seemly one at that. But for the fact that we are on the eve of a Presidential election and each party wants to get the vote of the Pacific Slope, this Senate would not be engaged in this debate." For years after the passage of the bill, the Chinese government filed protest after protest with our State Department, without even so much as receiving an acknowledgment. Our attitude toward China, as reflected by this legislation, was so severe that many foreign powers at the time suspected us of trying to provoke a war with her.

Not content with this state of affairs, Congress passed the notorious Geary Act of 1892 (again from political motives and again by a coalition of Southern and Western votes). This act continued the prohibition against further immigration for another ten years, but it also denied bail to Chinese in habeas corpus cases and required certificates of residence for all Chinese in default of which they could be deported. The passage of the act was denounced by the Chinese Minister in Washington as being "in violation of every principle of justice, equity, reason and fair-dealing between two friendly powers." During these same years, when Congress seemed determined to provoke a war with China, the Chinese were protecting American citizens and property rights and trade between the two nations was rapidly expanding. The effect of the Geary Act was to drive many Chinese out of this country and to terrify those who remained. Believing the act to be unconstitutional, the Chinese had not obtained certificates of residence; hence most of them were subject to deportation. Fortunately Congress had not provided for the actual enforcement of the statute, so that few deportations resulted, and subsequently its provisions were somewhat modified. In 1902 Congress indefinitely extended the prohibition against Chinese immigration and the denial of the privilege of naturalization. But further indignities were still in order. In 1924, Congress, despite strenuous protests from the Chinese government, insisted on making the terms of the Immigration Act of that year also applicable to Chinese, although further immigration had been stopped by previous legislation. Going one step further, Congress made it impossible for American citizens of Chinese ancestry to bring their alien wives into this country, thereby separating families and cementing the unequal sex ratio among the resident Chinese. In 1926, 1928, and 1930, resident Chinese groups vainly sought to have these provisions modified, but to no purpose. Many years previously, moreover, we had projected our exclusionary immigration laws into the Far East, by prohibiting further Chinese immigration into Hawaii and the Philippine Islands (1898). Mrs. Coolidge has succinctly summarized the entire development of the Chinese question in Congress as follows: "From suspension to restriction; from execution of treaty stipulations to flat prohibition of treaty compact, the movement went on until it culminated in the Geary Act, which reiterated and legalized the severer features of them all and added the requirement of registration. It was, in the words of Senator Hoar, progression from vinegar to vitriol." All but one of some eight anti-Chinese measures passed by Congress were passed on the eve of national elections and for avowed political purposes.

In the face of this extreme provocation, China steadfastly refrained from enacting retaliatory legislation. One reason for this, of course, was that China dared not act, having a weak and ineffectual government at the time. During these same years, however, we were holding China accountable, in the highest degree, for the protection of American life and property in the Orient. One sharp note after another was dispatched from Washington on this score. While China could not retaliate, nevertheless she did voice her resentment on more than one occasion. Mrs. Coolidge states, for example, that the exclusion indignities perpetrated upon the Chinese in this country "undoubtedly contributed to the accumulated resentment which found expression in the Boxer Rebellion." Mr. Wu has gone further and stated that the Boxer Rebellion was the expression of a spirit which, had China been stronger, would unquestionably have resulted in measures excluding all Americans from China. We sent warships and troops to protect out nationals in China; all China could do was to send us notes of protest. The verdict of history on this entire episode is likely to be

Theodore Roosevelt's: "In its effort to carry out the policy of excluding Chinese laborers, grave injustice and wrong have been done by this nation to the people of China, and therefore ultimately to this nation itself."

That we have a strong ally today in China is, in no small measure, due to the heroic activities of the Chinese residents in the United States upon whom we permitted to be visited for years on end every imaginable indignity. As early as 1890, these Chinese immigrants were supporting Dr. Sun Yat-sen with their "sweat" money. "The overseas Chinese," he himself said, "were the Mother of the Chinese Revolution." Both before and after the Revolution of 1911, according to General Tsai Ting-kai, the overseas Chinese contributed millions of dollars to patriotic funds. Being directly oppressed by foreign imperialism and being offended by the weakness of their government, they fervently desired to see China become a great progressive world power. They have been credited with a large share of the success of the General Strike in China in 1925 and of the northern expedition led by Chiang Kai-shek in 1926.[2] It was these same resident Chinese — the descendants of the despised "coolies" and "moon-faced lepers" of former years — who, during the period of Japanese aggression in the Far East, kept up an incessant protest in California; who picketed the Japanese consulates; who marched with banners in protest against the shipment of scrap iron, petroleum, and war supplies to Japan; who served, as few other groups did, to arouse America to the peril of Japanese militarism. Even before Pearl Harbor, West Coast Chinese had enlisted in China's Air Corps (Portland alone sent 33 trained pilots to Generalissimo Chiang Kai-shek). It was Los Angeles, California, that gave to the Chinese Air Force one of its greatest heroes, "Buffalo" Wong, who shot down more than 35 Japanese planes in the pre-Pearl Harbor days of Japanese invasion of China. Wong was shot down near Chengfu. His dying words, as reported in the press, were: "Tell America to send us some more planes . . . some good planes."

[2] See, generally, *Chinatown Inside Out* by Leong Gor Yun, 1936.

3. California Blackmail

How is it that a single West Coast state has been so consistently able to force its views upon the national government — to shape, in effect, the international policy of this country? One explanation, as I have suggested, is that California has cleverly made capital of our lack of unanimity over the Negro question. This was true throughout the period of the initial anti-Chinese legislation; but it also happens to be pertinent to later developments. California was largely responsible for the exclusionary provisions of the drastic Immigration Act of 1924. But the vote on this act was a national, not a sectional, vote. Had the nation actually been converted to the California point of view or were other factors responsible?

Here, again, the "nigger in the woodpile" is the Negro. Prior to the passage of the 1924 Immigration Act, which prohibited all further Japanese immigration and declared them ineligible to citizenship, Negroes had begun to move north. The years from 1918 to 1924 had witnessed a heavy northern movement of Negroes which, in turn, had served to make many Northern and Middle Western states race-conscious. Dr. Ray Lyman Wilbur pointed out in 1920 that "the redistribution of the colored race into the northern states due to war activities has brought before all thinking citizens the fear of adding another race problem to the almost insoluble one now faced by the United States. As long as the colored residents were confined largely to the south where they were understood and where a social system had been adopted by common consent (sic) that kept things on an even basis, this question was not a pressing one. The race riots in Chicago, Chester, Pennsylvania, and other places, are due to this redistribution and have had, in my opinion, a considerable effect." Had it not been for the fact that the Negro problem was becoming national in scope, there is good reason to believe that the Immigration Act of 1924 might have been defeated.

But there is still another explanation for the ease with which

California has successfully foisted its views on the national government. During the anti-Chinese agitation in Congress, this singular situation developed: the United States, with a strong national government, vehemently insisted that China, with a weak and ineffectual government, assume full responsibility for our nationals and their property in China. At the same time, however, this great nation of ours had to alibi to China that, owing to our system of government, it could not protect Chinese nationals or their property in America. In 1886, Secretary of State Bayard, while conceding that the outrages committed against the Chinese in this country were "shocking and inhuman in character," had to make the humiliating admission that, since the police power was vested in the states, the national government could take no effective action. Naturally this explanation made little sense to the Chinese minister.

Just why was the national government so impotent to safeguard treaty provisions? Here, again, we get back to the Negro problem. The express purpose of the Fourteenth Amendment, as Louis Boudin has demonstrated, was to make it possible for Congress to legislate for the protection of civil rights. But the courts had nullified the amendment and had declared the important provisions of the Civil Rights Statute unconstitutional. Hence the impotency of the national government. As to the extent of the indignities heaped upon the Chinese — which, incidentally, were far in excess of any ill treatment ever afforded Americans in the Orient — all one has to do is to refer to Chapter XV of Mrs. Coolidge's excellent book, *Chinese Immigration*. There the whole sorry tale of murder, robbery, and persecution is told in full, with the most convincing documentation.

Since the federal government was powerless to act, it had to yield to the blackmail of California. In other words, if Congress could not control the actions of individuals in California, it seemed advisable (and probably was) to exclude further Chinese immigration in order to avoid a repetition of these shameless attacks. Nor is this phase of the matter merely of academic interest today. In September 1925, the United States sent a note to China in which it stated, apropos of threats against American lives in the Orient, that

the government of the United States desire to impress upon the Chinese government the necessity for giving concrete evidence of its ability and willingness to enforce respect for the safety of foreign lives and property and to suppress disorder and anti-foreign agitation which embitter feelings . . . etc., etc.

Shortly after this note was despatched, anti-Chinese riots broke out in this country. They were not, properly speaking, so much riots as lawless raids by American police on Chinese settlements in Cleveland, Chicago, Boston, Philadelphia, and New York. In Cleveland, over 612 Chinese were arrested and a hundred places of business summarily closed.[3] Similar episodes have repeatedly occurred in this country.[4] While Chinese were cowering in their miserable Chinatown ghettos in this country, we were pompously lecturing China on its international treaty obligations.

In a closely knit world economy, there is a grave danger involved in permitting a single state or locality, on the basis of its deeply rooted prejudices or its real or imagined injuries, to dictate the foreign policy of a nation. On the entire problem of our relations with the Orient, as Dr. Eliot Grinnell Mears has said, "unquestionably sectional feeling has overshadowed considerations of international amity." The danger inherent in such a situation has been repeatedly pointed out by our elder statesmen. The late Elihu Root, in an address of December 12, 1906, said that no state should be permitted to endanger the international position of the nation. William Howard Taft wanted Congress to have more power to avoid possible embarrassments of an international character resulting from irresponsible state action. In 1913 we witnessed the amazing spectacle of William Jennings Bryan, then Secretary of State, coming as a supplicant to Sacramento, to plead with the Cali-

[3] See the *Nation*, October 14, 1925.
[4] See "The Chinese Boycott" by J. W. Foster, *Atlantic Monthly*, Vol. 97, p. 122.

fornia legislature not to embarrass this country by enacting further anti-Japanese legislation. President Theodore Roosevelt, in a message to Congress of December 3, 1906, stated: "I earnestly recommend that the criminal and civil statutes of the United States be so amended and added to as to enable the President, acting for the United States government, which is responsible in our international relations, to enforce the rights of aliens under treaties. It is unthinkable that we should continue a policy under which a given locality may be allowed to commit a crime against a friendly nation."

There is a still further reason why California was able to browbeat the nation on the Chinese question. The Chinese were not known to the nation; but they were known to Californians. The nation, as such, never did get an objective, scientific, factual account of the Chinese on the West Coast. That the nation never got the true facts is, in a large measure, due to the circumstance that we have permitted private pressure groups to determine our immigration policies. The arguments, for example, pro and con on the Chinese question were a hodgepodge of irrelevant nonsense and pseudo-anthropological theorizing. So long as the nation is unwilling to deal with problems of this character on a sound administrative basis, just so long will it be possible for special interest groups to confuse, bewilder, and bamboozle the American people. So long as the national government is powerless to protect the civil rights of all persons resident in the United States, and to adopt appropriate legislation for this purpose, just so long shall we be embarrassed by the untoward acts of irresponsible groups. And both of these considerations are as valid today as they were in 1900.

4. Chinatown

Quite apart from what has happened in the past, do we still have a Chinese problem in this country? If it were only past injustices that were involved, however grave these might be, it would seem rather pointless, in this chaotic world, to turn backward in time in order to find such episodes. But the fact is that we still have a serious resident Chinese problem which is directly related to the developments outlined in the prior sections of this chapter.

The number of Chinese resident in the United States declined from 107,500 in 1890 to 77,504 in 1940. Of this group, 30,868 are American citizens by reason of birth in this country. Being driven from the mines and from agriculture at an early date, they are, today, a highly urbanized minority. Approximately 80 per cent of them live in the Chinatown ghettos of such American cities as San Francisco, Los Angeles, New York, Chicago, Portland, Seattle, Boston, Philadelphia, Washington, Detroit, Baltimore, St. Louis, and Pittsburgh. The San Francisco Chinatown is, by all odds, the largest of these urban communities: 22 per cent of all the Chinese in the United States and 44 per cent of those in California live in this particular settlement. They have concentrated in urban problem areas, not because they have an innate relish for overcrowding, but because of external pressures. They have come together, in other words, for mutual aid and protection.

Owing to the restriction on immigration (and particularly to the Immigration Act of 1924 which made it impossible for citizen Chinese to bring their alien wives to this country), there is a sharply unequal sex ratio among the resident Chinese. According to Mr. Wu, in 1920 there were 695.5 Chinese males for every 100 Chinese females, or a ratio of something like 7 to 1. Gradually this disparity is being corrected; of the 1930 population, 59,-802 were males and 15,152 females. Again and again, the Chinese in San Francisco have petitioned the federal government to make it possible for them to bring relatives here from China, but to date no such modification has been secured.[5] In considering the unequal sex ratio it should also be kept in mind that California has a general miscegenation statute. Because of the ratio of the sexes and the fact that 80 per cent of the Chinese are urbanized, it might be assumed that they were a "vanishing race," doomed to ultimate extinction in this country. But such is not the case. For reasons that have not been fully explained, the resident Chinese, according to Dr. S. J. Holmes, represent the single exception in

[5] *Americans in Process,* by William Carlson Smith, 1937, p. 35.

this country of a mainly urban people with a reproductive rate well above replacement needs. Population figures indicate that they are actually increasing in numbers in this country. There is no likelihood whatever that they will vanish or disappear.

The passage of the Exclusion Act has resulted, over a period of years, in a definite pattern of geographical distribution of the Chinese. In 1870 nearly all the Chinese, 99 per cent in fact, were located west of the Rockies, most of them in California; but in 1920 only 59.4 per cent were located in the West. When the flow of immigration was stopped, the resident population began to scatter and to form "Chinatown" settlements in the large urban centers. It became necessary for Chinese businessmen to look to the American community in general for customers, and this tendency was the more marked because of the fact that the types of business in which they engaged were narrowly limited. Today many of these small businesses are in an extremely precarious position and an increasing economic insecurity has gripped virtually every Chinatown in the United States.

Over the years, too, there has been a marked occupational shift among the Chinese. In 1860, some 34,933 Chinese worked in the mines in California; but by 1870 only 17,609 were so employed and by 1920 the census listed only 151 miners. Generally speaking, the Chinese have "withdrawn from those jobs in which Americans compete and they are concentrated where no bitter voice is raised against them." More than 50 per cent of all the Chinese in the United States in 1920 were employed in restaurants or laundries. A similar shift is noted in other occupations: in 1870, some 2000 were engaged in general manufacturing; but in 1920 only 100 were so employed. At one time as many as 10,000 were employed in the railroads; today there are less than 488. In 1886 it was estimated that 30,000 worked as harvest hands in California; in 1920 only 3617 were so listed. While general trade has increased, it has been almost entirely restricted to Chinatown itself, with a few shops outside the district, such as curio, art, and antique shops. But, it should be noted, there is no competition in the exchange of luxuries. "The

Chinese," writes Mr. Wu, "have succeeded where personal service is a factor in success. But they have failed in the region in which America is supreme – in occupations which involve the application of machinery. They have failed to gain a foothold in the occupations in which they have competed with, and so replaced, the native stocks." It is for this reason that the Chinese question has lost its economic significance and that, as Mr. Schreike has said, "tolerant indifference to the Chinese has taken the place of hatred on the part of the Americans."

But tolerance is not acceptance, and indifference is not assimilation. So far as the Americans are concerned, the Chinese question may have lost its former urgent significance; but so far as the Chinese are concerned the problem has grown steadily more acute. Sociologically what has happened has been well summarized by Mr. Wu: "Something approaching commensalism," he writes, "has been brought about. The relations of the two races have become symbiotic rather than social. They live side by side, but they live on the whole in different worlds." For the most part, the relations between Chinatown and the American world are, as he notes, "cold, formal, and commercial." Nothing even approaching assimilation, in its fullest sense, has taken place. The life of the resident Chinese, writes Mr. Leong, "is not an unhappy life – most of the time. But it is neither Chinese nor American: it is Chinatown. It is a life led by the Chinese in spite of, rather than with the co-operation of, the Americans among whom they breathe and somehow find their living." They will become Americanized, he notes; but not Americans.

Not only are social relations between the two communities far from satisfactory, but conditions in the various Chinatowns themselves are wholly deplorable. The San Francisco Chinatown, because it is the largest and the oldest settlement, can well serve for illustration. At the height of the anti-Chinese fury in California, Chinatown was pointed to as conclusive proof of the hideous character of the Chinese. It was the superslum: "foul, uncanny, vicious, and a menace to the community . . . a sliver of space seven blocks long and three wide." Because of the enforced segregation with its resulting congestion, property values in Chinatown rose rapidly. The Chinese themselves have never been the beneficiaries, however, of this unearned increment in property values. Prior to the fire of 1906, Chinatown was owned by 150 property holders of whom only 33 were Chinese. The pre-fire Chinatown was, of course, a problem area. Due to the large number of single men, the absence of families, and the expectation on the part of many that they would ultimately return to China, overcrowding in the district became pronounced at an early date. An investigation in 1885 indicated that there were 14,552 bunks for single men in ten blocks of Chinatown. The fire of 1906 destroyed most of these old rookeries and the district was, to some extent, rebuilt. The frame structures were replaced; a sewer system was installed; and other improvements were made. But the district was rebuilt so rapidly, by force of necessity, that it was never properly reconstructed. It had to be rebuilt, moreover, on the old site, since restrictive clauses in property deeds generally barred the use or occupation of property by Chinese except in the ghetto section itself. As families became more common, one-room units were taken over by entire families. Property in Chinatown became increasingly profitable and rents rose rapidly. The problem of overcrowding and congestion was further aggravated during the depression, when many Chinese were driven into Chinatown from rural districts in an effort to seek employment or relief.

A legend prevails in San Francisco that the blessed fire of 1906 destroyed all that was ugly, sordid, and unhealthy about Chinatown. Suddenly it became, in the eyes of all proper San Franciscans, a "quaint" and "charming" place.[6] "Ladies," wrote Mr. Schreike, "do not mind going shopping all by themselves in the Chinese quarter. Dining in a Chinese restaurant is a form of recreation, and picturesque Chinatown stirs the imagination." Chinatown, after the fire, became "sanitary and clean," wrote a missionary in 1934.[7]

---

[6] See *Old Chinatown* by Arnold Genthe and Will Irwin, 1913; and *San Francisco's Chinatown* by Charles Caldwell Dobie, 1936.

[7] See *Orientals in American Life* by Albert W. Palmer.

In point of fact, Chinatown is still a slum — "San Francisco's main slum area" in the words of the San Francisco Housing Authority. Here is what the Authority had to say about the quaintness of Chinatown in 1941: —

Expansion in Chinatown is limited. Fifteen thousand Chinese live in an area five blocks by four blocks which is dedicated not primarily to residence but to shops, restaurants and institutions. Reports of the inconceivable conditions under which the Chinese maintain themselves are not exaggerated. Of the 3830 dwelling units in Chinatown approximately 3000 are totally without heating equipment. In all Chinatown there are only 447 homes acceptable by the Survey standards, and *all* of them are in a high rental bracket. Buildings constructed after the Fire to house single men on a bare existence basis — that is, containing tiny windowless rooms with hall toilets and kitchens and often no bath facilities anywhere — now house families in these same accommodations, sometimes as many as ten to a room. Some in the very heart of San Francisco have neither gas for cooking nor electricity for light but use wood and kerosene.

They live crowded together above the shops and below the sidewalks. Their windows, if they have any, look out on streets that are noisy until the early hours of the morning. The children lack adequate homes; they play in the streets at night or sit with their mothers and fathers at the workshops until midnight. As a consequence of these living conditions, the Chinatown tuberculosis rate is *three times* that of the rest of the city. Though the Chinese cultural tradition has helped to maintain morale so far, there are now numerous indications of discouragement and disintegration.

Three of every five Chinese families are living in one or two rooms, rooms usually so small as to deserve the appellation "cubicles."

Approximately 81.9 per cent of the Chinese-occupied dwelling units in San Francisco have been pronounced substandard, by contrast with 19.7 per cent for the rest of the population. The substandard rate for the Chinese is much higher, for example, than among the Negroes of San Francisco.

Not only is the housing problem serious, but it is extremely difficult to correct. Property values in Chinatown, because of the congestion, range from $2.50 to $3.50 a square foot; whereas the limit which housing authorities may spend, under the existing law, is $1.50 a square foot. It is largely for this reason that the plan of the San Francisco Housing Authority to build a $1,500,-000 project for the Chinese has had to be temporarily abandoned.[8]

Up to Pearl Harbor, the position of the Chinese in California was, indeed, remarkable. They were perhaps the oldest immigrant group in the state. Most of them, in fact, belonged to the second, third, and fourth generation. As a group they had lived in California much longer than, for example, the Armenians and the Portuguese. But they had failed to win for themselves a comparable place in the social, economic, and political life of the state. American-born Portuguese, Armenians, and Italians occupied conspicuous positions in the business, professional, and political life. Some of them are judges, mayors, legislators; and they even have their share of bank presidents. But there are no Chinese-American officials in California nor have there ever been any. This state of affairs was only the more remarkable by reason of the fact that the Chinese constituted a fairly good-sized minority and, as such, possessed considerable economic and political power.

The truth of the matter is that the Chinese have been the victims of a caste system not altogether unlike that which prevails in the Deep South. Speaking of the Chinese-American, Mr. Schreike observed that "his social status is fixed; there is a recognizable social distance." Earlier, in 1927, Mr. Wu had written that "if there is an obstacle which keeps the native-born Chinese from feeling completely at home in America, it is color." When confronted with this situation, the Californian has invariably given the stock explanation: "The Chinese are not assimilable." The facts, however, indicate that the Chinese have been the victims of a caste system which has been imposed upon them. It has been this caste system, rather than any inherent biological factor, which has prevented full assimilation. As a matter of fact the Chinese have actually changed biologically; it has been their social position which has remained static.

[8] See *New York Times Magazine*, an article by Tom White, February 2, 1941.

A class system is one in which, among other characteristics, there is social mobility. Members of a particular class can improve their status in society in a variety of ways — by marrying out of the group, by acquiring special skills and aptitudes, or, for that matter, by luck at the races. In a class society, movement is possible both up and down the status ladder. But in a caste system it is otherwise, and it is a caste system which has been imposed upon the Chinese. They cannot marry outside their own group and their social mobility is sharply restricted by the color line. They can attend schools and higher institutions of learning — there has been no discrimination here — but after graduation they can wash dishes. In the past, therefore, there has been both geographical segregation and occupational stratification. It may not have been the exact pattern of the Deep South but it was certainly cut from the same cloth. The pattern, moreover, tended to be self-perpetuating. When the Old Chinatown in Los Angeles was removed some years ago to make way for the new Union Station, many persons, Mr. Schreike among them, believed that the Chinese would be able to secure for themselves a more typical occupational and geographical distribution in the community. What actually happened, however, was that the Chinese moved a stone's throw from the old section and built a new streamlined and, if anything, more hideous Chinatown.[9]

In the past, the color barrier has been the main stumbling block in the lives of the American-born Chinese. Up to the end of 1938, the Oriental Division of the United States Employment Service in San Francisco reported that 90 per cent of its placements were for service workers, chiefly in the culinary trades. As late as June 1940 the service reported that, with few exceptions, most firms discriminated against Chinese in employment. This discrimination existed, moreover, despite the fact that most of the American-born Chinese are well educated and that many of them have received special training. It has not been at all uncommon for University of California graduates, with

[9] See also *Shake Hands with the Dragon* by Carl Glick, 1941, for a description of New York's Chinatown.

Ph.D. degrees and Phi Beta Kappa keys, to be forced to accept jobs as cooks and waiters. Even as late as 1941 it was estimated that there were at least 5000 young Chinese in San Francisco for whom "there seems to be no future worthy of their skills." [10] A few of these students had, however, made notable names for themselves. Dr. Chien-Shiung Wo, a very charming girl in her early twenties, has come to be recognized as one of the most brilliant young physicists in this country. Wherever these youngsters turned, however, most of them found, as Mr. Leong observed, "that social and racial prejudice and economic discrimination" were too much for them. "There is no likelihood," he wrote, "of improvement for generations to come." Instead of applying the skills for which they were trained, they were, as Mr. White observed, "washing dishes, carrying trays, ironing shirts, cutting meat, drying fish, and selling herbs."

Over a period of years, this situation has produced a serious crisis in Chinatown: the crisis of the second, third, and fourth generation. "Actually," wrote Mr. White in 1941, "only the face of Chinatown is bright. The heart of Chinatown is frustrated, perplexed, discontented, restless. It represents a 'melting pot' which has 'let the people down.' " Both the old and the new generation became highly skeptical, not only of the value of acquiring an education, but of American political ideals. "The younger generation," wrote Mr. Lim P. Lee, "shows marked political apathy." [11] For years the Chinese had been able to boast of one of the lowest crime rates of any ethnic group in this country. But by 1940 observers began to note the appearance of factors which were likely to make for a sharp increase in juvenile delinquency in the future. The old Chinese culture, which had held the people together and given them a set of genuine social values, began to disintegrate. The Chinese family itself began to show signs of disorganization, as the gap between parents and children steadily widened. A growing sense of frustration began to corrode the very core of these

[10] "Crisis in Chinatown" by Nate R. White, *Christian Science Monitor*, February 1, 1941.
[11] *Chinese Digest*, January 1940.

wholly admirable people. "The patience of the Chinese," wrote Mr. White, "is legendary. In the United States for ninety-two years they have endured hardship, racial persecution, social degradation, without complaint outwardly, without uprising, without inefficiency. But things are different in Chinatown today."

This mounting sense of frustration was, in fact, most noticeable prior to Pearl Harbor. In a prize-winning oration at Oregon State College, Miss Maxine Chin summarized the position of the second generation as follows: —

Because of our Occidental ways, if we return to China, we are looked upon as foreigners. There we are handicapped, since we neither speak real Chinese nor know modern Chinese culture. In the United States, likewise we are regarded as foreigners; because of the color of our skin we bear a double yoke. Because our parents and grandparents were ground into the depths of degradation by fear and intolerance, many of the younger Chinese have grown up fearing the white man, and allow themselves to be beaten into feeling inferior — so much so, that the majority of them cringe and creep back further into the black depths of Chinatown, afraid to come out and prove that they can be a desirable element in American society.

As you pass along the streets of Chinatown and look up at the buildings, strangely enough owned by Americans, tumbled-down and practically rotting at their bases, if you could but look inside and see the crowded conditions, climb up the stairs groping from one step to the next, see the dank, dark hovels that are rented as rooms with insufficient light, little electricity, ancient plumbing, and utter lack of sanitary facilities! Our primary thought is to cut loose the bonds that hold us to the mode of living that has characterized our people for generations. But at present we can only go back to Chinatown and become the little yellow people who roll the dice, deal the cards, mark the lottery tickets, serve the chow mein and noodles, occasionally do the laundry, and continue kow-towing to the Americans. When we do get jobs, we are often dressed up like museum pieces in native costumes. We do not want to be an outside group looking in.[12]

[12] *Chinese Press*, May 9, 1941.

After Pearl Harbor, however, a great change began to take place in Chinatown. The Employment Service reported that, in a year's time, the placement of Chinese workers in clerical and professional positions increased to about 38 per cent of total placements. Since Pearl Harbor more than 80 per cent of the placements have been in industries directly connected with the war effort. In a report given me under date of October 5, 1942, the Oriental Division of the Employment Service stated that it was "experiencing as much difficulty as the general office in finding competent workers for all types of jobs and an unemployed Chinese no longer need say that discrimination has barred him from utilizing his best skills." Chinese began to be placed in positions as stenographers, timekeepers, welders, carpenters, shipyard workers, and aircraft workers. From Chinatowns all over the nation, similar reports have been received. And, as the younger Chinese moved outward into the American community, antique shops and chop-suey restaurants and hand laundries began to close their doors. "No men to run it," announced Li Po, as he closed his Chinese restaurant in Los Angeles. No one knows, of course, whether these developments represent a permanent relaxation of the color barrier or mere temporary relaxation to meet an immediate need. But the Oriental Division of the Employment Service believes that "the proven success of these workers will no doubt continue them in their jobs after the war."

The difficulties that Chinese merchants have experienced in obtaining merchandise from China is another reason why the solidarity of Chinatown shows evidence of disintegration. A typical report, at the moment, is that of a merchant who has closed his antique shop and found employment in a war industry. Also the removal of restrictions in the United States Navy and Naval Reserve has attracted many Chinese volunteers.

Years ago Mr. Ng Poon Chew, one of the leaders of the Chinese community in California, observed that "perhaps in the future our American-born Chinese will have to look to China for their lifework." Most of those who returned to China in the past, however, reported that they were "confused" and "overwhelmed." Any number of them discovered that they had lost their familiarity with the Chinese language and that they were really out of place in China. Despite these handicaps, China has always had a strong appeal to the American-born Chinese. "To the young Chinese," wrote Albert W. Palmer, "a China in revolution, where almost anything may happen, offers excitement, opportunity, and possibilities of leadership." [13] That China is in the throes of a revolution and Japan is not probably accounts for the great interest that second-generation Chinese have shown in China in contrast to the lack of interest that second-generation Japanese have shown in Japan. "One thing is sure," writes Mr. William Hoy in a letter dated October 6, 1942, "those Chinese now in California and throughout the United States who are China-born will return to China as soon as the war is over and try their hands at business and seeking employment back in the old country. I have heard many Chinese tell me this." Even the boys who are enlisting in the Navy are doing so, in part, because they believe that, in the postwar world, "China must have a defensive navy and air force, to protect the contemplated merchant marine needed in delivering the raw materials she will swap in a free world market for the essentials of her industrialization." [14] They see, therefore, an opportunity to use their newly acquired skills in China.

Dr. T. K. Chang, Chinese consul in Los Angeles, believes that the new skills and experience being acquired by the Chinese in America may serve a triple purpose. In the first place, they will assist in dissipating the unacknowledged but very real prejudice which some Americans demonstrate toward all but Caucasians. In the second place, the new skills promise individual emancipation from the unwritten restrictions which in the past have confined the Chinese in the United States to a comparatively small list of business and employment activities. And, lastly, he believes that the acquired wartime trades will equip young Chinese-Americans with the potential ability to contribute to China's certain forthcoming industrialization, a process expected to rank

[13] *Our Racial and National Minorities*, 1937, p. 469.
[14] *Illustrated Daily News*, Los Angeles, September 19, 1942.

in historic importance with her past achievements in the arts, literature, and philosophy. Certainly the war has set in motion processes of far-reaching import insofar as the Chinese are concerned. "No longer," writes Rose Hum Lee, "do Americans think of the Chinese as mysterious Orientals from a little known land. Most of these Chinese living among them are fellow citizens. The rest of them, as well as their cousins in the old country, are Allies. *The crisis of December 7th has emancipated the Chinese in the United States. It is up to the American people to effect the emancipation by law.*" While this enthusiasm lasts, in other words, and before it abates, we should consolidate the gains which have already been achieved.

Considering the circumstances, it is indeed remarkable that the Chinese have fared as well as they have in this country. That they have been able to do so is a tribute to their faith in American democracy. It is also a tribute to those "Chinese cultural traditions," mentioned by the San Francisco Housing Authority, which, as much as anything else, have served to maintain morale in the face of the most discouraging prospects. Obviously the age-old solidarity which has prevailed in Chinatown has now been broken. At one and the same time, this is both a good and a bad omen for the future. If we do not capitalize upon the magnificent opportunity which now exists to afford these Chinese-Americans full participation in our cultural heritage, they will remain, as they have in the past, cultural outcasts. To insure that this will not happen, it is essential that the federal government intervene *now* for the purpose of consolidating these gains. The war has brought the Chinese out of Chinatown and we should lock the doors behind them. Intervention can take place at many levels: housing, training, education, employment opportunities, and in other fields. The objective should be to achieve assimilation at the level of full equality of social, economic, and political participation. A wise policy, however, would aim at preserving a measure of cultural autonomy. We need unity in the sense of a full and equal participation in the essentials of American industrial democracy; but we should also preserve diversity in the sense of freedom to maintain cultural traditions from which these people probably never can completely divorce themselves.

At the same time, we need to remove every vestige of racism from our statute books. The prohibition against Chinese immigration should be removed and the Chinese should be placed on a quota basis. The number who could enter this country on such a basis would be wholly negligible; and the stigma itself would be removed. Likewise, all resident Chinese aliens should be made eligible for citizenship on precisely the same basis as the nationals of all other countries (as recommended by President Theodore Roosevelt in 1906). Unless some such program is adopted, the old caste system will be reinstituted and we shall witness a growth in the number of so-called "marginal" men and women among the Chinese population — people who are, as Miss Chin observed, really without a country or a culture. It is worthy of note that the first step towards righting an old wrong — which is often the road to progress — has been taken in California. In its 1942 convention, the California League of Women Voters adopted the following resolution: —

> Recognizing the racial discrimination shown in several Asiatic Exclusion Acts passed by our government over a period of sixty years, the California League of Women Voters accepts its responsibility for education as to the history and effects of the Exclusion Acts leading toward effective opposition to racial discrimination in immigration laws.

Many resident Chinese are convinced that this ancient wrong will be righted. "Surely racial discrimination," writes Miss Rose Hum Lee, "should not be directed against those who are America's allies in the far east and are helping here in every way to win the war." [15]

5. Post-Mortem

Now that sixty years have passed since the Exclusion Act was adopted, just what can be said about the awful hullabaloo over the Chinese in California? Now that the tumult and the shouting have long since subsided, what can be said in retrospect about

[15] *Survey Graphic*, October 1942.

the long agitation that finally culminated in what is tantamount to total exclusion and the denial of citizenship? Admittedly California was genuinely fearful of the Chinese and this fear had its roots deep in the community. The movement against the Chinese was unquestionably a popular agitation. Such widespread public clamors are seldom wholly without foundation; the people are usually right, but often for the wrong reasons. Today it is possible to appraise the anti-Chinese movement with a measure of accuracy, not only because of the lapse of time, but because of some excellent latter-day research.

No one today can possibly deny that the Chinese made a remarkable contribution to the development of California. They made possible, in a brief period of time, a development that might otherwise have been retarded for years. Their labor was largely responsible for the early completion of the Central Pacific Railroad; they dug the ditches and reclaimed the marshlands; they harvested the crops and worked the abandoned claims in the mines. "Gap-fillers," as Mrs. Coolidge calls them, they fitted the existing shortages in the labor market with an exactness almost made to order. It is incontestable, in retrospect, that they were never a serious economic threat to any group or to any industry in the state. In the mines, for example, they worked only the "played-out diggings." And, while doing so, they paid to the counties of the state upwards of $5,000,000 in the form of a miner's tax which was assessed, in a highly discriminatory manner, against them alone. Recent research has seriously challenged the age-old assumption that the employment of the Chinese in California undermined the position of the "White-American" workman.[16] It is to be doubted, in fact, that the Chinese were ever in *direct* competition with any other labor group; their labor, in almost every respect, tended to *complement* rather than to *supplant* that of other groups. Actually there is good reason to believe that, by their presence, they tended to bolster up rather than to depress the wage standard for so-called "White-American" workers.

[16] See, for example, Dr. Varden Fuller's interesting report to be found in Vol. 54, LaFollette Committee Transcript, p. 19,823 et seq.

The circumstances which provoked the agitation against them were highly exceptional. "White-American" workmen were pouring into the state in tides of migration: in 1868–1869 some 59,000 workers entered California; in 1873–1875 approximately 150,000 arrived. With the Central Pacific Railroad completed in 1869 and a serious national panic in 1873, the labor market was badly disorganized and there were simply not enough jobs for those unemployed. Had there not been a single Chinaman in California during these critical years, virtually the same distress and unrest would have prevailed. That the whole theory of the Chinese as an economic menace was never sound, in point of fact, is indicated by the remarkable rapidity with which the argument against them was shifted from an economic to a so-called biological basis.[17]

The economic argument was, furthermore, extremely short-sighted. "The exclusion law," observes Mr. Wu, "which prevents aliens from coming in, cannot keep capital from going out. Competition between groups in the same economy is in the final analysis inevitable. If people are prevented from competing with one another in the same political region, their goods will still compete in the same world market." A tariff wall may protect the domestic market, but it cannot, in the long run, prevent the competition which, in a free society, must take place in the markets of the world. When the flow of Chinese labor was stopped, that of other groups such as the Japanese and Filipino was stimulated. And when these were stopped, in turn, the importation of Mexicans began. At the same time, American capital was seeking outlets throughout the Far East and in Central and South America and, in many instances, was actually seeking out the so-called cheap labor areas.

Justification for the California attitude exists; but it is not to be found in the realm of economic and biological speculation. The Californians knew, for example, that the movement of Chinese was being artificially stimulated. They knew that the passenger lines had developed a wonderfully profitable two-way traffic in Chinese labor, and that the "masters of foreign vessels

[17] See *Oriental Exclusion* by R. D. McKenzie, 1927, p. 15.

afforded every facility to emigration, distributing placards, maps and pamphlets with highly colored accounts of the Golden Hills, reaping enormous profits as the demands for passages and freights increased." They knew, too, that this entire migration was unsupervised, unregulated, and uncontrolled; and that the federal government showed an almost complete failure to appreciate or to deal with the consequences of this type of migration. That the state could, in fact, have absorbed, to the profit of all concerned, more Chinese than actually arrived prior to the Exclusion Law is today an obvious fact. But at some point the proper controls should have been established by negotiation with the Chinese government and some means should have been devised to assist in the process of adjustment. In default of any such approach, what subsequently happened was more or less inevitable.

America today has nothing to fear from China. In the China that is emerging from the war, an entirely new nation is discernible. It is a nation which, in a relatively short period, will become industrialized. Its standards of living will necessarily tend to approximate those prevailing in other industrialized nations. For if China is going to introduce Western industrialism, as Dr. Wu has said, "it cannot avoid the Western folkways, mores, and social organizations which are inherent in an industrialized civilization." If the bars against Chinese immigration were to be relaxed throughout the Pacific area, there is no likelihood that any nation or area would be overrun with immigrants. A relatively heavy migration to Australia and the Philippine Islands might take place, but both areas can, in fact, support a much larger population in the future than they have in the past. Furthermore, the problem of migration must necessarily be regarded, after the war, as a world problem to be handled by free negotiation and compact between all the nations of the world. No one nation should, therefore, fear inundation. In this world of the future, Chinese walls, such as those erected by English- and Spanish-speaking peoples around the rim of the Pacific against the Orient, can have no place. Having set in motion this wall-against-the-Orient, we should take the initiative in its removal. There will be no place in the future for unilateral treaties and one-sided agreements. Either we adjust our ideas to this new situation or, as Pearl Buck has said, we will permanently ally the Far East against the West.

CHAPTER III

The Forgotten Mexican

SHORTLY after Mexico declared war against the Axis, President Camacho, in a broadcast in Spanish, urged his compatriots in this country "to forget the war of 1846" and reminded them that the United States and Mexico are now allies. That the War of 1846 should still be an active memory among Mexicans, particularly along the border, will doubtless strike many Americans as slightly fantastic. Yet in Mexico maps are still in use, in some of the schools, which carry an overprint designating the territory along the northern border as "territory temporarily in the hands of the United States." It is significant that President Camacho should have addressed his appeal to Mexicans living in the United States. For it is this large group of Mexicans who are, perhaps, most conscious of the memories of the past and most susceptible to anti-American propaganda.

"No other group of aliens in our midst," writes Dr. W. Rex Crawford, "presents a dichotomy so marked as the heterogeneous population loosely labeled Latin Americans."[1] The visitor from South America is lionized in Washington; but "the Mexicans of the southwest, whether they be newly arrived or descendants of older Spanish-speaking settlers, are a submerged, isolated, or forgotten population, whose presence is felt as a weight, a problem, an annoyance." This same dichotomy has frequently puzzled Mexicans in the United States. "When one sees the great sums spent to reconstruct the Spanish missions and other buildings of the Latin-American occupation," writes Jovita Gonzalez de Mireles, "one cannot help but wonder at the inconsistency of things in general. If Anglo-Americans accept their art and culture, why have they not also accepted the people?"[2]

[1] *Annals of the American Academy*, September 1942, p. 123.
[2] *Our Racial and National Minorities*, 1937, p. 509.

When we broadcast Good Neighbor programs in Spanish, it seldom occurs to us that there is a sizable Mexican population in our midst and that the Good Neighbor Policy might very well start here, at home, within our own borders. If the Good Neighbor Policy is to succeed, then we must promptly reconsider the problem presented by this Mexico that lies within the United States. For here is the real, the living, the historical frontier of Latin-American relations. No matter how generous we may be south of the border, our good intentions will be wasted unless we meet the acid test of applying at home what we preach abroad. Unless our domestic attitudes are brought into conformance with our foreign policy, then we risk the charge of inconsistency on still another score. For, as Dr. Crawford states, "when a government changes its policy toward a group of nations, its citizens are likely in their private lives to perpetuate for some time the former attitudes. . . . This lag may lead to the curious and most unfortunate result that the honored guest of the government, if his color be a little dark, is made the object of racial prejudice and discriminatory treatment." It was only a few years ago, as I recall, when the Marine Band, participating in the farewell ceremonies in Washington on the occasion of the departure of a representative of Haiti, played "Bye-Bye Blackbird." The very fact that this lag must be overcome creates the opportunity for a vast improvement in living conditions among resident Latin Americans.

1. Scope of the Problem

No one can state, with even a pretense of statistical accuracy, the number of Mexicans residing within the United States. For years the counts made by the two governments, of movement back and forth across the border, have been in violent disagreement and complete reconciliation of these figures has never been achieved. The problem is further complicated by the fact that, with Mexicans, the distinction between native-born and foreign-born is utterly unrealistic (particularly in the Southwest where the bulk of the Mexicans reside). In Texas and California, for example, the rule obtains that "once a Mexican, always a Mexican." Immigrant stocks of high visibility and low economic status retain their minority status over long periods of time, even though, by birth or naturalization, they may have acquired citizenship. The National Resources Planning Board has stated that the number of Mexicans or persons of Spanish-speaking ancestry in the United States is "about 3,000,000." [3] It is currently estimated that at least 2,000,000 Spanish-speaking people reside in the states of Texas, Colorado, California, Arizona, and New Mexico; and some observers have placed the total for the United States as high as 3,500,000. A special enumeration of the 1940 census listed 1,861,400 people who designated Spanish as their mother tongue, that is, "the principal foreign language, if any, spoken in the home of the person in his earliest childhood." Of this group, the census classified 714,060 as "native-white, foreign, or mixed parentage"; 718,980 as "native white–native parentage"; and 428,360 as foreign born. But there are excellent reasons to believe that these figures minimize the number of Mexicans or Spanish-speaking people in the United States. One reason for the undercount of Mexicans is that the census of 1940 classified Mexicans as "white," in accordance with the procedure followed prior to 1930. Ethnically this procedure may be and unquestionably is sound practice; but sociologically it makes little sense.

Mexicans in the United States may be classified in several different ways: by geographical distribution; by status; and by length of residence. Geographically they are concentrated in the Southwest. The 1940 census showed 1,633,220 living in the South and the West; and only 228,180 living in the North. As to status, Mexicans may be divided into alien and citizen groupings: approximately 500,000 are aliens and the rest are citizens. With respect to length of residence, Mexicans can be regarded as falling into two categories: immigrants and established residents. The size of the immigrant group can only be approximated. According to Mr. Daniel T. Valdes, approximately 1,000,000 Mexicans emigrated to the United States between 1910 and 1930; and, since 1930, some 300,000 have returned to

[3] *The Problems of a Changing Population*, 1938, p. 224.

Mexico.[4] Roughly speaking, therefore, the immigrant group would number around 700,000. In considering the size of the immigrant group, however, it should be kept in mind, as noted by Dr. Crawford, that "if they move back and forth over the frontier with considerable freedom (as they did prior to 1929), their assimilation and approximation to the standard of living of the receiving country is further retarded, although their experience may and usually does have the effect of making them dissatisfied with permanent return to the lower economic level of their country of origin." There is every reason to believe, as pointed out by Dr. Crawford, that the bulk of the Mexicans now living in the United States are here to stay.

From the point of view of cultural adaptation, Mexicans should be classified into a number of distinct "problem groupings," recognizing, of course, that these groupings frequently overlap. It is convenient, therefore, to think of Mexicans as falling into the following categories: the long-resident Spanish-Colonial group, all of whom are citizens; the fairly recent immigrants, most of whom are aliens but who have American-born children who are citizens; and, lastly, older immigrant groups who have become stranded in a number of urban areas.

The Spanish Colonials are primarily concentrated in New Mexico and in the contiguous San Luis Valley in Colorado. Immigration from Mexico has contributed relatively little to the population of New Mexico; in 1930, for example, there were only 16,406 foreign-born Mexicans in the state. By and large, Mexican immigrants have avoided the long-colonized settlements of Spanish-speaking people in New Mexico and Colorado. The number of persons listing Spanish as the mother tongue in these two states in 1940 was as follows: New Mexico, 221,740; Colorado 92,540. Of these totals, the numbers of native whites of native parentage were, respectively, 192,800 and 71,800. In other words, the Mexican or Spanish-speaking population of both states shows a high percentage of native born of native parentage, indicating long residence in this country. These percentages are sharply at variance with those of two other states,

<hr>

[4] *The Spanish Speaking People of the Southwest,* 1938.

California and Texas, both of which have a large Mexican population. According to the 1940 census, there were 416,140 people listing Spanish as the mother tongue in California, of whom, however, only 63,700 were native white, of native parentage. In Texas there were 738,440 Spanish-speaking residents of whom 272,080 fell in the native-white, native-parentage category. The distinction between the Texas-California group and the New Mexico group implies far more than mere comparative length of residence. The group in New Mexico, in addition to long residence in one locality, possess a deeply rooted culture and self-contained economy. They "belong," so to speak, to the landscape and the region; whereas those who have lived for years, and even generations, in Texas and California do not evidence anything like the same degree of cultural, social, or economic solidarity. It is necessary, therefore, to regard each of these groups separately.

2. Mexican Immigrants

Of the Mexican immigrants, most of whom are migratory workers, much has been written. The general circumstances surrounding their recruitment, the manner of their distribution, and details on living and working conditions, have been carefully documented in excellent studies by Dr. Manuel Gamio and Dr. Paul S. Taylor.[5] *In Factories in the Field* and *Ill Fares the Land*, I have already given a detailed account of the vast armies of Mexican migratory workers who follow the crops throughout the Southwest and as far north as Michigan, Montana, Indiana, and Ohio. No point would be served in repeating here the material to be found in these two volumes and in the sources indicated.

Two general considerations, however, should be kept in mind concerning Mexican migratory workers. In the first place, they are a highly mobile group, many of them being more or less habitual interstate migrants. Their very mobility has served to

---

[5] See also *Mexican Migratory Workers of South Texas*, by Selden C. Menefee, WPA, 1941; "Transient Mexican Agricultural Labor" by Lawrence Leslie Waters, *Southwestern Social Science Quarterly*, June 1941.

retard, if not altogether to prevent, opportunities for adjustment and assimilation. In the second place, wherever they go in their long and endless peregrinations, they are socially ostracized and sharply set apart from the resident white communities. For example, approximately 93,100 Mexicans are contract sugar-beet workers. Practices in the sugar-beet industry have long required that the Mexican family migrate as a group, since all or most of the members of the family must work in the fields. (Similar practices are followed in most of the other crops in which Mexicans are employed as agricultural migrants.) As a consequence, the Mexican immigrant continues to speak Spanish, to live among his own group, and to follow his own mode of living. Not even in the most superficial sense does he have an opportunity to become acculturated. These large migratory movements are, moreover, fed from certain central points, such as Los Angeles, El Paso, Denver, and San Antonio, from which the labor is recruited. In these wintering communities, the Mexican migrant lives in a Mexican shacktown, continues to speak Spanish, and remains set apart from the larger community. It has been pointed out, *ad nauseam*, that the Mexican migrant is ill-housed, ill-clothed, and ill-fed. His children are retarded in the schools, and in many areas they do not even attend schools. From every point of view, Mexican migratory workers (most of whom are fairly recent immigrants) constitute a definitely disadvantaged submerged class in our society. They are the victims of a well-organized caste system which dooms them to restricted types of employment, visits upon them a complex and comprehensive system of social discrimination, and makes for chronic maladjustment. This system, moreover, tends by its very nature to be self-perpetuating.

The well-being of these Mexican migrants, who number close to a million men, women, and children, is a matter of the utmost concern to the furtherance and the permanence of the Good Neighbor Policy. Their plight is well-known to Mexican officials. Dr. Manuel Gamio, the historian of Mexican immigration to the United States, is today a highly placed official in the Mexican government. Every "incident" affecting these people has immediate repercussions in Mexico. The significance of the group, in terms of our international relations, is self-evident. In 1928 Dr. Robert McLean estimated, for example, that one eighth of the population of Mexico was residing within the United States. The destiny of these million expatriates cannot help but be a matter of continuing concern to the Republic of Mexico, particularly when the people are so close to Mexico geographically, culturally, and linguistically. Our continued neglect of their well-being not only threatens to jeopardize the Good Neighbor Policy, but materially weakens the national defense effort. Pro-Fascist groups, such as the *Sinarquistas*, have consistently addressed their propaganda to the deep-seated unrest and latent hostility among these people.[6] In an article in the Mexican weekly *Hoy*, of September 20, 1942, a writer states that the Mexicans who went to the United States and later returned are completely useless. They have no energy, he states. "The United States was the *trapiche* (sugar mill) which squeezed out their juice; they returned only *bagazo* (sugar mill waste)." Antagonisms engendered over a period of years cannot be eliminated overnight by a few radio broadcasts in Spanish and occasional gestures of good will. The problem of the Mexican in the United States is, moreover, merely one phase of our general color-caste system; and, as such, it is deeply rooted in American society.

That we have so long been blind to the development of this general color-caste system is largely due to the fact that we have failed to correlate its various phases. In the course of the general westward shift of population, a geographical segregation of racial "color groups" has taken place in the United States: the Negro in the South; the Mexicans in the Southwest; and the Orientals on the Pacific Coast. Oriental and Mexican immigration brought to the Southwest and the Pacific Coast a racially colored population which, over a period of years, has come to be fitted into a status system not distinguishable, in all respects, from that which prevails throughout the Deep South.

The parallel between the Oriental on the Pacific Coast and the

[6] See statement of Ernesto Felix Diaz, *Los Angeles Times*, October 15, 1942.

Mexican in the Southwest is, in many respects, most striking. The growth of large resident elements of both groups was, roughly speaking, somewhat parallel in point of time, with the Mexican element emigrating in large numbers later than the Orientals (principally from 1910 to 1930 but dating from 1900). Just as each successive wave of Oriental immigration — Chinese, Japanese, and Filipino — met with an increasingly hostile resistance, and ultimately with exclusion, so the pattern has developed in the case of the Mexican. As tides of Mexican immigration swept northward across the border, a strong reaction swiftly developed. The argument against them shifted rapidly from the familiar contention that they constituted unfair economic competition to the equally familiar contention that they were "a racially undesirable element." This general sentiment crystallized in the early twenties in the movement to exclude them altogether, just as the Orientals had been excluded earlier. Both the Box Bill and the Harris Bill were designed to restrict Mexican immigration by placing it on a quota basis. While neither measure passed, nevertheless the objectives sought to be accomplished were, in fact, realized. With the creation of the Border Patrol, the strict enforcement of the immigration laws, and by tacit agreement on the part of both countries, all further Mexican immigration virtually ceased in 1929. Thus the final outcome of the anti-Mexican agitation roughly approximated the outcome of the anti-Oriental movement on the Coast. The arguments in favor of and opposed to Mexican immigration followed the familiar pattern of a confused hodgepodge of pseudo-sociological and bogus anthropological nonsense that characterized every hearing on Oriental immigration. In both cases, the issues were kicked around by special-interest groups, with the government of the United States, as such, having virtually nothing to say in the course of the debate and no voice in the outcome.

This singular lack of national concern over a problem of such magnitude as Mexican immigration is, in retrospect, almost incredible. For the movement of over a million Mexican workers to the United States in such a short period of time has been rightly characterized as the most significant mass movement of population between two republics of the Western Hemisphere. It has been a movement fraught with the utmost consequences, not only to the people involved, but to existing relations between the two republics. Although this migration was of enormous social and economic significance, its direction and use, as Mr. Ernesto Galarza has said, was *left to chance* and the self-interest of individuals interested in the exploitation of human labor. "Friendly co-operative international action," remarks Mr. Galarza, "was taken by the governments of the United States and Mexico with regard to the exchange of goods, the adjustment of boundaries and the flow of water, but never, so far as I know, with regard to the flow of working men, women, and children." Just as we utterly ignored the initial migration itself (until we were forced to stop it in the course of a clumsy and irritating display of national self-interest), so we have neglected its continuing consequences. No effort whatever has been made, on a national scale, to assist these immigrants in their adjustment to a radically different environment. Culturally, racially, linguistically, Mexican immigrants are sharply set apart from the general population. Instead of assisting in a process of gradual acculturation, we have abandoned the people to chance and circumstance. And thereby we have permitted the extension to them, as a group, of a caste system which had its origins in a semi-feudal slave economy and which has never been obliterated in the United States. In this system they remain embroiled to this day.

It is interesting to note that Mr. Galarza makes almost the same suggestion, for a proper administrative approach to the problem of Mexican immigration, that Dr. Bruno Lasker made, at an earlier date, in reference to Filipino immigration. "I want to suggest," said Mr. Galarza, speaking on behalf of the Pan-American Union to the members of the Tolan Committee, "that the time has come for the creation of a joint international agency, composed of representatives of the United States and Mexico, to develop and carry out a long term program of resettlement, rehabilitation and regulation of migration between the two republics. This program would be based upon the normal needs of agriculture north of the border, the further development of the land program of Mexico, the utilization of Mexican land resources, with possible United States capital or a joint international fund, and the technical knowledge and skill of citizens of both Mexico and the United States who understand this problem from every angle."

The whole problem of Mexican immigration, about which so much was said and written and so little done between 1920 and 1930, has once again become a lively issue. As our manpower crisis deepens, it is altogether probable that we may be forced, once again, to relax the border regulations and to permit the large-scale importation of thousands of Mexican workers. We are already in the process of admitting 3000 Mexicans for agricultural employment; and thousands more will probably be imported if the war continues. All the more reason, therefore, to concern ourselves with the million or more Mexican immigrants now in the United States, and with the creation of a sound administrative approach to the entire problem. The admirable way in which current importation of Mexican labor is being handled only demonstrates the soundness of such an approach.[7]

3. Mexican Settlements

In order to emphasize some of the special problems that have arisen in connection with Mexican immigration, it might be well to examine a few typical situations. There are, for example, probably upwards of 75,000 Mexican immigrants who today are marooned, so to speak, in urban industrial centers. The Mexican immigrant never secured a strong foothold in American industry, largely by reason of the fact that, in point of time, he arrived on the scene rather late. He arrived in Chicago and Detroit, for instance, even later than the Negro migrant from the Deep South. Despite this fact, however, there are sizable Mexican colonies in such communities as Chicago, Detroit,

[7] See "Migration — the Democratic Way," *Christian Science Monitor*, October 15, 1942.

Flint, Gary, and Bethlehem. The Mexican colony in Chicago numbers upwards of 20,000 today.[8] While relatively insignificant, these Mexican colonies in large urban industrial areas constitute a serious problem. The repatriation movement of the depression had its genesis in the determination of such communities as St. Paul and Chicago to get rid of their Mexican relief cases. In these urban areas, the Mexican immigrant is at a distinct disadvantage, even by comparison with the American Negro. He has had slight industrial experience and finds almost insuperable obstacles in the way of adjustment to this particular type of environment. Isolated as he is from large centers of Mexican population, what remains of his traditional culture rapidly disintegrates and he presents a serious problem of personal and group disorganization.

Much the same situation exists in the urban communities in the Southwest from which Mexican workers are recruited for employment in agriculture. San Antonio may be taken as a typical urban community of this variety. It is estimated that 100,000 or more Mexicans reside in San Antonio for at least a portion of the year. They constitute more than one third of the total population of the city; and some have placed the estimate as high as 65 per cent. While Mexicans have lived in San Antonio for years, even for generations, nevertheless they have not achieved that deep-rooted social solidarity which prevails in New Mexico. The San Antonio Mexicans are, for the most part, rootless semi-urbanized workers. That they constitute *the social problem* of San Antonio has long been acknowledged. "There is no disagreement," states the Public Welfare Survey of San Antonio of 1940, "with the notion that the Mexican problem is as difficult as a city ever had to cope with. Whatever their number — 40 per cent or more or less — they admittedly comprise the most needy segment of the community. Many of them are dependent upon one form or another of public assistance, and in this community that is a meagre subsistence indeed. The worst housing conditions in the city are on the West Side in the heart of the Mexican district. The highest amount of illiteracy is to be found among them. Family life is broken down

[8] See *The Mexican in Chicago* by Robert C. Jones and Louis R. Wilson.

among them more than in any other group because more children and more mothers work. More Mexican children are out of school than of any other segment of the population."

Approximately 56 per cent of the dwellers in substandard housing are Mexicans; over 55 per cent of all juvenile arrests in 1938 were of Mexican children; the city's high death rates for infant mortality and tuberculosis are primarily attributable to the high rates among the resident Mexican population (72 per cent of all tuberculosis deaths in San Antonio are among Mexicans). The Mexican infant mortality rate, 120 per 1000 live births, is one of the highest in the nation. Almost nine tenths of the city's 14,462 illiterates are Mexicans, the proportion of illiteracy for the group being 15.7 per cent. Over 3000 Mexican children of school age have never entered the public schools of San Antonio. The percentage of Mexican youngsters graduating from high school is extremely small; the number who enter college negligible. Among the Anglo-Americans the tuberculosis death rate is 52.8 per 100,000 population; among the Latin Americans it is 302.7. Accompanying this general situation is, as might be expected, a serious problem of social discrimination which belies the fundamental concepts of the Good Neighbor Policy.

The Mexicans object to the use of the term "white" in such a way as to exclude Mexicans. They prefer to call whites of European extraction "Anglo-Americans" or "Anglos." The Mexicans are conscious of such Spanish blood as they may have, and are not ashamed of their predominantly Indian blood. They jealously guard against any move that would set them apart from the self-styled "white race."

The Mexican is nevertheless segregated from the rest of the community almost as effectively as the Negro. He is not kept apart from the Anglo-Americans in lavatories, waiting rooms, and public vehicles by law as is the Negro, but his poverty and low wages segregate him in the poorest sections of the city, in the day coaches of the railroads, in the balconies of the less pretentious theaters, and in the cheapest restaurants. These circumstances tend to perpetuate the social handicaps under which the Mexicans are forced to live.[9]

[9] *The Pecan Shellers of San Antonio* by Selden C. Menefee and Orin C. Cassmore, WPA monograph, 1940, p. 51.

In measuring the seriousness of such a problem, it should be kept in mind that, whereas Mexicans constitute a large racial minority in San Antonio today, at their present rate of increase they will soon become a racial majority. Nor has the war, and the resultant stimulation of employment, altogether changed the situation. According to W. F. Montavon of the National Catholic Welfare Conference, there are 20,000 or more Mexicans in San Antonio living in swamps in miserable huts and utter destitution.[10]

As a matter of fact, the present war has only served to bring to the surface tensions and pressures which have long been repressed within the Mexican immigrant group. The character of the problem has, in fact, radically changed. Since the Mexican is the newest of the large immigrant groups (the fourth largest in the United States), a large second generation born of parents of Mexican nationality is only now coming to maturity.[11] Unlike their parents, this generation knows nothing of Mexico. They have been born, reared, and educated (after a fashion) in this country. But they come from Spanish-speaking homes, they live in Mexican shacktown slums, and, as a group, they are violently maladjusted. As youngsters they have been denied many educational and recreational facilities, while, at the same time, their appetite for the excitements of American life has been inordinately stimulated. The traditional restraints of family, culture, and church have little application to them as a group. Mexican family life and Mexican culture have become disorganized and chaotic, while the Church has ceased to be a dominant influence in their lives. Social discrimination has, also, served to make them extremely race-conscious. In a sense, therefore, this second-generation group presents the real problem so far as the Mexican immigrants are concerned.

Just how acute the problem actually is may be illustrated by reference to the situation in Los Angeles County. Some 219,000 Mexicans reside in the County of Los Angeles, of whom 36,410 are between the ages of six and seventeen. From grammar-

---

[10] *New Republic*, August 24, 1941.
[11] See *Recent Social Trends*, Vol. I, 1933, p. 562.

school days on, these Mexican youngsters have formed "gangs" and have indulged in their share of petty crime. There are Mexican districts in Los Angeles in which it is possible to find a case of juvenile delinquency in almost every family living in the neighborhood. With the loosening of traditional restraints occasioned by the war, these *pachuco* gangs have engaged in open internecine warfare. In the first week of August 1942, two murders and a number of serious assaults resulted from inter-gang strife. In an effort to check further outbreaks, the police, in one master raid, arrested over 300 Mexican youngsters. "The biggest roundup since prohibition days," commented the *Los Angeles Times.* Evidencing no understanding whatever of the background of the problem, police officials, juvenile probation officers, and even the juvenile court judges have announced a highly repressive campaign in which the "kid gloves are off." This terroristic campaign has rapidly spread throughout the county and has had echoes in most of the citrus-belt Mexican communities and even in San Diego. In the course of the investigation, police officials discovered that Mexican gangs were well organized; that each gang had its own uniform — that is, wore black shirts or green shirts; and that in the background of the whole movement were elements of conscious political motivation. At the very moment when Vice-President Henry Wallace and a representative of President Camacho were exchanging Good Neighbor greetings on the steps of the State Building in Los Angeles, the local press was featuring stories of "Mexican Gang Warfare." Shortly afterwards it was reported that the United States monitoring service had recorded "a deluge of broadcasts from Germany to Latin America exploiting the predicament in which Mexicans in Los Angeles find themselves." [12] In view of existing conditions, it was positively embarrassing to hear Vice-President Wallace state, as he did in Los Angeles on September 16, 1942, that "California had become a fusion ground for the two cultures of the Americas." For the essence of the problem in California is that no such fusion has taken place.

[12] *The Americans,* October 19, 1942, p. 3.

In all of these situations — in Chicago, San Antonio, Los Angeles — the problem is not merely that of bad housing, inadequate educational and recreational facilities, and a serious public health condition. Nor is it merely a question of restricted employment opportunities and social discrimination. These are, in large part, but symptoms of cultural maladjustment. By concentrating upon unrelated aspects of the problem we are somewhat in the position of not being able to see the forest for the trees. What the Mexican problem involves is long-standing cultural conflict rather than individual maladjustment. That this is the heart of the problem becomes abundantly clear when the old Spanish-speaking settlements in the United States are examined. In the areas where these settlements are located no social discrimination exists and employment opportunities are not monopolized by white Americans, yet the evidence of cultural maladjustment, and its resulting social problems, is overwhelmingly apparent.

4. The Hispanos

It comes as something of a shock to most Americans to realize that New Mexico is predominantly a Spanish-speaking state. With a population of 531,818 in 1940, some 221,740 New Mexicans listed Spanish as their mother tongue. In 1940 Dr. Sigurd Johansen estimated that 49.1 per cent of the population of the state consisted of Spanish Americans, or *Hispanos* as they are called. Both Spanish and English are official languages in the state of New Mexico. In each of 15 out of 31 counties, Hispanos comprise 50 per cent or more of the population and these 15 counties have almost three fifths of the entire population. In each of seven counties, the Spanish-speaking people constitute more than 80 per cent of the population. These New Mexico Hispanos are not recent immigrants; on the contrary, 90 per cent or more are descendants of the early Spanish colonists.

For the most part, the Hispanos are concentrated today as yesterday in the Rio Grande Valley and along the numerous tributaries of the river. Here is, perhaps, the oldest agricultural settlement in America; the Pueblo Indians have practised agriculture in the valley for over a thousand years. The initial conquest of New Mexico began, of course, with Coronado's exploration of the Rio Grande in 1540. The establishment of Spanish colonies in the valley dates from 1598. Following the Indian uprising of 1692, the area was again conquered and new settlements began to appear: Bernalillo in 1700; Albuquerque in 1706; Los Lunas in 1716; Tome in 1739; and Belen in 1742. The early Spanish colonists brought with them a highly integrated pattern of social life, built largely around the church and the family. As New Mexico was virtually isolated from the rest of the world, and from its main currents, events, and developments from 1540 to 1846, this pattern of social life became firmly imbedded in the region. Not only was Spanish culture deeply implanted in the valley, but the people themselves became in time, as they remain today, a homogeneous, genetic aggregation. As Mr. John Russell has pointed out, these Hispanos "are alike physically and in behavior. Born in the same region, they came from parents alike in race, and in physical type. Although there has been considerable intermarriage with the Indian tribes, at present the descendants seem to have taken on characteristics which differentiate them from the Indians. They learn the same language and have similar cultural forms. Thus, they think alike, talk alike, differing only as individuals, but more alike in their social behavior than different. They are race conscious and possess a distinctive historical and traditional background." The New Mexican's whole life, as Dr. George Sanchez has said in his truly remarkable book, *Forgotten People: A Study of New Mexicans*, "revolved around a primitive agricultural economy which stifled initiative and which gave little hope for the future. New ideas from the outside world rarely reached him. His language, his customs, and his technology remained those of sixteenth century Spain."

Following the War of 1846, the United States acquired, in addition to a vast domain, a sizable alien population who overnight became citizens of this country, at least in name. At the time of the annexation of New Mexico, the population of the state was approximately 61,547 and, for the most part, consisted of the descendants of the original Spanish colonists. Recognizing that these people constituted, at the time, a distinct ethnic group, with their own language, culture, economy, and law, just how did we go about the business of incorporating them *as a people* into the main current of American life and culture? Just what methods were used to adjust this primitive society to the American society of the times? The Treaty of Guadalupe Hidalgo (1848) carefully defined borders and boundaries; it stipulated a price to be paid for the territories annexed; but it contained only vague and general provisions for the individual rights of the peoples inhabiting these lands and no provisions whatever for the protection of the society of which they were a part. The treaty, as Dr. Sanchez observed, failed utterly to make provision for the rights of these people as a society. On the contrary, it was blandly assumed that somehow, by chance or otherwise, the social reality would adjust to the juridical reality established by the treaty. But, to quote Dr. Sanchez, "the New Mexican is not yet an American culturally, the Treaty of Guadalupe notwithstanding."

We did not even bother to organize a territorial government in New Mexico until 1851; and the state was not admitted to the Union until 1912. Prior to 1890, there was virtually no public school system in the state. Even after a school system was established, it remained for years utterly inadequate from the standpoint both of organization and of techniques. As late as 1903, more than half of the school population was not in attendance in the existing schools. Over 24 per cent of the native white males of voting age were illiterate in 1900; and according to the Census of 1940 there are 26,488 residents of the state, twenty-five years of age or older, who have not completed one year of school. In making belated land grants for educational purposes, Congress never bothered to appraise its responsibilities to the native people of the region. "It failed to take note of the fact," writes Dr. Sanchez, "that these people were, in effect, subject peoples of a culture and of a way of life radically different from that into which they were suddenly and unwittingly thrust by a treaty. The government also failed to appreciate the fact that the territory lacked the economic resources, the leadership, and *the administrative devices* necessary to launch an effective program of cultural rehabilitation." As a consequence, the Hispanos were utterly unprepared to meet the problems of social change which arose both before and after statehood was acquired. Nor are they much better prepared today, for, as Dr. Sanchez has said, "they breathe their own cultural inadequacy. They are unprepared to act in their new environment — unprepared because of centuries of isolation. They have no tradition of competition, of education, or of western civilization beyond the sixteenth century."

Despite the fact that the Hispanos constitute a numerical majority in New Mexico and that they are all citizens, nevertheless the great masses of their people remain a severely handicapped social and economic group. Although they clearly hold the balance of political power in New Mexico, and are actively interested in politics, their cultural inadequacy frustrates an effective use of this power.[18] As Dr. Sanchez has said, "their status is one of privation and want, of cultural inadequacy and of bewilderment. Neglected for more than two hundred years as Spanish colonials and Mexicans, their cultural situation was not greatly improved by the territorial regime. In fact, the little improvement that took place through the limited educational efforts that were made in their behalf was more than offset by the social and economic decline that resulted from the influx of new peoples and of a new economic order."

Wherever the highest proportions of Spanish-speaking people reside in New Mexico, there you will find the highest illiteracy rates, the worst public health conditions, the worst housing, the lowest income levels, and the most poverty. A few figures tell the story: —

In 1930, 13.3 per cent of the population of New Mexico was illiterate.

Children from Spanish-speaking homes constitute one half of the

[18] See the chapter on New Mexico politics in *Rocky Mountain Politics*, Albuquerque, 1940.

school enrollment, but make up less than one fifth of the enrollment in the twelfth grade.

Of almost 60,000 Spanish-speaking children enrolled in schools, more than half are in the first three grades.

As the percentage of Spanish-speaking population increases, educational opportunities decrease.

New Mexico, with a death rate of 13.8, has almost 3 deaths more per 1000 population than the national average.

The counties with the highest death rates are uniformly those where the Spanish-speaking people constitute more than 50 per cent of the population. In Mora County, almost 80 per cent of the deaths were from *unknown* causes!

The counties with the largest Spanish-speaking population are also the poorest counties — the higher the percentage of Spanish-speaking people the lower the per capita assessed valuation.

Compared with a national rate of 57 deaths per 1000 live births, New Mexico had a rate of 118 — the highest in the nation.

Tuberculosis death rates are the highest in the nation in New Mexico.

In 1930, the percentage of illiteracy in New Mexico was over three times as high as in the entire United States.

These figures tell their own story, and further comment would be superfluous.

In summarizing the responsibility for this sorry state of affairs, Dr. Sanchez writes: "The generally inferior status held by the native New Mexican today is, in large measure, a result of the failure of the United States to recognize the *special character* of the social responsibility it assumed when it brought these people forcibly into the American society. Granting them technical citizenship did not discharge that responsibility." The problem is not political; it has much deeper implications since it involves, basically, the problem of cultural contact. Again and again Dr. Sanchez has occasion to emphasize the *special character* of the problems, both specific and general, faced by the Hispano. It was, therefore, childishly naïve to expect that adjustment between two societies and cultures so fundamentally different would automatically result after annexation.

Far from recognizing the special character of the problem

(which would have indicated at once the necessity for a special-ized approach), we have consistently pretended that no such problem existed. The resultant failure of policy may be variously illustrated. In the first place, as Dr. Sanchez observes, no or-ganized effort was ever made to compile and to assemble the available information which, had it been done, would clearly have indicated the special character of the problem involved. "Isolated agencies," he writes, "and individuals have made re-searches and, on occasion, have inaugurated action programs of limited scope. At no time, however, have these efforts been co-ordinated nor has joint study ever been given to the various phases of the minority problem of the area."

From the point of view of educational policy, no recognition has ever been made of the special character of the problem in New Mexico. The Spanish Americans of New Mexico are not in the same situation as the other racial minorities in the United States. Most immigrant groups in America are distant from the countries in which the culture of their race and language flour-ished. But the Spanish American of New Mexico, as Dr. Antonio Rebolledo has pointed out, is "the racial continuation of the great Spanish-American family of the American continent, be-ginning in Cape Horn and ending here. New Mexico is the geo-graphical prolongation of Spanish America in United States territory." [14] Furthermore, Spanish has always been spoken in the state; and annexation in no wise changed the situation. Spanish, one might almost say, is indigenous to the region. But it has only been of recent years that serious consideration has been given to the possibility of bilingual instruction, particularly to make use of Spanish as an initial instrument to retain child-hood experiences and to acquire transferable concepts. The Spanish-speaking child comes to the public schools without a word of English and without "the environmental experience upon which school life is based." That such a child is likely to be retarded is, therefore, a foregone conclusion. As Dr. Sanchez states, "the use of standard curricula, books, and ma-terials among these children is a ridiculous gesture." Bilingual

[14] *New Mexico Quarterly Review*, February 1942, p. 27.

instruction does not signify neglect of English; on the contrary, it would establish the basis upon which a real and workable knowledge of English might be predicated. Preliminary instruction in Spanish, in the schools, is a necessary complement of standard instruction in order to achieve ends that cannot be gained by the use of English. Through Spanish, also, government programs, in public health and in agriculture, could be brought home to the people in the most immediate and practical way. Ultimately, as Dr. Rebolledo has said, "through Spanish will come the consciousness of his [the individual's] own worth, the affirmation of his own personality, and the desire for social refinement and spiritual culture that will elevate him in his own estimation and enhance his prestige among the other racial groups of the state."

When New Mexico was annexed, we made the gratuitous assumption that its economic resources would enable the people to attain standards of living such as prevailed elsewhere in the United States. But we made no such assumption in the case of the American Indian, the Filipino, or the Puerto Rican, who also were subject peoples. Recognizing his cultural disabilities, we threw special safeguards around the American Indian. But although the Hispano was in much the same position as the Indian, we failed to recognize his status and the proper measures for his incorporation into American practices and institutions were never taken. No one protected the Hispano in his property rights or set up special schools for his guidance or gave special attention to his peculiar agricultural problems. On the contrary, as Dr. Sanchez has observed, "instead of safeguarding him in his land and water rights, government has inadvertently deprived him of those rights through taxation, through the expansion of Indian lands, and by placing him at the mercy of unrestricted economic competition."

After the advent of the New Deal, general economic rehabilitation measures were attempted in New Mexico, but again without any effort being made to understand the special character of the problems involved, particularly their cultural aspect. Policies suitable for agricultural rehabilitation in Iowa were stupidly applied in the Tewa Basin of New Mexico, where 85 per cent of the farming is subsistence noncommercial agriculture. Every loan was individually conceived, every rehabilitation plan was an individual plan; every farmer was regarded as distinct and so was his neighbor; each failure was a special case and likewise each success. Every problem was regarded as "unitary, discrete, and exceptional." No effort was made to understand that it was a collective adjustment which the economy of the region required and that it was the entire economy which was deficient. To make loans repayable with interest to these subsistence farmers was economic suicide. Naturally such rehabilitation measures failed as they were destined to from the outset.

"What happened to the Spanish-speaking people," writes Mr. Allen Harper, "was inevitable in the circumstances, and it is probably true that, looking at the ensuing havoc from the vantage point of the present, it is lamentable that some special protection should not have been provided by our federal government. Perhaps, as some believe, a kind of wardship like that by which the Indians have benefited should have been thrown around them in the difficult transition of readjusting their way of life to the conditions which were inherent in the advent of frontier expansion. No such special protection, however, was extended. There ensued social and economic dislocations, injustices, losses of land, and a general worsening of the Spanish-speaking peoples' economic and social position within the framework of frontier and territorial conditions." To appreciate the aptness of this expert comment it is necessary to take a look at the havoc which has been wrought in the village agricultural economy of New Mexico.

Before turning to the villages, however, two qualifications should be noted to what has been previously said in this section. American economic and cultural penetration of New Mexico had begun prior to 1846; in fact, the beginnings of the move to incorporate New Mexico into a continental economy may be traced to the developing Santa Fe trade of the 1820's. Annexation, therefore, merely accelerated a process already well under way by 1846. In the conflict that subsequently ensued, and which still continues, no question is involved of the inferiority of one culture by comparison with the other. Technically the Anglo culture may have been more efficient (a debatable point); socially the Hispano culture was probably superior. Hispanos might, in fact, have competed with Anglos successfully, if annexation had not also involved an enormous shift of power. This shift in economic power may be variously illustrated. In 1827, some 240,000 sheep were counted in New Mexico; in 1860, 830,000; in 1880, 4,000,000. The increase in the number of sheep merely represents the increasingly important role played by large-scale Anglo enterprise in New Mexico. With the development of large commercial cattle and sheep operations, huge investments of capital from "the states" and even from foreign countries were made in New Mexico. Underlying the entire shift in power, and basic to the whole problem, was the manipulation of Spanish land grants effected by the so-called "Santa Fe Ring," an unholy alliance of Anglo lawyers and power politicians. That land grants were corruptly and dishonestly manipulated can be readily demonstrated by reference to an article by George W. Julian, who became Surveyor General of New Mexico in 1885.[15] In appointing Julian, President Cleveland stated that he was anxious to break up the "ring" in New Mexico Territory. In the fight that followed, however, the "ring" bested Mr. Julian.[16] "Cultural inadequacy," therefore, does not tell the whole story.

5. Village Life

Along the Rio Grande River in New Mexico, and its numerous tributaries, are located some of the most fascinating and fabulous villages in America. In such villages as Nambe, Chimayo (founded in 1692), Cundiyo, Cordova, and Truchas, one can visit today communities which have remained almost wholly unaffected by world developments during the last two hundred years. Inhabited by the descendants of the original Spanish

---

[15] "Land Stealing in New Mexico," *North American Review*, May 1887.
[16] See Twitchell, *Old Santa Fe*, 1925, p. 411.

colonists, these villagers still speak the Spanish of the time of Cervantes. To visit the villages is not only to form an intense admiration for the people themselves, but to become deeply impressed with the integrity of their social life and of their culture. For these are really living peoples and theirs is a genuine folk culture.

Many of these villages are the outgrowth of community land grants made at the time of the Spanish conquest; some of the grants are, in fact, still administered by elected trustees on behalf of the entire community. In making these grants there was much overlapping and boundaries were not clearly defined. But the people themselves never regarded titles as important; they have always had a sense of the value of use and occupancy, but never a sense of the value of individual ownership. Isolated farmhouses are rare in New Mexico; the pattern is everywhere — in the Spanish-speaking areas — that of the village or semi-communal type of agriculture. All of the Hispano villages are laid out in accordance with a similar pattern. There is the plaza, from which the four principal streets lead outward; and then the building lots, or *solares*, for the settlers' homes. Around the villages are the *zuertes*, or agricultural plots, on which the people raise their own corn, wheat, beans, squash, and fruit. Beyond the small irrigated plots is (or rather was) the *ejido*, or town common, used for grazing stock and as a source of fuel and building wood; and beyond the *ejido* is the *dehesa* or community pasture. During both the Spanish and the Mexican period, no taxes were levied on land, taxes being laid only on the products of the land and being payable in kind. In these villages, a distinctly self-sufficient noncommercial agriculture was practised. Grains were milled in the community-owned or private mills; cloth was woven from wool and cotton in the home; footwear was manufactured by village craftsmen, as were also tools, cooking utensils, and other household goods. Trade was limited and money was virtually unknown. Lost in time and in space, these villages acquired the character of a distinct racial and cultural society. While there was some intermarriage with Indians at an early date, there has been virtually no intermarriage within the memory of the oldest living inhabitants.

The degree of social compactness which still prevails in these villages is, indeed, amazing. The hold of village, family, and church is still very strong. The village of Cundiyo, with a population of 122 people, is entirely made up of persons with the surname of Vigil. Village and family are, in many instances, almost synonymous terms. So close are family ties, in fact, that to remove or to resettle one family might conceivably interfere with or even threaten the existence of the social structure of a particular village. Because of the old-established social controls that still prevail, thievery and plundering are almost unknown and crime of any sort is most exceptional. Custom, rather than law, rules their lives. So strong is the sense of community among these people that individuals are identified as much by the community in which they live as by family name. "To be born into a community is to inherit an identification with it that is never forgotten." [17]

Most of these villages are still isolated; many of them are extremely difficult to find and can only be reached by barely passable roads. There are few automobiles, scarcely any radios, and no telephones. In studies that have been made, it has been found that 85 per cent of the villagers, in these typical settlements, receive no outside mail. An "Anglo," in fact, is seldom seen. Agricultural machinery, as such, is virtually nonexistent, and most of the available implements are handmade. Old water-driven stone mills, incredibly ancient and crude, are still in use. In many of these villages may be found some of the most interesting specimens of church architecture in America. Some of the villages themselves are indescribably picturesque and lovely. Truchas, at 8000 feet elevation, perched on the edge of a 500-foot canyon wall, presents one of the most fantastic sights in America. That such a village actually exists in America is essentially incredible.

With the advent of United States sovereignty and the en-

[17] See *Culture of a Contemporary Rural Community*, by Messrs. Leonard and Loomis, 1941.

suing influx of an "Anglo" population, intense pressures were brought to bear upon the Spanish-American settlements. New concepts and new values, difficult enough in themselves to grasp, were injected into the villages; and were beclouded, as Mr. Harper has observed, by the difference in language. With American sovereignty there also came new laws, a new land system, and a money tax. "There came," as Mr. Harper writes, "eastern and English capital seeking investment. Large sheep and cattle enterprises developed and commercial trading was introduced. There came also the Anglos, seeking more than a mere subsistence livelihood. There came the dry farmers. There came the homesteaders who settled out on the range near desirable water holes, to whom the highway was the connecting link with store, church and school, instead of the village." There developed the usual sharp frontier practices, the same unsavory trafficking in land grants that occurred in Texas and California, and the same shady real-estate deals and manipulations. Many of the original land grants were not validated; others were sold for taxes. In area after area in New Mexico, the Hispanos lost their once vast holdings. The mesa lands were taken up by homesteaders and large sheep and cattle concerns; the forests passed into the hands of American investors and were soon despoiled; the community grazing and pasture lands drifted out of Hispano use and control. For a century, now, there has been a continuous sharpening of the competition between commercial and noncommercial users of the resources of the region. As this competition has sharpened, the Hispano has been driven inward upon his limited village resources. He has lost virtually everything except the village lot itself and a small plot of irrigated land. This he holds onto with amazing tenacity, refusing to sell it to the Anglo or to mortgage it. Having no system of primogeniture, village holdings have, through inheritance, become minutely divided and subdivided. The average holding per family today is between three and four acres. Usually the lands are divided into narrow strips running at right angles to the irrigation ditch or canal. As the Hispano has been driven inward upon the village itself, the pressure of population upon resources has intensified.

The average number of persons per square mile in New Mexico, in 1930, was 3.5, but in the irrigated areas this density reaches 500 persons per square mile.

For many years the villagers managed to survive, in the face of intense competition for land, by seeking employment outside the area. Prior to 1930, it was estimated that as many as 10,000 Hispanos (usually one person in every family) sought outside seasonal employment: in sugar beets and potatoes; in the mines and on the railroads; in the sheep camps of Colorado and Utah, Wyoming and Montana. But estimated seasonal earnings for the entire group dropped from around $2,000,000 in 1930 to less than $350,000 in 1937; while the number of migratory workers fell from 10,000 to around 2000. With no outside employment available, the number of persons residing in the villages increased and, during the depression, there was a decided movement of population back to the villages. The population of many has, in fact, actually increased in this manner. In most of the villages today there are not enough available resources to care for more than one fourth of the present residents. When efforts have been made to expand the land base, as by the creation of the Rio Grande Conservancy District in 1927, the resultant increase in taxes and assessments forced a majority of the small landowners and villagers to part with title to their tiny holdings and join the ranks of the landless. The Rio Grande Conservancy District added 100,000 acres of cultivable land; but it was a positive curse to the villagers, for here was a type of collectively imposed debt which they could not escape.

The pressure of population upon resources even began to be reflected in the diet of the Hispano. In the circumstances in which he found himself, the planting of beans and grain offered two distinct and not inconsiderable advantages: such crops could be consumed alike by animals and by human beings and they were easily grown and readily stored. The brilliant research of Dr. Michel Pijoan has shown what disastrous effects this dependence upon a diet high in carbohydrates has had upon the Hispano. In villages studied by Dr. Pijoan the incidence of rickets, in the first decade of life, was found to run as high as 84 per cent. He found, also, that only about 60 per cent of the children reach adult life. To keep these undernourished children in school is, according to Dr. Pijoan, a kind of cruelty. They lack the energy to learn. Most of the villages, of course, have no hospitals or any readily available medical service. In any number of villages studied by the Soil Conservation Service, in an admirable piece of research directed by Mr. Hugh Calkins and Dr. Eshref Shevky, it was found that about 90 per cent of the births were delivered by midwives.

Why, under these circumstances, do the villages refuse to migrate? Why, it will be asked, do they stay in such poverty-ridden areas? Many of the people freely admit that they would be much better off were they to migrate. But the explanation for their refusal to leave must be sought, as Messrs. Leonard and Loomis note, "among such subtle factors as the attitudes and values of the people, the importance of community and religion, the integration and solidarity of the family, and the place of the individual in it all." Social solidarity in these villages was such that, in the face of the most intense competition, they could and did resist change for years. As a matter of fact, the external pressures seemed to have had the effect of increasing rather than decreasing this social cohesiveness. But their resources are now so low that most of the villagers realize that change is imminent. And this change they fear since, to many of them, it means the abandonment of many cherished values and customs which have given meaning, purpose, and dignity to their lives. Only within the last ten years, in fact, has this remarkable social solidarity shown visible signs of disintegration. "Among the people of this area today," write Messrs. Leonard and Loomis, "is to be found a growing feeling of futility, a general sense of inability to cope with circumstances as they exist."

Of recent years, however, some observers have noticed numerous indications that the Hispano culture pattern is in process of change, perhaps of disintegration. In the past, geographical isolation resulted from the absence of open-country population around the Hispano villages; cultural isolation resulted, in part, from the language barrier. Gradually both types of isolation have been broken down and a degree of inter-group cultural exchange has developed. This process would now go forward rapidly, if it were not for the inertia which prevails. "The lack of opportunity to satisfy new wants and desires," writes Dr. Sigurd Johansen,[18] "has resulted in a feeling of dissatisfaction on the part of many children and young people. Family solidarity is also feeling the effect of the influence of outside contacts. Family mores are no longer as binding as they once were." Similarly there is evidence that the influence of the Church — once a strong factor in group solidarity — has become less effective, particularly insofar as the younger people are concerned. New patterns might be readily superimposed on the existing culture, if this culture were to be used as the basis upon which to proceed. But haphazard weakening, at different levels, of the existing culture tends to destroy its capacity for adjustment. So violent have been the social changes which have occurred of recent years that, in the opinion of Dr. Johansen, the mechanisms do not seem to exist in the culture of the Spanish-American people by which an adjustment might be made. "New forces," he writes, "must be brought into play if the problems of these people are to be solved." To some extent, the people themselves recognize this necessity, as witness the program of the League of United Latin American Citizens (formed in 1929).

6. Promise and Realization

Faced with this situation there are, of course, many Americans who will say that the threatened liquidation of the Spanish American and his culture was predestined from the outset; that no noncompetitive economy can possibly survive in the midst of our competitive American economy; and that the sooner these anachronistic islands, these isolated and compact communities, disappear the better for all concerned. But such a view is not only partial; it is amazingly shortsighted. As a matter

[18] "The Social Organization of Spanish-American Villages," 1942, an unpublished paper.

of fact it is of the unmost importance that the essentials of this culture and this way of life be preserved. Preservation naturally implies adaptation and change, and the introduction of superior techniques; but all of this can be accomplished while preserving the enduring values which adhere in these communities. That there are such values is self-evident; otherwise these communities would have gone to pieces fifty years ago. The best proof of the statement is to know the people themselves, for to know them, even to see them, is to form a great admiration for their sense of personal dignity, their charm of manner, and the social values which they have kept intact. There are elements in their agriculture which we can, in fact, study with great profit. For with the possible exception of the rapidly disappearing Mormon villages, the Hispano villages represent the last vestiges of a semicommunal form of agriculture in America. Here most of the tools and implements, primitive as they may be, are nevertheless owned, used, and shared in common. Here the villagers live and work together as a compact social group, planting, cultivating, irrigating, and harvesting their crops together. These villages should be preserved, not as antique representations of a forgotten way of life, but as a pattern of a rural living which has much to commend itself to us at the present time. The almost complete absence of class distinctions in this society should also be noted. Today life is stagnant in the villages and most of the people are sustained by one form or another of public relief and assistance. But if we were to give serious consideration to the task of assisting in the total readjustment of the entire area and economy — as a working and functioning whole — its people and their culture, to our technology, culture, and economy, then these villages might take a new lease on life; conceivably they might endure for another three hundred years. But this can only be done if we realize the special character of the problem itself and if we desire the special administrative techniques to assist in such a process of creative adjustment, involving as it does the revitalizing of the existing culture and economy.

New Mexico, like Hawaii, has much to teach the entire nation on the score of racial tolerance. Indians, Hispanos, and Anglos have lived side by side in the Rio Grande Valley for years and, so far as social relations are concerned, tolerance prevails. There is no miscegenation statute in New Mexico; nor has there ever been one. Because of the large resident Hispano population, social discrimination has never been tolerated. Both Indians and Mexicans (including native-born Hispanos) have free and equal access to public institutions, hotels, barbershops, and places of amusement. In this respect, the situation is totally at variance with, say, Texas and California practice, where the rankest social discrimination prevails. This favorable social milieu is, indeed, a national asset of inestimable value, if we would only appreciate its true significance. For New Mexico, which is a predominantly Spanish state, is really the key to the problem of permanently improving Latin-American relations and in bringing about a real *rapprochement* between the two cultures of the Western Hemisphere.

All one needs to do, in order to appreciate New Mexico's possibilities in the field of Latin-American relations, is to listen to the words of Dr. Joaquin Ortega of the University of New Mexico: —

I am convinced [he writes] that New Mexico has a significant contribution to make to *national* and *international* understanding.

Nationally, New Mexico should lead in offering norms for the solution of difficult problems of adjustment presented by the minority of over three and one-half million people of Spanish descent and speech who live within our borders. These problems are aggravated by intolerance on the part of some members of the dominant Anglo-Saxon group, and the concomitant resistance on the part of the dominated to lose their identity to an unkind people. When a so-called "superior" culture wants to superimpose itself upon another, it must do so persuasively, for otherwise the "attacked" culture in a natural move of self-assertion and self-preservation (which is, by the way, the measure of its strength) instead of acceding to assimilation maintains stubbornly its own practices. Here in New Mexico lives the most cohesive Hispanic population in the United States, the one most faithful to a long and uninterrupted tradition of identification with the soil. Here in New Mexico the Hispanic population still wields political power and can in good measure be the master of its destiny. Here in New Mexico one encounters fewer antagonistic attitudes — far from perfect as the situation is — than in other states. Fraternity among the various groups in the Southwest may be impossible. Human nature is recalcitrant. Let us strive just for the good old American principle of *equal opportunity*, which today hardly exists. That will be a sufficient goal. The population of New Mexico ought to lead in a policy of *rapprochement*. By working out this cultural adjustment in a generous and rational manner, New Mexico could perform a great service to the Union, and receive for it a commensurate reward.

Internationally, New Mexico is destined to be the bridge between the two Americas. This state is the shortest route to Mexican good will. To work in close harmony with Mexico and heal the open sore created in the Pan-American body by the distressing situation of Mexican citizens and Mexican descendants in the midst of our vaunted democracy is more important now than ever, for Mexico is a key country in our defense, and Mexico exerts a profound intellectual influence in Latin America, particularly so in the Caribbean region. The job is at the same time one of intrinsic social justice and of sound international politics.

This point of view is by no means restricted to academic circles in New Mexico. While it is not understood by all of the Hispanos, it is something which most of them feel. And it has also found eloquent political articulation by Senator Dennis Chavez of New Mexico, himself an Hispano. In a statement issued on June 13, 1942, Senator Chavez called upon the nation to put a stop to racial intolerance and pointed out that the time to do so is now most opportune. "Our nation," he said, "is now involved in a tremendous war for existence and in this titanic struggle most of the Latin-American nations are allied with us. We are all brothers in the fight for the four freedoms. How, therefore, can equality of race and equality of opportunity be denied us *within the United States?*" Proof of the valor and heroism of the Hispano, in fact, needs no emphasis. German radio programs against the United States directed to Latin-American listeners have no effect whatever in New Mexico. In 1898 we fought a war with Spain, and the Hispanos of New

Mexico — with the memories of the War of 1846 still vivid in their minds — actively supported the United States against their mother country. No one felt called upon to suggest in 1898 that we should incarcerate all resident Latin Americans; and no one had cause to doubt their loyalty. In this war, the 200th Coast Artillery and the 515th Coast Artillery, composed largely of men from New Mexico, covered the retreat of General MacArthur's army from Manila to Bataan, and those who survived are, today, in Japanese prison camps.

The loyalty of these Spanish-American villagers in New Mexico beggars description. In a remote and isolated village in northern New Mexico, in 1942, I saw an old man, who spoke not a word of English, walking from village to village, selling defense bonds. I had had occasion, moreover, to learn something about the poverty that exists in these same villages. But the old Hispano told me that he had no trouble selling defense bonds and stamps. "They all buy some," he said. Allen Harper thoughtfully jotted down the notes of a conversation that he had with a young Spanish American hitchhiking in New Mexico. "I am going to my village in Taos County," he said, "to say good-by. I am the last of my family — my mother and my father are dead. My brother — I am very glad now — they thought he got killed out there some place; but now the War Department has sent me a telegram, saying that's not so — he's alive. I think I'm going out there, too, just where my brother is, then we can fight together. We got to fight — we got to win this war — maybe we die for liberty — maybe not — but we got to fight — we got to win." This boy epitomized, as Mr. Harper has said, the spirit of the Spanish Americans of New Mexico. "Their loyalty springs," he writes, "not from benefits bestowed by United States citizenship, but from the promise inherent in our democracy and our institutions. They have faith in that promise, in spite of almost a century of being 'forgotten.' Now is the time to implement promise with realization."

CHAPTER IV
Our Japanese Hostages

I F the problem of colored racial minorities in the United States was complicated prior to December 7, 1941, it has become doubly complicated in the last year. Today we have over 100,000 Japanese — men, women, and children — in protective custody. They have been uprooted from their homes, transported to assembly centers, and from there moved into relocation settlements — all in the space of less than one year. Already their lives have been violently disrupted and it would be a brave prophet indeed who would predict their future. Involved in the whole problem of these resident Japanese are issues fraught with profound import, not only in relation to the war itself, but to American democracy. By deciding upon the policy of evacuation, the government has in effect become the trustee for Japanese holdings on the West Coast running into the millions of dollars, and has assumed a continuing responsibility for the welfare of these people. Further complications already loom large as the West Coast states have begun to take action designed to prevent the return of the Japanese evacuees after the war. Here, therefore, is one of the knottiest minority problems which this country has ever faced.

1. The Time and Place

Historically Japan always opposed the emigration of its people. From 1638 to 1854 it was an offense punishable by death for any Japanese to emigrate; during the same period the building of all ocean-going boats was forbidden by imperial decree to make certain, as Dr. Ruth Benedict has said, "that Japan would preserve her policy of isolation." In 1884 this policy was reversed, at the behest of the Hawaiian Sugar Planters Association. From 1884 to 1907, Japanese steadily migrated to Hawaii, and in time the stream of out-migration came to have other destinations: Canada, the United States, South America. While Japanese emigration to Hawaii took place over a long period, most of the Japanese came to the mainland in a comparatively brief span of years. In 1890 there were only 2039 Japanese in the United States: in 1900 there were 24,236, in 1910 72,157. A great many of the original immigrants came by way of Hawaii; but over a period of years the number of Japanese in California who had come directly from Japan showed a marked increase.

No other immigrant group ever settled in America under more adverse circumstances than the Japanese. In the first place, the timing of the movement was most unfortunate in that Japanese immigrants began to arrive in California in large numbers just at the time when Japan, emerging from its so-called "youthful period," was beginning to loom large as a great power in the Far East. Japanese immigrants, therefore, came to be associated with the rise of Japanese nationalism. To the folk mind of California, they appeared as the spearhead of an actual Japanese invasion. The uneasiness which their presence occasioned only increased as Japanese nationalism became more menacing.

Not only did Japanese immigrants come at the wrong time, but they came to the wrong place. Out of 126,947 Japanese in the United States in 1940, 112,353 resided in the states of Oregon, Washington, and California (88.5 per cent of all those in this country). Of this group in turn, 93,717, or 73.8 per cent of the total, resided in California. Over a period of years, in fact, the concentration of Japanese in California steadily increased. If Japan be regarded as the "frontier" nation of the Orient, as Dr. Inui has suggested, and if America be regarded as the "frontier" of Western Europe, then it was inevitable that these two frontiers should eventually establish direct contact. But it was unfortunate that this initial contact should have been established in California. In 1900 California was primarily rural; its institutions were newly formed; its social heritage was largely that of a frontier community; and it evidenced marked manifestations of a frontier psychology. Long isolated from the rest of the country, California had developed a strong in-group feeling against all out-groups and this feeling was particularly intense where Orientals were concerned.

Overrun with newcomers from other parts of the nation, California has, also, long been a paradise for political demagogues. It is a state where sharp contrasts between rich and poor have long prevailed and where class consciousness has long been manifest. This strong current of class consciousness has tended to blend, in a curiously complicated manner, with race agitations. In all anti-Oriental movements in California, organized labor has played an important part and has, on more than one occasion, permitted resentment against its natural enemies to be diverted against Oriental immigrants. Furthermore, Japanese immigrants arrived in the state at a time when its resources were being rapidly monopolized — when it was becoming an area of closed rather than of open resources.

David Starr Jordan once said that California "is one of earth's male lands" — a state where public opinion is of the outdoor, stentorian, rough-and-tumble variety. "Californians," said Chester Rowell, "are vividly conscious of their position as the warders of the Western mart," given to invest their fight against the Oriental with all "the significance of a new Thermopylae." It has never been in the Californian's nature to go at things in a moderate way. As Julian Street once remarked: "He likes antagonism. He feels the need of it. He must have something to combat — something to neutralize the everlasting sunshine and the cloying sweetness of the orange-blossoms and roses." In any case, California in the years from 1900 to 1907 was a most unlikely place for the frontiers of Japan and America to make their first direct contact.

Almost from the moment of their arrival (the first anti-Japanese mass meeting was held in San Francisco on May 7, 1900), the Japanese were involved in the crosscurrents of previous anti-Oriental agitation. And no sooner had they arrived than tension between the United States and Japan began to develop. Faced with a hostile public opinion, restricted by official and unofficial discrimination, they have been the victims of a deepening international crisis from the time of their arrival. The constant strain, the almost uninterrupted anxiety, of this experience has been reflected in the life of every Japanese immigrant in this country. When the definitive history of these immigrants is eventually written, it will be found that they never had a chance to work out a real way of life for themselves; that they were, in effect, hostages from the time of their arrival. Under a cloud from the outset, their entire experience in this country has been punctuated by a series of crises. Except for a few brief years, they have been under fire from 1900 to 1941.

2. Years of the Yellow Peril

Apparently stimulated by the Russo-Japanese War, a major attack against the Japanese in California was launched in 1905 by the *San Francisco Chronicle*. The attack culminated the following year with the passage, by the San Francisco Board of Education, of an ordinance requiring the segregation of Oriental children in a single school. There was no problem in San Francisco at the time, since there were only 93 Japanese children of school age in the city. The sponsors of the ordinance never bothered to conceal the fact that their real intention was to start a process of discrimination which would eventually lead to the exclusion of further Japanese immigration. A minor motive behind the move was the desire of Mayor Eugene E. Schmitz to divert public attention from his notoriously corrupt administration. When the Mayor declared that, if necessary, he would lay down his life battling the Japanese, the *Los Angeles Times* commented: "It is a notable fact that His Honor has never laid down anything of value. His promise, however, would almost reconcile anyone to a war with Japan."

The timing of the ordinance could not have been more provocative. Japan had just emerged triumphant from the Russo-Japanese War and a turning point in Japanese-American relations had been reached. Furthermore, Japan had just contributed, through the Red Cross, more than $100,000 for the relief of victims of the San Francisco earthquake and fire. When confronted with this ordinance, the federal government, in order to give Japanese residents the protection of treaty provisions, was forced to file injunction suits seeking to restrain the enforcement of the ordinance. These suits never came to trial. For on March 14, 1907, President Theodore Roosevelt by executive order had stopped further Japanese immigration from Mexico, Canada, and Hawaii; and at the same time had negotiated the Gentlemen's Agreement of 1907. Mollified by these measures, the anti-Oriental forces agreed to withdraw the ordinance.

But these same forces could not be long appeased: almost immediately they launched a campaign against the Gentlemen's Agreement. This agreement had two weaknesses: an unofficial document, its provisions were not made public out of deference to Japanese sensibilities; and also it permitted the importation of so-called Japanese "picture brides." In 1900 women constituted only 4 per cent of the resident Japanese; but this percentage rapidly increased after 1907 (reaching 34 per cent in 1920). As the sex ratio came into some sort of balance, the number of native-born Japanese children increased. This rapid increase in births greatly alarmed the Californians. Just as Prince von Bülow had remarked of the Poles that "they breed like rabbits," so the same charge was made against the Japanese. If the birth rate had been adjusted to age levels, it would have been found that the Japanese rate was not much higher than that of the native population. Despite the fact that, as Raymond Leslie Buell pointed out, the Gentlemen's Agreement had "worked admirably and entirely achieved its purpose," the continued influx of Japanese women kept the issue alive. Seeing that the Californians continued to be agitated by sensational "picture-bride" stories, the California Japanese on October 29, 1919, *voluntarily petitioned* the Japanese government to deny further passports to Japanese women. In February 1920, Japan stopped issuing such passports, but Congress went ahead in 1924 and passed the Exclusion Act.

As early as 1909, California had started to legislate the Japanese out of the state (seventeen anti-Japanese bills were introduced in that year alone). After a lull in such activities oc-

casioned by the desire to obtain federal funds for the Panama
Pacific Exposition, the anti-Oriental forces launched a new
attack in 1913. Despite the protest of President Wilson and the
intervention of Secretary of State Bryan, the legislature passed
an Alien Land Act. The proponents of this measure were not
primarily concerned with the land problem; the author of the
bill stated, at the time, that "the fundamental basis of all legislation upon this subject has been, and is, race undesirability."
The bill was cunningly drafted since it was made to turn upon
the "ineligibility-to-citizenship" issue and consequently was
upheld by the courts.

With Japan our ally in the first World War, economic antagonism to the Japanese practically ceased. As industrial expansion stepped up labor demands and farm workers left rural
districts to seek factory employment, the Japanese were eagerly
sought as farm laborers. Anti-Japanese feeling, however, flared
up momentarily in 1914 at the time of the Zimmermann affair
when the Kaiser coined the phrase "the yellow peril" and
sought to provoke trouble between this country and Japan. It
flared up again in 1915 at the time of the signing of the Sino-
Japanese Treaty. Anti-Japanese feeling was again noticeable
when, at the Versailles Peace Conference, Japan, supported by
China, sought a declaration on racial equality (eight powers,
including the United States, Great Britain, and the British
Dominions, voted against the proposal).

Wartime hostilities had hardly ceased before anti-Japanese
agitation surged forward again. A new alignment of forces was
noticeable, however, after the war. Organized labor, for the
first time, was divided on the issue. A new element had also been
injected into politics, namely, the American Legion, which was
determined to keep America for the Americans. While further
Japanese immigration had virtually ceased and while the Japanese
issue itself was not of much urgency, nevertheless the agitation
was resumed upon, if anything, a broader basis. "The general
antipathy among sections of the public," wrote Dr. Payson
Treat, "which were not directly affected by the presence of
the Japanese settlers must be ascribed to the distrust aroused

and the almost universal criticism of the conduct of Japanese officials and people in China, Korea, and Siberia. The innocent Japanese in California are paying the price for their government's errors." Many sections of the public thought that a war between Japan and the United States was not unlikely and, as this feeling developed, opinion crystallized not so much against the Japanese as against Japan. In 1920 a Congressional committee of inquiry visited the Coast (on the eve of a national election); Senator James Phelan raised the issue of "white supremacy"; and the people of California adopted a new and far more stringent Alien Land Act, as an initiative measure, by a vote of more than three to one.

In November 1921, the Washington Naval Conference convened and the ink was hardly dry on the signatures to the agreement (widely regarded as a great triumph for American diplomacy) before the Supreme Court handed down its decision in the famous Ozawa case (November 13, 1922). This case, involving a graduate of Berkeley High School who had spent three years at the University of California, held that a Japanese was not a "white person" and was therefore ineligible to citizenship. As soon as the decision was handed down, the anti-Oriental forces went to work to secure the adoption of an immigration act which would bar all aliens "ineligible to citizenship." While the Immigration Act of 1924, which contained such a provision, was pending before Congress, Secretary of State Hughes stated that he feared the adoption of the act "would largely undo the work of the Washington Conference on Limitation of Armament, which so greatly improved our relations with Japan." Led by Senator Henry Cabot Lodge, the jingoes in Congress seized upon this remark and a statement by the Japanese Ambassador about "unfortunate consequences," and, orating at length about racial superiority, proceeded to pass the bill. President Coolidge, with stated reluctance, then signed the measure. The consequences of the passage of this bill can, in retrospect, hardly be exaggerated. Ambassador Woods, our representative in Tokyo, immediately resigned; and, in this country, Ambassador Hanihara also resigned. Prior to the bill's adoption, the fifteen leading newspapers of Tokyo published a joint declaration against the measure; and some thirty American university presidents joined in a statement pointing out that the bill was certain to have fateful consequences. As late as 1929, Viscount Shibusawa reminded the Institute of Pacific Relations that the passage of the bill, so far as Japan was concerned, was "not a closed incident." It would be difficult, in fact, to imagine a bill better calculated to further the hand of the militarists in Japan.

Even after the passage of the bill, incidents continued to multiply. In 1925 a mob of American citizens forcefully deported a small group of Japanese workers from their homes in Toledo, Oregon. Suits were later brought against the parties responsible and damages collected. Here, again, the weakness of our national government in the protection of rights guaranteed by the Constitution and by treaty was glaringly revealed. "Japan," stated one observer, "does not understand the explanation that the United States cannot chasten the State of Oregon. An anomalous situation continues. The nation continues to make treaties which the states or their citizens are to violate and the best the Secretary of State can do will be to explain our Constitution and ask Congress to vote compensation to the injured aliens and their families." After 1930 there was another momentary lull which abruptly terminated when tensions again developed in the Far East.[1] Thereafter developments were increasingly ominous; the Sino-Japanese War broke out in 1937, in 1940 Japan joined the Axis, and on December 7, 1941, Japan attacked Pearl Harbor.

I have by no means catalogued even the more important incidents which occurred between 1900 and 1940. Every disturbance in relations between Japan and the United States only further agitated the situation in California; and every disturbance in California only complicated the international situation. With the exception of only a few years, therefore, the Japanese in California were constantly involved in a rapidly developing international crisis. Under an increasing barrage, they were kept

[1] See my article in the *Nation*, June 26, 1935, "Once Again the Yellow Peril."

constantly on the defensive. They never knew what fresh turn of events, entirely beyond their control, might threaten them with disaster. Maligned in the newspapers for years on end, forced to defend themselves against the most unprincipled attacks, and tested every day of their lives by the most trying provocation, it is indeed remarkable that they even managed to survive.

3. Assimilation: California Style

If no other immigrant group ever faced such difficulties as the Japanese encountered in this country, it can also be said that no group ever conducted themselves more creditably. For the most part these early Japanese immigrants were young, unmarried men, in their best working years. They came to this country not as religious or political refugees, but as hardworking immigrants anxious to better their condition. Trained and experienced farmers, they were by no means an illiterate peasantry. Most of them had the equivalent of an eighth-grade education. They showed, from the outset, great eagerness to adopt American ways. They quickly adopted American clothes; they cut their hair like Americans; they adopted an American diet, used American furnishings in their homes; and tried to act like Americans. The Immigration Commission consistently paid tribute in its reports to the eagerness with which the Japanese tried to adjust themselves to their new environment. "The progress of the Japanese," reads one report, "is due to their greater eagerness to learn, which has overcome more obstacles than have been encountered by most of the other races, obstacles of race prejudice, of segregation, and wide differences in language." They even changed their religion in their eagerness to become Americans (in 1914 converts to Christianity in California were running as high as five hundred a year).

In every way they tried to deport themselves in a creditable manner. There was no crime problem among them (nor has there ever been one); and they paid their debts. Even during depressions, they were never dependent upon public relief or assistance. When objections were raised to the type of homes in which they lived in rural areas, they quickly pointed out that, since they could not own the land, it was hardly fair to expect them to build fine homes. Nevertheless they organized a "Better Homes and Garden Campaign" and brought about a measure of improvement in rural housing. In the Hood River Valley, in Oregon, they sought repeatedly to get the American farmers to appoint a committee so that the two groups might sit down together and iron out existing difficulties. (The offers were invariably refused.) Their cleanliness was, and is, proverbial. The truth of the matter is that their remarkable adaptability militated against them. Dr. R. E. Park has, in fact, admirably summarized their worth as immigrants. "Precisely because of their historical traits of allegiance and organization," he wrote, "the Japanese are capable of transforming their lives and practices more rapidly than any other group. . . . They are inclined to make more far-going concessions than any other group in order to overcome American prejudice and secure status here. . . . Whether we like them or not, no other foreign-language group is so completely and intelligently organized to control its members, and no other group has at all equaled them in the work of accommodating themselves to alien conditions."

It is difficult in retrospect to re-create the social atmosphere in which the Japanese found themselves in this "danger zone." For forty years on end, crisis followed crisis; one investigation succeeded a prior investigation; one campaign ended only to find another launched; and the newspaper attack was continuous and remorseless. They were discriminated against in almost every walk of life; no session of the legislature passed without the introduction of some anti-Japanese bills. Sounding off about the Japanese became a legislative pastime in California. One legislator called them "a bandy-legged set of bagabooes — miserable craven Simians — degenerate rotten little devils"; they were "skulking," "servile," "immoral," "treacherous," "sneaking," and "insidious." While they were never physically mistreated as were the Chinese (the Japanese consulates were quick to lodge protests), nevertheless the atmosphere in which they lived became poisonously prejudiced against them.

While creating this kind of atmosphere, the Californians continued to repeat the dogma "Once a Jap, Always a Jap," and to urge the contention that they were biologically unassimilable. The doctrine of their unassimilability was raised to the pinnacle of an official state policy and consistently applied in practice. In actuality, however, the Japanese were adapting themselves even biologically. It has been repeatedly demonstrated (by Dr. H. L. Shapiro, Dr. Inui, Dr. Ichihashi, and others) that the children of Japanese immigrants differ from their parents physically as well as culturally. They are taller, larger, and heavier than children born and reared in Japan (an observation confirmed by the Department of Health in California). As a result of better dental care, the shape of their mouths is different. Despite these observed facts, however, the doctrine of their biological unassimilability remained, as one observer said, "inexorable, conclusive, and unchangeable."

4. The Economic and Political Argument

That the theory of unfair economic competition was never the real basis of the opposition to the Japanese in California may be variously demonstrated. At the outset a large number of Japanese were employed as domestic servants. In California from 1900 to 1930, domestic service was essentially noncompetitive employment. Even in this field, as Dr. Millis demonstrated, the higher wages paid Japanese tended to raise, not to lower, existing wage rates. In railroad construction, lumbering, and mining, the Japanese never constituted a serious threat to local American labor. In urban trade, the Japanese were confined, by reason of organized boycotts, largely to providing goods and services to their own people (who were frequently discriminated against in non-Japanese stores and services). Furthermore, as the Tolan Committee reported, "the typical Japanese business was small, requiring a small capital investment, having a small volume of annual transactions, and directed by a single proprietor with the aid of his wife or by two partners." Over a period of years, the amount of capital, but not the number of employees, tended to increase slightly. Over a period of years, also, Japanese stores began to be patronized by Mexican and Filipino customers; but accompanying this expansion in patronage the proportion of American-made goods in the stores increased. By and large, Little Tokyo never competed with Main Street.

In agriculture the Japanese were originally used to replace, not to displace, the Chinese as field workers. As Dr. Varden Fuller has demonstrated, they constituted a complementary source of labor supply. By 1910 wages paid Japanese farm workers were frequently higher than those paid any other nationality group. In this same year, the Labor Commissioner of California reported that "Japanese or some form of labor of a similar character, capable of independent subsistence, quick mobilization, submissive of instant dismissal and entailing no responsibility upon the employer for continuous employment, is absolutely necessary in the California orchard, vineyard, and field, if these vast industries are to be perpetuated and developed." (His report was promptly suppressed.) Not only were they deemed necessary for the expansion of California agriculture, but their presence as farm laborers tended to bolster up wages in nonagricultural types of employment.

Prior to the passage of the Alien Land Act, the Japanese did make rapid progress as farmers. In 1905 the land owned by Japanese constituted 3.9 per cent of the land they operated; but by 1925 this percentage had risen to 13.9 per cent. As a matter of fact, it was the advance in status of Japanese from farm laborers to farm operators that made it possible for them to bring their wives to this country and that also encouraged them to remain in the state. But once they had married and established families, it became increasingly difficult for them to return to Japan (which was probably their original intention). It should also be pointed out, as the *San Francisco Chronicle* observed, "that the most striking feature of Japanese farming in California has been the development of successful orchards, vineyards, or gardens on land that was either completely out of use or employed for far less profitable enterprises." The Japanese, in effect, made their own place in California agriculture. They pioneered in the production of many crops; they reclaimed desert and swamp lands; and, in the Northwest, they converted cut-over timber lands into prosperous berry-growing areas. The Japanese uniformly forced prices for farm land up, not down, and greatly increased the amount of rent received by American landlords. At the time the Alien Land Act was adopted in Oregon, an American farmer testified: "We have not heard of any land being sold at a sacrifice because of the presence of the Japanese." With reference to the situation at Florin, California, Alice Brown, a vineyardist, testified in 1921: "There never has been a farm sold to get away from a Japanese neighbor. On the contrary, white families are coming in all the time and erecting homes." In quoting sensational statistics about Japanese-operated farms in California, the anti-Oriental forces seldom took the trouble to point out that most of these lands were operated on a cash-rental basis. The Alien Land Act was designed not to protect the American farmer (who was getting along very well indeed) but to stop further Japanese immigration.

The economic argument, in fact, so frequently backfired upon those who used it that by 1920 it had been generally abandoned. Thereafter the argument was actually used in reverse — that is, those who advocated further restrictions said that they were doing so *against* their own economic interests; that "dollars and cents" had nothing to do with the matter anyway; and that they were interested in "larger issues." By 1920 Japanese immigration had virtually ceased. If the Japanese had been placed on a quota basis in 1924, instead of being excluded as ineligible to citizenship, it would have meant restricting immigration to 2 per cent of the number of foreign-born individuals of Japanese nationality residing in this country in 1890. The Japanese quota would, therefore, have been about one hundred a year. That such a small annual influx could have constituted a serious threat to the economic interests of native-white Californians is incredible (almost two million American citizens migrated to California between 1920 and 1930).

Politically the Japanese were suspect because they were "too clannish" and well-organized; but they were no more clannish or well-organized than their white neighbors. The history of some of these anti-Oriental organizations is, moreover, quite interesting. Mr. W. L. Mackenzie King, now Canadian Prime Minister, charged in 1908 that the powerful Asiatic Exclusion League of North America had been subsidized in part by the Hawaiian Sugar Planters Association in an effort to check the further migration of Japanese plantation workers from Hawaii to the mainland. It was not until *after* this organization was formed (1908) that the local Japanese organizations merged to form the Japanese Association of America. "Nothing so easily establishes solidarity within a group," said William Graham Sumner, "as an attack from without." In general the pattern was everywhere the same — namely, that the Japanese organized for mutual aid and protection.

The Japanese were also suspect politically because they sponsored Japanese-language schools. Any number of American educators, however, endorsed the idea of the schools, as making for a closer tie between parent and child, and also as essential to future employment in export-and-import firms. It is indeed difficult to read anything subversive into the frankly expressed wish of Japanese parents that their children should know something about the history and culture of Japan. It is probably true, however, that some of these schools used text material that, on the score of patriotism, was objectionable. In Hawaii the Japanese themselves sponsored legislation to bring the vernacular schools under state regulation. And many people have forgotten that in December 1920 the Japanese Association of America suggested that California should enact similar legislation. In fact, such a bill was passed in California only to be held unconstitutional in the courts in 1927. What has also been forgotten is that, in Oregon, the Japanese were finally successful in getting one public school to form a Japanese-language class.[2] Parochial schools teaching foreign languages to immigrant children have long been tolerated in America. Furthermore the average time spent by Japanese youngsters in vernacular schools was only three or four years. That these schools were, in fact, unsuccessful has been

[2] *The History of the Japanese People in Oregon,* by Marjorie R. Stearns, 1937, p. 68.

proved by the discovery of the Army that only 15 per cent of the younger generation can speak Japanese and that only 5 per cent could pass a test in reading and writing Japanese.

Another score on which the Japanese were politically suspect was that of dual citizenship. The Japanese Nationality Code has always been predicated upon the doctrine of *jus sanguinis* — namely, that a child is Japanese if its father is a Japanese national at the time of its birth. Under the Fourteenth Amendment, we have always followed the doctrine of *jus soli* (except in so far as our own nationals abroad were concerned) — that persons born in this country are citizens of the United States. That there are two such conflicting doctrines of nationality may be readily explained: countries having a heavy out-migration — the population exporting countries — almost uniformly followed the doctrine of *jus sanguinis;* while countries of heavy in-migration — the population receiving countries — follow the doctrine of *jus soli.* There is nothing peculiar, therefore, about the rule followed by Japan (it has been adopted in many European countries). What we have forgotten is that the Japanese on the West Coast *themselves petitioned* Japan in 1914 to modify its law. The law was, in fact, modified, in March 1916 and in December 1925, so as to make it possible for Japanese residents, born in this country, to renounce any claim of dual citizenship. It is a little difficult to see how such a claim could arise in practice, since we have never recognized the principle of dual citizenship. In any case, after 1925 many *Nisei* (American-born) did renounce Japanese citizenship (those born subsequent to December 1, 1925, were automatically released from such a claim); but it is estimated that about a third of them failed to do so.

The relationship between Japanese nationals in this country and the government of Japan always aroused American concern. For Japan, as Mr. Schreike observed in 1934, has long "displayed an extraordinary solicitude" for its nationals abroad. That it recognizes such nationals as colonists is shown by reports issued on the Japanese in Hawaii and the United States. The Japanese government was always quick to lodge protests over mistreatment of or discrimination against its nationals, and to defend them.

I have no doubt that some of the extremely active publicists in this country, both American and Japanese, who rushed into print on all occasions to defend the resident Japanese were, in fact, subsidized by Japan. One of the men most active in "defending" the Japanese in the 1920's has subsequently been indicted as an unregistered agent of the Japanese government. A minister who testified before the Tolan Committee in 1942 in defense of the Japanese has subsequently been exposed as a former agent of the Japanese government. Unquestionably there were elements in Japan who were not at all unwilling to keep the pot boiling in California. For every manifestation of racial prejudice in California served to strengthen the hand of militarism in Japan. But this much should be observed: we had it in our power to have terminated any overzealous interest of Japan in its nationals. Had we made it possible for the resident Japanese to become citizens, then Japan would have had no basis upon which to protest. Furthermore it should be pointed out that no nation in all history has been more aggressive about protecting the rights of its nationals abroad than the government of the United States.

5. The Real Case

If the biological, economic, and political arguments raised against the Japanese were lacking in substance, what, then, was the real basis of anti-Japanese agitation? One of the commonest mistakes made by Japanese protagonists in California was to charge, as all of them did, that anti-Japanese agitation was caused solely by unscrupulous political demagogues who, in most cases, obviously did not know what they were talking about and who habitually made false, misleading, and inaccurate statements. Now it is true that the Japanese issue, like the Chinese, became hopelessly mired in the muck of California politics. But politicians do not invent political issues: the issue must first be there. "The legislation against Oriental labor," said Miss Eaves (the ablest student of the problem), "sprang from the people." No amount of rationalization can ever obscure this fact. The people of California felt, and quite rightly, that the federal government had been derelict in its responsibilities in having permitted, in the first instance, a large Japanese settlement to develop in the state, and in not having attempted to regulate, control, or supervise additional immigration. For all the Californians knew a steadily increasing volume of Japanese immigration might have continued for an indefinite period. It was the absence of *a federal policy*, as much as anything else, that justified popular apprehension. Furthermore, California, as a West Coast state, was properly concerned by the unmistakable evidences of aggressive intentions on the part of the Japanese government. Residents put down the morning's newspaper, which told of further Japanese aggression in Manchuria or Korea, only to observe the industrious Japanese farmer next door. "The more powerful Japan became," said Dr. Inui, "the more conspicuous became the anti-Japanese agitation and the more readily Japan's foreign policies became involved." The fact is that both the resident Japanese and the resident Californians were the victims of a developing international crisis to which a tragic outcome was more or less implicit from the outset.

Californians, moreover, felt that the unsolved Negro problem in the South should be a warning to them. Until we had solved this problem, or had indicated an ability and willingness to solve it, there was a measure of justification for the belief that it was bad policy to admit further "colored" people to the United States. The analogy between the Negro and the Japanese was, perhaps, the most effective instrument in the hands of the rabid anti-Oriental leaders. These leaders always have been, and still are, race purists. As late as 1942 the California Joint Immigration Committee (sponsored by the Native Sons and Daughters of the Golden West, the American Legion, the State Federation of Labor, and the California Grange) informed the Tolan Committee that this nation made a "grave mistake in granting citizenship to the Negroes after the Civil War." [3] This is not to imply that the organizations sponsoring the committee endorse such a statement; they do, however, sponsor the organization which made the statement. Apart from such people, however, there

[3] Part 29, Tolan Transcript, p. 11,085.

were many sincere and fair-minded citizens of California who supported the anti-Japanese movement because they wanted to prevent a race problem from arising in the state. One finds this sentiment repeated throughout the agitation over a period of many years. The Japanese problem, it was said, "will make the black problem of the South look white"; it was "a menace as great as the Negro question in the days of the Civil War." "We have learned a lesson from the experience of the Southern states," said an editorial writer in the *San Francisco Bulletin;* "our race problem is in the future. We can prevent it from developing further if we act firmly and sanely now and put aside the counsels of doctrinaires and academicians." The Japanese publicists only made matters worse by attempting, in a thoroughly shameless manner, to dissociate themselves from the Negroes. "It is absurd," said Mr. Kawakami in 1921, "to speak of the Japanese question in California in the same breath as the Negro question in the South. Intellectually and physically, socially and individually, and in their respective cultural and historical backgrounds, there is no similarity between the two races." In an effort to save themselves, some Japanese were not above slandering Chinese, Negroes, Filipinos, Indians, and Mexicans. In retrospect it cannot be said that the strategy was particularly effective.

6. *Little Tokyo*

On December 7, 1941, about 55 per cent of the Japanese on the West Coast were living in urban communities and, within these communities, were concentrated in Little Tokyos. The Alien Land Acts, even though they were not effectively enforced, had tended to drive the Japanese into urban areas. Here they were forced into Little Tokyo, not only by economic pressures, but by a comprehensive system of "race restrictions" in grant deeds which made it impossible for them to secure for themselves a more typical distribution throughout the community. What they had succeeded in doing was "to survive and encyst themselves in the body politic." That they had managed to survive, or, stated another way, that they had decided to remain here, is explained by the fact that they had found a niche for themselves in our economy.

Of the Japanese on the West Coast, some 22,027, or 43 per cent of those gainfully employed, were employed in agriculture. But some 11,472 (24 per cent of those gainfully employed) were engaged in wholesale and retail trade which, for the most part, was largely confined to the distribution of Japanese-grown agricultural produce. Thus the dependence of the Japanese upon agriculture was much greater than would appear on the surface. About 17 per cent of those gainfully employed were to be found in service industries — domestic service, cleaning and dyeing, barbershops, restaurants, and hotels. Here, again, many of these people were dependent upon agriculture since they catered primarily to the Japanese community. Very few Japanese were to be found in manufacturing or in construction industries. Those engaged in the professions were, of course, dependent upon the patronage of the Japanese community.

The narrow economic base upon which the entire Japanese community was dependent may be shown by an examination of the Japanese in California agriculture. In 1940 there were some 5135 Japanese-operated farms, with a total of about 226,094 acres of land which, including buildings, were valued at $65,781,000. The average acreage of Japanese farms had been reduced by the operations of the Alien Land Act: from 80.1 acres in 1920 to 44 acres in 1940; from a total of 361,276 acres in 1920 to 226,094 acres in 1940. While most of these farms were small, Japanese production, intensive in character, was quite substantial. In 1941 the Japanese grew about 42 per cent of the produce crops raised in the state; and this production was valued at around $35,000,000. Although they operated only 3.9 per cent of the land in farms and harvested only 2.7 per cent of all cropland harvested, they produced from 50 to 90 per cent of such crops as celery, peppers, strawberries, cucumbers, artichokes, cauliflower, spinach, and tomatoes. By and large, the Japanese had acquired a near monopoly on the production of fresh vegetables on a small-acreage basis for the large urban markets on the West Coast. They figured only slightly in the production of stable crops which are grown on a large-acreage basis by mechanized methods; and, except in Washington and Oregon, they figured only slightly in the large-scale production of produce crops for out-of-state shipment.

This monopoly on the fresh-vegetable market was strengthened by the fact that the Japanese had reached out and organized wholesale and retail outlets for Japanese-grown produce. Thus in 1941 there were some 1000 Japanese-operated fruit and vegetable stores in Los Angeles employing around 5000 people (mostly all Japanese), and doing a business of $25,000,000 a year. The industry had been thoroughly integrated from the fields to the wholesale markets to the retail outlets. The Little Tokyos were primarily service centers for people engaged directly or indirectly in, or otherwise dependent upon, this single industry.

By 1941 the Japanese population had outgrown this narrow economic base. There were too many Japanese service trades and retail stores, and too many Japanese in the professions, to be supported by the income available in the Japanese community. Little Tokyo was faced, in fact, with a serious economic crisis. Many of the retail stores had been able to survive because they catered to the peculiar tastes and buying habits of the older or *Issei* generation. As this generation began to die off (their median age was 50.1 years), stores were faced with the necessity of changing the character of their merchandise in order to hold the patronage of the younger generation. To the extent that these stores began to cater to the Americanized tastes of the second generation, they came into direct competition with large chain-store organizations. For years prior to 1941, observers had noted the high incidence of business failures and bankruptcies in Little Tokyo. "The Japanese business shops have a good front," one merchant told Frank Miyamoto, "but when you get inside, you find out how bad the whole thing is." Many of these businesses were behind the times; offered inferior merchandise; and were badly managed.[4] Of 138,834 Japanese in the United States in 1930, 50.2 per cent were foreign-born; but of 126,947

[4] See Schreike, p. 36.

Japanese in 1940, only 37.3 per cent were foreign-born. Without their realizing it, therefore, a death sentence had been imposed on Little Tokyo before December 7, 1941.

External pressures served, however, to keep Little Tokyo intact. Refused service in beauty shops, barbershops, hotels, and restaurants, Japanese had to patronize concerns operated by members of their race. Being ineligible to citizenship, the first generation took no part in community affairs outside of Little Tokyo. The Alien Land Act made it difficult for Japanese families to take deep root in rural communities. Miscegenation statutes barred intermarriage. Restrictive legislation, at the same time that it set the Japanese apart, stimulated national self-consciousness among them. Both Dr. Inui and Mr. Schreike observed that the first-generation Japanese became noticeably more nationalistic after the passage of the Immigration Act of 1924. The number of foreign-language schools, for example, immediately increased. If the Japanese tended to remain apart in California, said Dr. Inui, "it is because of restraint, economic deprivation, social ostracism, and political discrimination. As nationalism is stirred by restraint upon a given nationality, so racialism can also be awakened by the same process."

Such factors, however, fail to account entirely for Little Tokyo's most conspicuous characteristic, namely, its powerful internal solidarity. Japanese have, as Frank Miyamoto has said,[5] a strong sense of the meaning of the family, the community, and the nation. These group realities have special significance to them since "the whole of their culture is integrated like a mosaic." It was this traditional feeling (very pronounced among the first generation), as well as the necessity for developing their "optimum competitive strength within the American economy," which served to set them apart. The cleavage in the age grouping occasioned by the Exclusion Act (which resulted in an abnormal population pyramid — too many young people, too many old people, and a paucity of middle-aged people) fixed control in the hands of the first generation who were naturally influenced more by Japanese cultural traits than the second gen-

[5] *Social Solidarity Among the Japanese in Seattle*, 1939.

eration. Little Tokyo was made up, moreover, of people who belonged to the same social class. Most of them were lower middle class, with only a few capitalists and only a few working-class families. "Among the Japanese," writes Mr. Miyamoto, "there is apparently an ingrown feeling that the relationship between two members of their own nationality is an entirely different thing than the relationship between themselves and other nationalities." (This feeling was probably intensified by the external pressures previously mentioned.) Social distance grew with the years until the relationship between the two communities became essentially symbiotic. "Social contacts," wrote Dr. Edward K. Strong, Jr., in 1934, "between whites and Japanese have been largely restricted to those in school. . . . Neither race knows the other and each leads its distinct social life." The fact that many Japanese used English inefficiently indicated to Mr. Miyamoto that they had learned the language from books: not from daily conversation with English-speaking people. This strong in-group feeling was heightened by the increase in the power of Japan. It served to tie the Japanese communities to the consulates and through the consulates to the Japanese government — a development which the second generation (whose median age was nineteen years) was powerless to prevent.[6] Thus the Japanese communities, under the dominance of the first generation, committed themselves in support of Japanese aggression in China. Just to the degree that these communities were economically self-sufficient, to that extent were they set apart.

Little Tokyo had within it, however, the seeds of its own dissolution. Of the Japanese evacuated from the West Coast (112,353), some 41,000 were aliens or *Issei*, but 71,000 were American-born (*Nisei*) and therefore citizens. Prior to December 7, a sizable number of these *Nisei* had graduated from college and had found a place for themselves in Little Tokyo. The first graduates fared moderately well; but as others reached maturity they found it extremely difficult to find a place for

[6] For an interesting description of Japanese organizations on the West Coast written by a Japanese-American see the article by M. Fujita in *Sociology and Social Research*, January–February, 1929.

themselves. Little Tokyo, in the nature of things, could only support a limited number of doctors, lawyers, and journalists. This saturation point had been reached long before December 7. With an average intelligence comparing altogether favorably with the general average, these youngsters were well-educated and extremely ambitious. Inevitably, therefore, they found themselves more and more in conflict, first, with their parents, and second, with the system which denied them equal opportunity with other Americans.

The second generation was separated from the first generation linguistically, culturally, politically. From a wide acquaintance among them, I state categorically that the overwhelming bulk of the second generation were Japanese only in appearance. As Michio Kunitani told the members of the Tolan Committee:—

We are Americans, not by virtue of our birth in America, but by virtue of the social and cultural forces in America. . . . We are Americans, not by mere technicality of birth, but by all the other forces of sports, amusements, schools, churches, which *are in our communities* and which affect our lives directly. Some of us are Yankee fans; some of us are Dodger fans; some of us like to sip beer; some like to go up to the Top of the Mark (the Mark Hopkins Hotel); once in a while we enjoy Jack Benny; we listen to Beethoven; and some of us even go through the *Congressional Record*.

For years the second-generation youngsters had faced many barriers. There were few barriers as such in the schools and colleges (where the Japanese Americans were well liked and frequently elected to class offices), but after graduation they found it increasingly difficult to find employment. Despite these difficulties, however, Dr. Strong found, after quite elaborate studies made in 1934, that "practically none expressed a desire to go to Japan." Even the *Kibei* — those who had received part of their education in Japan — complained that in the Orient they were regarded as "aliens" and "foreigners." Those among the *Nisei* who had visited Japan almost uniformly stated, as did one youngster interviewed by Dr. Strong: "I felt out of place in

Japan. Everything seemed so strange to me. I was really afraid to go about alone because I could not read the signs and I was afraid I would get lost. The Japanese also made comments about me. They commented on my dress and my ways. . . . The modernness of the capital surprised me, but like a true Angeleno, I compared everything I saw with some corresponding thing in Los Angeles, and said to myself: 'We can beat that in Los Angeles.'" That the second generation had precipitated a serious crisis in Little Tokyo is indicated by many developments which were apparent prior to December 7. It is interesting to note that Dr. E. S. Bogardus, writing in the summer of 1941, observed that the rift between the two generations was steadily widening. "Sometimes the chasm grows so great," he said, "whether owing to the developing tension between Japan and the United States or to other matters is not always clear, that second-generation boys and girls are joining the ranks of American delinquency. Recently a tendency toward delinquency is noticeable" — and this among a people that previously had one of the lowest crime rates of any ethnic group in America.

While outwardly Americanized in every respect, the *Nisei* were by no means thoroughly acculturated. One Japanese woman complained that, with the weakening of parental control, the second generation had been cut loose from any guiding influence. "The Japanese," she said, "*lack something* in their background that makes them peculiarly unresponsive to forces that reach American young people." Many observers noted the lack of social adjustment.[7] And the *Nisei* themselves were painfully aware of the predicament in which they found themselves. Dr. W. C. Smith, who has made excellent studies of the second-generation problem, quotes one youngster as follows:—

"We belong to two groups, the Japanese and the American. In ancestry and physical appearance we are Japanese, while in birth, education, in ideals, and in ways of thinking we are American. Nevertheless, the older Japanese will not accept us into their group because, as they see us, we are too independent, too pert, and too

[7] See B. Schreike, p. 38.

self-confident, and the Americans bar us from their group because we retain the yellow skin and flat nose of the Oriental. Thus we stand on the border line that separates Orient from Occident. Though on either side of us flow the streams of two great civilizations — the old Japanese culture with its formal traditions and customs and the newer American civilization with its freedom and individualism — the chance to perceive and to imbibe the best things from each has been withheld from us."

Such, in general, was the situation existing prior to December 7, 1941. It represented, to some extent, a purely temporary equilibrium. Within a narrow orbit the Japanese were tolerated; but outside this narrow orbit they were hedged in by all manner of restrictions, race prejudice, discriminations, and economic controls. At the same time they were subject to powerful influences in American life, such, for example, as the movies, which operated within Little Tokyo. A dry rot, of a sort, had begun to corrode the foundations upon which Little Tokyo was built.

7. *Post Pearl Harbor*

The attack on Pearl Harbor came as a stunning — a paralyzing — blow to the Japanese on the West Coast. I witnessed their reaction at first hand and know whereof I speak. A few people in the Japanese communities, notably the young anti-Fascists, had foreseen that war was inevitable. They had been infuriating their elders for years by denouncing Japanese militarism and warning of the debacle to come. There were, in fact, many telltale signs on the horizon. For example, the motorship *Hikawa Maru* came to Seattle in November 1941, prepared to take a thousand passengers to Japan. The circumstances of its arrival and departure clearly indicated that this was, so to speak, a last-minute chance for those to leave who desired to do so. (As a matter of fact, the ship sailed with two thirds of its passenger space unoccupied.) Still the vast majority of Japanese firmly believed that war would be averted. The consternation that seized Little Tokyo on December 7 could not have been simulated: it was obviously genuine. Many members of the community were still in a daze at the time of the Tolan Committee hearings in February and March, 1942, as their conduct clearly indicated.

It would serve no purpose, here, to retrace the steps which led up to the decision, made by the military, to evacuate all Japanese residents from the three West Coast states (I have described these steps in detail in an article in *Harper's* for September 1942, and in a long report published by the Institute of Pacific Relations). Suffice it to say that, between March 2 and June 8, 1942, 100,000 Japanese — men, women, and children, citizens and aliens, grandparents, parents, and children — were moved from their homes into temporary assembly centers, and between June and November they were moved from the assembly centers into some ten relocation centers in California, Arizona, Idaho, Utah, Wyoming, Colorado, and Arkansas. With the exception, therefore, of a few institutionalized cases, all the Japanese have been removed from the West Coast or placed in protective custody in centers located in California. The California Japanese population, for example, has dropped from 93,717 on December 7, 1941, to around 20,000 (representing those in the Manzanar and Tule Lake relocation centers).

It would also serve no purpose to debate the question of whether or not total mass evacuation should or should not have been ordered. The fact is that the decision was made by the military and it is to be presumed that it was dictated by good and sufficient reasons. The decision, however, has created an enormous problem. The civil liberties of upwards of 71,000 American citizens have been suspended without due process of law; property losses running into the millions of dollars have been sustained; and the government, at an initial cost of $70,000,-000, is now attempting to resettle these evacués. The seriousness of the problem is indicated by the fact that, in the relocation centers today, there are really three generations: the first generation (aliens), the second generation (citizens), and the third generation (also citizens). The first generation have really no basis for complaint: in time of war nations are allowed great latitude in dealing with enemy aliens. But the second, and particularly the third, generation present an entirely different problem.

Fortunately the War Relocation Authority (created by executive order of the President) has done and is doing a creditable job in its effort to relocate these people. Not only are their physical needs being satisfactorily met in the relocation centers, but, within general limitations, their civil liberties have been protected. As the manpower shortage has increased, the WRA has been able to place thousands of Japanese in new employment outside the prohibited zone. Today some 9000 Japanese are working outside the centers: as farm workers, as stock feeders, as sheep herders, as irrigators, turkey pickers, hotel employees, section hands, and miners. Their use as sugar-beet workers unquestionably saved the sugar-beet crop this year in such states as Utah and Idaho. By next year, it is estimated that perhaps 25,000 will have been relocated in permanent employment outside the centers, free of any restrictions, and with their rights fully restored. "Our first concern," Mr. Dillon Meyer, Director of WRA, has said, "is not the postwar period, but the problem of relocating residents outside the centers before the war is over." Within less than a year, the program has come to a full circle: evacuation, movement to assembly centers, transferral to relocation centers, relocation itself. If the manpower shortage continues, it is reasonable to assume that, before the war is over, virtually all of the Japanese will have been relocated. No longer concentrated in Little Tokyos, they will be scattered in small groups throughout the inter-mountain region. It is unlikely that they will ever return, en masse, to the West Coast. With Little Tokyo a ghost town, the isolation of the Japanese belongs to the past. The "cyst" has been removed, but has it been absorbed?

What will happen after the war is an open question. Already a movement is under way to exclude the Japanese altogether from the United States after the war. This movement has taken two forms: a rather vague expression of an intention to deport all Japanese; and a more specific plan to deprive the second generation of American citizenship, if necessary by constitutional amendment. A bill introduced by Senator Stewart of Tennessee purports to authorize the detention of all persons of Japanese descent for the duration of the war; a bill by Senator Holman of Oregon seeks to deprive the *Nisei* of American citizenship. It is too early to predict the fate of these and other measures now pending.

In most of the areas where they are working at the present time, the Japanese are being well received despite a rhetorically violent opposition at the outset. When an economic reality (labor shortage) collides with a subjective emotion (prejudice), the economic reality usually emerges triumphant. But the real test will come, of course, when the war is over. Whatever barriers it may raise in the future, the war will certainly have removed some barriers that, in the past, have retarded assimilation. Until Japanese militarism had been liquidated, until the Far Eastern crisis had been settled, it was chimerical to have expected a satisfactory solution to the Japanese problem. With these issues settled by the war, then the Japanese would seem to face a tolerably hopeful future. A few may decide to return to Japan (1250 evacués have signed up with WRA for repatriation), but the majority will unquestionably want to stick it out. This majority has already demonstrated its patriotism and loyalty. "I would say," testified Mr. Milton Eisenhower (formerly director of WRA) before a Congressional committee, "that from 80 per cent to 85 per cent of the *Nisei* are loyal to the United States. I just cannot say things too favorable about the way they have co-operated under the most adverse circumstances." When coupled with the fine effort they are making in relocation centers, this kind of assurance should go a long way toward winning for the Japanese a much wider range of acceptance after the war. The war has, also, forever broken the dominance of the *Issei;* it has shattered the isolation of Little Tokyo; and, violently and crudely, it is bringing the Japanese into the main current of American life. If American democracy overcomes its *laissez faire* attitude toward race problems and demonstrates an ability to cope with such questions, then it is likely that some of our fixations on race may be profoundly modified. It should also be remembered that the federal government has now assumed responsibility for the welfare of these evacués; it can hardly abandon them, therefore, until some moderately satisfactory solution has been effected.

What will happen to them after the war is, of course, a question that will have to be answered by the American people. In deciding what answer they will give, it might be well for them to ponder a statement made some years ago by Dr. Edward K. Strong, Jr., of Stanford University. "The slow onward march toward political democracy," he said, "has been marked by one struggle after another, because equality could not be recognized in the presence of some seemingly essential difference. Finally it was realized that women could vote even though they were not men. Similarly, progress is being made toward industrial democracy. But cultural and racial democracy we do not yet have in America, and, until we do have it, our democracy is painfully and tragically incomplete. Progress is also slow because we all assume so absolutely that our own views are the only true ones; hence all differences are signs of inferiority. We must learn that practical equality can exist with essential differences and that differences do not imply inferiority. Whether we like it or not, the world is getting smaller every year. . . . Nations should view each other as neighbors and must learn to live with one another. One way for the citizens of these countries to learn how to do this is to travel and meet other people. Another way is to know them as personal neighbors at home. Apparently the latter is harder and more disagreeable than the former. The point here is: is there not genuine value in the learning? Is there not value in having different social cultures before one's eyes?"

CHAPTER V

Hawaii: Island Outpost

PRIOR to the attack on Pearl Harbor, *Fortune* magazine called the attention of the nation to the peculiar vulnerabilities of our two most strategic outposts: Hawaii, at the crossroads of the Pacific, and Puerto Rico, the sentinel of the Caribbean. The strong defenses of both island outposts were, at that time, being materially strengthened and consolidated. What *Fortune* feared, however, was the internal situation in both islands. The major weaknesses of Hawaii, it pointed out, were the large resident Japanese population and the two-crop economy (sugar and pineapple). These two weaknesses are, of course, intimately related, for if the two-crop plantation economy had not acquired a stranglehold in the islands, the Japanese would never have been in Hawaii. *Fortune* pointed out (August 1940) that Hawaii had to import 95 per cent of its rice — the staple food of its predominantly Oriental population — from the mainland; and that, in fact, 60 per cent of its food came from the West Coast. In Puerto Rico, on the other hand, *Fortune* noted (February 1941) "the inexorable fact that defense of the region surrounding the Panama Canal is intertwined with all the psychological factors affecting Mr. Hull's Good Neighbor Policy," particularly so in Puerto Rico itself because of the circumstance that the language, the culture, and the traditions of the Puerto Ricans are only slightly less Latin-American today than they were in 1898. Likewise *Fortune* noted that "whenever the United States makes a mistake in Puerto Rico, Berlin short-waves the information to Uruguay and Brazil." These basic weaknesses in both outposts were only emphasized by the fact that, prior to the attack on Pearl Harbor, Hawaii and Puerto Rico were, with Alaska, involved in a race to see which would first be admitted to the Union as the forty-ninth state. The circumstances constituting their vulnerability are, in fact, closely interrelated and may be attributed, in large measure, to our failure to formulate any clear-cut national population policy. The present war has only served to underscore this weakness. The war is also rapidly working profound changes, not only in the internal economy of both Hawaii and Puerto Rico, but in their relationship to the national government. The racial problem in both islands has, as a consequence, ceased to be a matter of local concern. To see this problem in proper perspective requires a rather detailed analysis of the complex racial pattern existing in Hawaii.

1. Ethnic Laboratory

To a degree that is largely unknown to the average American, our national policy on minority groups, particularly those of Oriental ancestry, has become unbelievably complicated by the intermixture of races in Hawaii. The Hawaiian Islands are occupied today by what, from the point of race and cultural differences, is, according to Dr. Robert E. Park, "the most thoroughly scrambled community in the world." Twelve different racial categories are listed in the census figures. From Europe have come Germans, Galicians, Russians, Poles, Portuguese, Scandinavians, and Spaniards; from the Orient have come Chinese, Japanese, Filipinos, Koreans, and South Sea Islanders; and from Puerto Rico have come the hybrids of our other island outpost. "Mixed?" queried a young girl of Dr. Park. "Yes, I am a kind of league of nations in myself." During the brief period of sixty-two years, from 1875 to 1937, the islands have been literally repeopled with alien races. More people have been imported to Hawaii during this period than were living there in 1875 at the time of Captain Cook's first visit. To appreciate the national and international complications which this racial intermixture has created, it is merely sufficient to point out that all persons born on the islands are citizens of the United States.

For the most part, this amazing influx of peoples to Hawaii has never seriously concerned the citizens of the mainland. A number of explanations may be offered to account for this singular indifference. The islands are 2100 miles from San Francisco. Being unrelated and detached from the mainland has served to hide them, so to speak, from public opinion in this country. Although the islands have important economic ties with the mainland, particularly with California, even the West Coast has been content to ignore racial policies developed at such a distance from its shores. Immigration to Hawaii, unlike that to the mainland, has been closely supervised and controlled by the sugar planters, which has served to minimize disturbances that, otherwise, might have aroused public opinion here. Throughout the whole period of intensive immigration to the islands, the sugar interests have been extremely sensitive to mainland opinion. As a consequence they have created one of the most efficient public-relations mechanisms of its kind in the world.[1] Through this agency they have been consistently able to allay, divert, and mystify mainland concern over the increasingly complex minority problem in the islands. Almost every book written about the islands of recent years, according to the *New Republic*,[2] has been subsidized by Bowman, Deute & Cummings, public-relations advisers to the Hawaii Sugar Planters Association. As a result of this deluge of propaganda, most Americans have been induced to take an extremely romantic view of the islands. The lush vegetation, the hula dancers, and the beach at Waikiki have served as a wonderful "cover-up" for the shenanigans of the sugar planters. Quite apart from these considerations, the melting-pot thesis has, to some extent at least, been vindicated in Hawaii. There is little "race feeling" as such. But the war has brought the isolation of the islands to an abrupt and permanent termination. The presence on them of 150,000 Japanese is no longer a matter of indifference to the mainland. The Pacific Ocean has suddenly become a large pond and Hawaii seems at our doorstep. Pearl Harbor has served to rivet American attention on the islands and all of Mr. Bowman's skill and cunning in manipulating public opinion cannot alter this fact.

[1] See *Hawaii: Restless Rampart*, by Joseph Barber, Jr., 1941, Chapter III, for details.
[2] January 27, 1941.

Even prior to December 7, some areas in this country had become concerned over the future of the islands and had begun to interest themselves in their internal affairs. Californians had come to realize that Hawaii was a steppingstone to the mainland for many Oriental immigrants. A large number of the contract employees imported to Hawaii were "industrial excursionists," determined to get to the mainland if possible. Between 1900 and 1910, approximately 40,000 Japanese and about 8000 Spanish and Portuguese left the islands for California; and from 1910 to 1930 thousands of Filipinos likewise left for the West Coast. The increasing agitation for the admission of Hawaii to the Union as a state has also served to arouse mainland interest in its racial composition. On November 5, 1940, about 46,000 of some 84,000 registered voters in Hawaii said they were in favor of statehood (23,000 opposed it and about 15,000 failed to vote). Recent Gallup polls indicate that opinion in this country favors Hawaii's admission as a state by two to one. As this issue becomes of increasing urgency, the more will public opinion here be concerned over Hawaii's curiously mixed population.

There are still other reasons for the belief that we can no longer regard what happens in Hawaii as a matter of indifference in terms of our mainland race problems. Whether Hawaii is admitted as a state or not, it would seem obvious that we must recognize the inconsistency of treating particular groups in one manner under the American flag in Hawaii and in a diametrically opposite manner under the same flag on the mainland. Today, for example, virtually every Japanese on the West Coast is in protective custody; but the Japanese population of the islands remains in full possession of its prewar rights and privileges. This inconsistency becomes the more striking in view of the fact that the Japanese population in the three West Coast states constituted but 1 per cent of the total population; whereas the Japanese in Hawaii constitute 37 per cent of the total population. While differences may be noted in the Japanese problem in Hawaii, by comparison with the mainland, these hardly account for two such sharply divergent policies. In appraising the policy of evacuation, it might be noted that no acts of sabotage have been reported in Hawaii since December 7, 1941.[3] It is possible, therefore, that Hawaii has something to teach the mainland on the score of race relations. For it is, as Mr. Albert Horlings has stated, one of the greatest anthropological laboratories in the world.

2. The Inborn Tide

Annexed in 1898, Hawaii became "an integral part" of the United States in 1900. Annexation, however, merely gave formal recognition to what had long been an accomplished fact, for American domination of island affairs dates back to 1820. American interests had become so thoroughly entrenched by 1900 that annexation involved no major changes. The government merely recognized the *status quo* and assumed that no special action on its part was needed for the protection, for example, of the natives. Other native races under American jurisdiction — Indians, Eskimos, Chamorros of Guam, Virgin Islanders, and Filipinos — were given some measure of special attention and protection, but not the Hawaiians. One reason for this singular lack of concern is that, by 1900, the major part of the damage had already been done.

At the time of Captain Cook's second visit to the islands, in 1778, there were about 300,000 natives in Hawaii. Population was, at that time, more or less stabilized. The natives had developed, over a long period of years, a culture and a subsistence economy which met most of their needs. When this culture came into contact with Western civilization the most frightful havoc was wrought to native life. It was not necessary to shoot the natives; for, unlike the American Indians, they were extremely pacific. "The Hawaiians," said one observer, "can lie down and die the easiest of any people with which I am acquainted." Today there are only 22,636 natives left. The decimation of native population between 1778 and 1900

[3] See the correspondence and affidavits in the Findings and Recommendations of the Tolan Committee, May 1942, pp. 48–58; and "The Japanese in Hawaii" by Blake Clark, *New Republic*, September 14, 1942.

was catastrophic. As a people they simply collapsed under the impact of an alien culture and economy. "Within a century and a half following the visit of the first white men to the islands," writes Dr. Andrew W. Lind, "the native population had diminished to about one-tenth of its pre-European size; and the first half of this era alone witnessed a decline of 72 per cent." [4]

Neither before nor after annexation were any governmental safeguards thrown about the native culture and economy. With the inevitable collapse of that culture and economy, the natives died. Nor was an attempt made to throw legal protection around native land tenure, such, for instance, as Great Britain afforded the Fijians when Fiji became a crown colony in 1874.[5] In a historical fortnight, the Hawaiians were stripped of their landholdings. Such lands as are still owned, in whole or in part, by Hawaiians are administered by trust companies (controlled by the Big Five) who charge exorbitant fees for a trusteeship that, by right, should have been assumed by the government.[6] Formerly Hawaii had a subsistence agricultural economy; today 90 per cent of its cultivated lands are developed to two plantation crops: sugar cane and pineapples. Approximately 65 per cent of its working population is employed in these two crops. Virtually no attempts have ever been made to rehabilitate the native population or to resettle it on the land. In 1920 a feeble attempt was made along these lines by the creation of the Hawaiian Homes Commission; but the lands set aside for native homesteads were quickly diverted to sugar cane and pineapples. No special protection has even been afforded the natives in such an obviously necessary particular as public health. On the contrary, a general hospital established by Queen Emma Kaleleonalani for the treatment of the natives ended up by becoming a private institution from which Hawaiians and part-Hawaiians are generally excluded. The necessity for special public-health measures is quite

[4] *An Island Community*, p. 94.
[5] See *Fijian Frontier* by Laura Thompson, 1940.
[6] See Barber, p. 239, for details.

obvious: according to Mr. Barber, the death rate among native Hawaiians is twice as high as the national average; their birth rate is well below the national average; their infant mortality rate is eight times as high as the national average; their maternal mortality rate nearly twice as high. Possessed of few worldly goods, these remaining natives are described as "desperately poor, dragging out a hand-to-mouth existence through fishing and raising a few vegetables." For the most part, they have been pushed back into the marginal crevices, where they have found a kind of haven. "Few dollars pass through their hands," writes Mr. Barber; "indeed they, more than any other island group, are responsible for the fact that the average per capita effective buying income of Hawaii is less than $275, lower than all but three or four states in the Union." The American Indian, it would seem, has fared well when compared with the natives of Hawaii.

The year 1850 marked the turning point in the affairs of the islands. In that year, non-Hawaiians constituted only 2 per cent of the population; but by then the plantation system had become firmly entrenched. In 1850 the first indentured labor law was enacted and two years later the first batch of Chinese contract workers arrived. From then on the proportion of non-Hawaiians steadily increased: from 10 per cent in 1872 to 45 per cent in 1884 and to 86 per cent in 1930. Today Caucasians constitute less than one fifth of the population, and, since birth rates among this group are the lowest in the islands, they will probably constitute numerically a still lower percentage in the future. From 1850 until 1930 immigrants were imported in a seemingly endless procession, particularly after 1876 when a reciprocal trade treaty with the United States gave an added impetus to sugar production. To illustrate the magnitude of this migration, suffice it to say that plantation interests have spent a total of nearly $20,000,000 in importing upwards of 400,000 workers from 1850 to date. Nor does this total represent all that was spent in stimulating immigration, since a Bureau of Immigration was established in the local government in 1864 which, in turn, spent large sums. Recruitment of workers has been a continuous process since, after annexation, it became extremely difficult to hold labor on the plantations. Prior to annexation, plantation workers were held in a kind of semi-feudal bondage and could not breach their contracts of employment. The law forbidding the importation of contract employees, which became effective after annexation, never bothered the sugar interests. They kept on importing workers until 1934. Labor turnover on the plantations has always been extremely high. Imported workers, after annexation, deserted their contracts, moved into Honolulu and Hilo for non-plantation jobs; and some of them returned to their homelands or moved on to the West Coast. The movement of Oriental immigrants to Hawaii rapidly set in motion a tide of immigration from the same sources which went directly to the mainland. More and more Japanese and Filipinos, for example, began coming directly from the Orient to California. Patterns of immigration were thus established which have had, in the course of years, international significance. In the development of these patterns, however, the government of the United States had little to say. It was exclusively the work of the sugar plantations of the island; and the government, by ignoring the situation, permitted a state of affairs to develop which, to this day, has plagued the United States.

The first racial element to be imported to Hawaii were the Chinese. Prior to 1900, when the Chinese Exclusion Law became effective in Hawaii, some 46,000 Chinese had been brought to the islands. A considerable number of the original Chinese immigrants eventually returned to the Orient; and only a few went on to the mainland, since most of the Chinese in California had gone directly to the Coast immediately after the discovery of gold in 1849. There are today about 28,380 Chinese in the islands, 84.91 per cent of whom are American citizens by reason of birth in Hawaii. As rapidly as circumstances permitted, the Chinese left the plantations and moved into the towns and cities where they became actively interested in the small retail trade. In 1939, only 674 Chinese were employed as plantation workers. There is also today, of course, a large Chinese-Hawaiian population. Since most of the original Chinese who came to the islands were single men, many of them took Hawaiian brides. Today 71 per cent of the Chinese are concentrated in Honolulu. Despite its widely publicized racial *aloha*, miniature ghettos have developed in Hawaii. The census of 1866, according to Dr. Lind, revealed a concentration of 74 per cent of all of Honolulu's Chinese within the restricted Chinatown; seventy years later most of the Chinese in Honolulu were still living within an area of half a square mile, including and surrounding the old Chinatown. The period of Chinese importation was, generally, from 1852 to 1900.

In their efforts to get immigrant workers who were "racially cognate" with the Hawaiian people, the sugar interests ranged far afield. From 1868 to 1885, they imported about 2448 South Sea Islanders; but this importation was soon dropped as the workers recruited did not prove satisfactory. Between 1878 and 1886, some 17,500 Portuguese were imported, principally dark-skinned immigrants from the Azores and Madeira. In 1900 about 6000 Puerto Ricans were imported, most of whom had been recruited from among the mud-flat slums of San Juan. From 1906 to 1913, approximately 8000 Spaniards were imported, most of whom subsequently moved on to California. During the period when Spaniards were imported, Spain prohibited emigration. As a result of this policy, the sugar interests had to smuggle the bulk of these workers out of Spain by way of Gibraltar. I have seen first-hand autobiographical accounts of how these peasants fared on their trip around the Horn, crowded as they were in rotten old crates for months en route. The whole traffic, in fact, was strikingly similar to the Middle Passage of the period of African slavery. The Gentlemen's Agreement of 1907 and the Immigration Act of 1924 greatly stimulated the importation of Filipino workers. From 1906 to 1930, approximately 120,000 Filipinos were imported to the islands. None of this large-scale recruitment of immigrants has been checked, supervised, or officially approved by the government of the United States and much of it has gone on since 1900. The government simply did not concern itself with the labor policies of the sugar planters and permitted these interests to people the islands as they saw fit.

In their labor recruitment activities, as Mr. William C. Smith has pointed out, "the planters guarded well their interests lest they lose control. When the large influx of Chinese in the early days of sugar production endangered the scheme, they brought Portuguese and Japanese to checkmate them; and later, when the Japanese became dangerously numerous, they relieved the tension by the importation of Koreans, Puerto Ricans, Spanish, and more Portuguese." [7] Once the Philippines and Puerto Rico were taken over by the United States at the close of the Spanish-American War in 1898, the planters were able to tap the very large labor pools in these outlying possessions without encountering immigration restrictions.

Because of its great significance, the importation of Japanese to the islands requires some special comment. The sugar interests were interested in Japanese labor from an early date; but they encountered — and this fact should be emphasized — strong opposition on the part of the Japanese government. The first Japanese who came to the islands (147 in 1868) were, according to the protests of Japan, "piratically stolen," or kidnaped. As a result of an official Japanese note of protest, most of these initial immigrants were returned to Japan. It was the conjunction, however, of American capital and Japanese labor that eventually created the plantation economy of the islands. The Reciprocity Treaty of 1876 between Hawaii and the United States really opened the islands for American capital, as it also brought about American domination in Hawaii's internal affairs. The Reciprocity Treaty, on the other hand, as Dr. Lind has observed, also was the economic occasion for the Hawaiian-Japanese Labor Convention of 1886, which, for the first time, "officially opened the doors for the emigration of Japanese laborers to the outside world." Prior to 1886, there existed in Japan a "fixed prejudice against foreign emigration in any form." In bringing about a change in policy on the part of the Japanese government, it was the sugar interests of Hawaii who took the initiative and who,

[7] *Annals of the American Academy*, September 1942, p. 42.

in effect, pleaded with Japan for a relaxation of its policy against emigration. It is Hawaii, therefore, as Dr. Lind writes, "that has the distinction of having initiated the emigration of Japanese laborers to foreign lands during the modern period, and during the forty years of the movement it received the largest single body of workers that Japan sent to any foreign land." The agreement signed between the Hawaiian government and Japan coincided with the passage of the Chinese Exclusion Act in this country in 1882. The agreement, signed in Tokyo, provided for the importation of Japanese contract laborers for a term of three years to work in the islands at wages of nine dollars a month and a food allowance of six dollars per month for agricultural employees. Under the terms of this agreement, approximately 180,000 Japanese laborers migrated to Hawaii. The Gentlemen's Agreement of 1907 was conspicuously silent on the question of further Japanese immigration to Hawaii. As a matter of fact, Japanese continued to migrate until the passage of the 1924 Immigration Act. We owe it to the plantation sugar interests of Hawaii, therefore, that today there are some 617,988 Japanese in the Western Hemisphere. Implicit in this migration of workers were developments of the most profound implications for the peace of the world. Yet the whole movement, as such, was ignored by the United States, which, in its *laissez faire* attitude, failed to concern itself with population policies. To argue that Hawaii was not under American rule in 1886 is to beg the question; for it was most certainly under complete American dominance at the time. Thus it was, as Dr. Lind observes, "that the same events which opened wider doors for the importation of American capital and Japanese labor to Hawaii also brought to a clearer focus the role which each of these emerging powers was to play in the Pacific for decades to come."

Today there are 153,539 Japanese in the islands, 37.31 per cent of the total population, of whom 116,584 are citizens (73.93 per cent of the entire group). Like the Chinese before them, they have shown some tendency to leave the plantations; in fact, in 1939, only 13,460 were employed as plantation workers. As pointed out previously, some 40,000 of the number originally imported moved on to California as soon as their contracts of employment were at an end. What, then, has happened to the remaining Japanese in Hawaii — that is, those who are not still employed on the plantations?

To appreciate what has happened to them it is necessary to keep one or two general considerations in mind. In the first place, Hawaii is controlled by what is, perhaps, the most air-tight economic oligarchy in the world. The so-called "Big Five" of the islands — American Factors, C. Brewer & Company, Ltd., Alexander & Baldwin, Castle and Cook, Ltd., and T. H. Davies & Co., Ltd. — control not only the cane and pineapple plantations, but virtually every business of any importance in the islands. A reference to the testimony of Mr. E. J. Eagen, before the House Committee on the Labor Board and the Wagner Act, May 3, 1940, will show, in detail, how far-reaching is this control. It includes transportation, banking, hotels and restaurants, public utilities, lands, the wholesale trade, and almost every local industry. When Japanese immigration to Hawaii was restricted in 1907, the local Japanese protested bitterly. They contended that it left them at the mercy of their employers, since it checked the gradual increase of Japanese laborers on the one hand, thereby reducing Japanese purchasing power in the islands, and at the same time left the sugar interests free to engage in still further mass importation of other groups, in particular Filipinos, and to pit one race against another. In an effort to improve plantation working conditions, the Japanese went on strike in May 1909. The strike lasted for months and cost the planters an estimated $2,000,000. In 1920 the Japanese plantation workers again went on strike and again the strike was suppressed only after considerable sums had been spent by the planters. Both of these strikes resulted in a sharp increase in the importation of Filipino workers, the policy of the planters being to supplant the Japanese as swiftly as possible. As a consequence, the Japanese were in this predicament: they were being replaced as plantation workers; they could not enter the general commercial or industrial field since these fields had long since been pre-empted by the Big Five; and, despite a keen desire on their part to secure small agricultural freeholds, "the difficulties in the way," as Dr. Lind points out, "have been well-nigh insurmountable." These difficulties consisted, of course, primarily in the land and credit monopolies held by the Big Five.

Hedged in from all sides in this manner, the Japanese turned to the small retail trade. Here they encountered little opposition, for, as John Williams has pointed out, "the retail market was chicken feed anyhow, compared with the wholesale agencies. The Hawaiian capitalists sewed up every agency by interlocking directorates of practically every company in Hawaii. The capitalists weren't worried overmuch about the expanding Japanese retailers; after all, the capitalists were in Hawaii to make fortunes." [8] The consequence is that today the Japanese constitute 56 per cent of the servants and personal attendants in Hawaii; 53 per cent of the fishermen (prior to Pearl Harbor); 43 per cent of those in manufacturing and mechanical trades; 42 per cent of the tradesmen and storekeepers; and 23 per cent of the small truck farmers. [9] Always thrifty and industrious, they have prospered in their new field, as witness the fact that they constitute 47 per cent of the depositors in Hawaii's banks and their deposits amount to 30 per cent of the total. In terms of dollars, the Japanese savings total some $15,000,000 and their real and personal property holdings are valued at another $25,-000,000. [10] In carving out this new field for themselves, the Japanese were forced to become more and more race-conscious, to organize their own community in self-defense, and, in effect, to create a community within a community. Prior to Pearl Harbor, this well-organized Japanese community was steadily growing stronger. They held, in 1941, one seat in the Hawaiian Senate and six seats in the lower house. The same complex of forces that tended to make them race-conscious and organization-minded tended also to tie them economically to Japan (two thirds of their savings were, for example, in Japanese banks in 1941). It also gave the older generation a tight hold on the

[8] *PM*, August 10, 1941.
[9] Barber, p. 136.
[10] *PM*, August 6, 1941.

Nisei, or younger generation. The *Nisei*, owing to their race and color, are definitely handicapped in the "white American" business and social world; consequently the *Issei* have had little difficulty in holding these youngsters within the orbit of the Japanese community. Much the same pattern existed in California.

For this general state of affairs we have no one to blame but ourselves. We permitted it to come into being; and ours is the responsibility for the fact itself. If the Japanese communities on the West Coast constituted a military hazard, then most certainly the Japanese community in Hawaii is a greater hazard, not only because of the great strategic importance of the islands and the greater percentage of Japanese, but because the Japanese community as such is even better organized in Hawaii than it was on the West Coast. Yet no large-scale precautionary measures have been taken in Hawaii despite repeated warnings.[11] Congressional delegate Sam King has been working assiduously to convince Congress that no action should be taken against the Japanese in Hawaii; and some months ago Mr. John McClory, Assistant Secretary of War, announced that the resident Japanese in Hawaii were indispensable to its economic life as well as to its military defenses. In these statements and in the silence in the general press on the Japanese problem in Hawaii, it is possible to read the powerful influence of the sugar interests, bent as always upon ruling Hawaii as they see fit, and determined in this emergency to hold fast to sugar cane and pineapples, the *status quo* and the Japanese.

As pointed out previously, some 120,000 Filipinos have been brought to Hawaii since 1906. While many of them have returned to the Philippines and thousands have moved on to California, the number still remaining is substantial. There are today about 52,810 Filipinos in Hawaii, of whom 16,201 are American citizens and 36,609 are aliens. Unlike the other groups, they have not shown a marked tendency to leave plantation employment. In part this is owing to the fact that they are the newest

[11] See "Hawaii's 150,000 Japanese" by Albert Horlings, *Nation*, July 25, 1942; and a series of articles by John Williams in *PM*, August 3, 4, 5, 6, and 10, 1941.

immigrants in point of time. At present about 43,170 Filipinos are to be found on the plantations. After the Gentlemen's Agreement of 1907, the plantation interests were somewhat restricted in their recruiting activities. At that time, as observed by Dr. Bruno Lasker, the only two large potential reservoirs of labor were Puerto Rico and the Philippines. Because they were both under the American flag, these "countries seemed free from the danger of being suddenly closed by restrictive immigration laws." Theoretically, the Filipinos were imported to Hawaii "as temporary labor, and not as a scheme of settlement"; [12] that is, according to the sugar interests. But most of them have remained, and there is little likelihood that those now there will depart. Mr. Kilmer O. Moe has interviewed many who, after a return to the Philippines, have come back to Hawaii to stay. "For the most part they were disappointed with their old home villages." [13] What was intended by the planters as a temporary expedient has turned into a permanent settlement, with resultant social problems almost as aggravated in Hawaii as in California. For example, the ratio of men to women, among Filipinos in Hawaii, is 20 to 1. It is not surprising, therefore, to discover that 60 per cent of the murderers incarcerated in Hawaii are Filipinos nor that they constitute one third of those arrested for rape. [14] The *Voice of Labor*, published in Honolulu, bluntly summarized one phase of this problem in its issue of October 21, 1936: —

Thousands of Filipino workers frequent houses of prostitution because the sugar planters have failed to provide them with a normal social life. Sugar planters can marry but Filipino workers can't. The Lord's Anointed forgot to import women for them. That is why a Filipino laborer must pay two days' wages for a visit to a prostitute. It was much cheaper to provide prostitutes for Filipinos than to provide Filipinos with wives, a home, and a normal social life.

That the Filipinos have occasionally rebelled against these conditions is a matter which the race theorists of the islands, con-

[12] *King Cane: The Story of Sugar in Hawaii,* by John W. Vandercook, p. 62.
[13] See *Interracial Marriage in Hawaii* by Romanzo Adams, p. 259.
[14] *Filipino Immigration* by Dr. Bruno Lasker, p. 192.

cerned only with the fact that there are no race riots or lynchings as such, consistently overlook. They forget that, as *Fortune* pointed out, the race problem is a labor problem, and, conversely, that the labor problem is a race problem. In the great strike of Filipino plantation workers in 1924, five policemen and fifteen strikers were killed. After this strike thousands left the island for California only to have their places taken by still newer recruits from the Philippines. Pablo Manlapit, who led the 1924 strike, returned to the islands in 1937, and once again tried to organize the field workers, only to be "banished" from the islands. As to the present working and living conditions of Filipinos in the islands, a reference to the following sources will give the facts: *Filipino Plantation Workers in Hawaii*, by Edna Clark Wentworth (1941); report by Henry A. Rudin, for sixteen years Welfare Director of Waialua Plantation, in the *Voice of Labor*, August 17, 1936; *Labor in the Territory of Hawaii*, by James H. Shoemaker (1936). Nor have we heard the last of Filipino labor in Hawaii. When the Philippine Islands Independence Act was passed, which restricted further Filipino immigration to the United States (fixing a quota of fifty a year), the sugar interests had a proviso written into the bill that, under certain circumstances, Filipino labor might still be imported to Hawaii. Under the Filipino Repatriation Act of July 10, 1935, Filipinos resident in the United States were offered free passage back to the Philippines; but this act applied only to those Filipinos on the mainland — the same offer was *not* extended to those in Hawaii. On August 23, 1941, Mr. D. M. Yap, formerly attached to the Philippines Commonwealth staff in Washington, announced that he had been asked to investigate the feasibility of importing more Filipinos to the islands to meet the demands for labor. While the war has made such importation impossible, there is reason to believe that it may be resumed in the future.

Despite the fact that Filipinos constitute a large portion of the population of Hawaii, they have never formed a compact community. Lacking cultural integration in the Philippines, they have been seemingly unable to create strong social organizations. "There is a lack," writes Mr. Roman R. Cariaga, "of any

principle of organization among the Hawaiian Filipinos powerful enough to knit them together in larger wholes." [15] Tagalogs
quarrel with Visayans and Visayans war with Ilocanos. "Disputes occur between factions and their leaders. Often organizations with the same objectives compete, as it would seem, unnecessarily." Organizations spring up like mushrooms and die
away as quickly. "Being highly disorganized, the struggle for
social position in the Filipino community is intense. When an
individual rises, the others endeavor to pull him down."

"When the Filipinos came to Hawaii," writes Mr. Cariaga,
"and to the mainland of the United States, they thought and
felt about many things in the same way as a westerner; they
had in varying degree a philosophy of social equality, liberty of
action and freedom of worship. As an immigrant, however, the
Filipino was thrown into an American community which was
unaware of his thoughts and ambitions, longings and desires
for the new and better life which he was assured he would find
in the territory. His physical characteristics belied his western
heritage, and he met economic and social restrictions and tabus.
Conflict arose in his mind and serious problems of social adjustment emerged. As long as he remained within the fold of his
own racial grouping, he was safely harbored. But in Hawaii
such isolation was impossible. Whatever move he made, he encountered Americans, Japanese, Chinese, Koreans, Hawaiians,
and others, each with their varying customs. As the latest comer
he had a hard time winning his way anywhere other than in the
socially lowest strata of the society. Barriers arose before him,
causing him frequently to be disillusioned, discouraged, and
even hopeless. Confused, he naturally tended to blame the
Americans for making him believe what he was not allowed to
enjoy. . . . Although Filipinos have contributed substantially
to the economic welfare of the whole community they are not
yet considered integral to the social whole."

In another connection, Mr. Cariaga states: "Hawaii for most
Filipinos of the immigrant generation is at present a *half-world*,
a mechanical existence as a means toward an end, money, which

[15] *The Filipinos in Hawaii*, 1937.

will bring social prestige upon return to the ancestral area. . . . The vast majority of plantation men, while they may take a passing interest in foreign experience, have their hearts focussed on the homeland and their energies bent upon acquiring capital to invest in Philippine soil." While they have sent large sums back to the Philippines, nevertheless most of them are hopelessly involved in a credit system with the operations of which they remain unfamiliar. "They are more likely to remain in Hawaii," writes Mr. Cariaga, "struggling on rather than return to show their failure. . . . The man who has failed, unless deported to the Philippines, or drawn by exceptionally strong home ties, does not go back." The longer they stay in Hawaii, the more likely they are to marry and raise families. In 1930 there were 11,217 Filipino children under fifteen years of age in Hawaii. These children likewise show signs of cultural maladjustment: 22.5 per cent of Filipino boys and girls between the ages of ten and twenty were listed as illiterate in the 1930 census.

In addition to the groups I have mentioned, there are some other miscellaneous "importees" in Hawaii. Between 1909 and 1912, the Bureau of Immigration of Hawaii, at a public expense of $178,000, imported 2056 Russians from Manchuria. There are also approximately 6707 Koreans (of whom 4355 are citizens); and a present Puerto Rican population of 7639, all of whom are citizens. And, lastly, there are the important "mixed blood" groups: 20,507 Caucasian-Hawaiians, all of whom are citizens, and 20,360 Asiatic-Hawaiians, all of whom are citizens. There are also, of course, as previously noted, 21,268 Hawaiians. The Hawaiians and part-Hawaiians increased 26.4 per cent from 1930 to 1940: from 50,860 to 64,310. It is these latter groups that are of extreme importance, since it has been through intermarriage that the native Hawaiians have survived and now seem to be on the increase. "The neo-Hawaiian amalgam of Polynesian and foreign stocks," notes Dr. Lind, "seems destined finally to inherit the earth." If one disregards recent increases in Army and Navy personnel in the islands, the combined Caucasian strength has remained almost exactly one fifth of the total population for the last twenty years. Mixed bloods are unquestionably expanding at the expense of the so-called pure bloods. At the same time, the alien element is rapidly receding into the background. In 1896 only 10.3 per cent of the Chinese were native-born and citizens, while in 1940 the percentage was 86.89. In 1896 only 8.5 per cent of the Japanese were native-born, while in 1940 their citizenship (identical with nativity) rose to 77.9 per cent.

3. Racial Aloha

The various races in the islands are in the process of becoming one people.[16] As the base of the population pyramid becomes increasingly made up of mixed or hybrid stock, a new type of American citizen is being created, a type quite unique in the American scheme of things. Just as the Negro in the United States differs in important respects from the Negro in Africa, so the intermixture of groups in the islands is creating new types, new features, new characteristics. The end result of this intermixture, as can already be seen, is the creation of a new amalgam. What is happening in Hawaii, in this respect, has world-wide significance. For the intermixture taking place is, perhaps, a forecast of what is likely to happen throughout the Pacific area in the future. Despite the barriers that have been erected against the migration of Orientals, some 17,000,000 people of Asiatic origin are today living outside Asia proper. The intermixture taking place in Hawaii may, therefore, well be indicative of a new world amalgam. For with the world becoming more and more a single economic unit, and with the development of air transportation, the peoples of the East and the West are certain to be brought into increasingly closer relations and, out of these relations, intermixture will result.

That this new amalgam of races has been created in Hawaii with a minimum of friction and in a brief historical period certainly calls in question some of the heavy pseudo-anthropological theorizing of former years. By and large this amalgamation has come about with slight, if any, friction. All observers seem to agree that there is no race prejudice, as such, in Hawaii. This is

[16] See *The American Empire*, 1940, paper by John Wesley Coulter, p. 393.

not to say, of course, that race prejudice does not exist; but rather to say that it does not exist officially. "The race mores of Hawaii are, or tend to be, the mores of race equality" is the way Dr. Romanzo Adams puts it.[17] There is no race prejudice in the practised rituals of race relations. Such prejudice as does exist is covert, unofficial, and quiescent. The most striking manifestation of the fact itself consists in the circumstance that, as Dr. Adams has said, "in Hawaii public sentiment is not opposed to interracial marriage." There has never been, for example, a miscegenation statute in the islands. There have been no lynchings in the islands; race riots are unknown; and no fixed patterns of segregation have developed. The same spirit of admirable racial *aloha* exists in the public schools. Teachers belong to all races and nationalities. The schools themselves are open to all and free to all. The children of the different nationalities mingle freely together in the schoolroom and on the playground; and there is no segregation within the school system. "Big Business" and the key administrative and executive posts are, of course, reserved for the whites or *haoles,* who constitute about 9 per cent of the population; and the economic life of the islands is completely dominated by this group. But non-whites nevertheless engage in a wide variety of trades, occupations, and professions. There have been Chinese and Japanese legislators in Hawaii, and even one Negro. No politician would dare raise the racial issue in the islands. And, by contrast with California, there is a large measure of social equality.

"Why," Dr. Adams has asked, "this freedom in Hawaii? Why, in Hawaii, did the people of British and American origin fail to set up the obstacles that are so commonly found where English-speaking people have established contacts with the darker races?" The key to this problem is the matter of interracial marriage. For, as Dr. Adams has said, "any sort of social control able to prevent interracial marriage for a long time cannot fail to create a caste system." No such controls have ever existed in Hawaii; and for a number of obvious reasons. In the first place, the native Hawaiians had not created a tightly knit

[17] See *When Peoples Meet,* 1942, p. 257.

social system at the time of American penetration of the islands; there were, for example, no tabus on intermarriage. Since the sex ratios, as between Caucasians and Hawaiians, were so one-sided, Hawaiian women began to marry non-Hawaiian men. This one-sided aspect of the matter is still observed, since more Hawaiian women marry outside the group than men, with the result that there are three times as many single men as single women among the Hawaiians. Slavery, as such, never existed in Hawaii, so that there was no antecedent pattern of slave relations. The early missionaries to the islands were from New England, and, as such, they were opposed to slavery and, for practical reasons, were favorably disposed to economic and social alliances with the natives. Also, Hawaii remained nominally independent for some years after Captain Cook's memorable visit. It became, therefore, necessary to curry favor with the natives in order to win important economic concessions. The early non-white immigrants were, for the most part, young unmarried men: Chinese, Filipinos, Koreans. Given this fact and the absence of tabus on intermarriage, racial intermixture was inherent in the situation. The creation, in this manner, of an important "mixed group" served to break down any remaining tabus. The mixed group has served, over a long period of years, as a liaison between whites and non-whites. Then, too, as Dr. Adams has observed, "race prejudice is most effective where there are just two racial groups." With so many different racial groups involved, it became extremely difficult to erect a single race doctrine or a single set of racial controls. No one group, in other words, was dominant. Long controlling every phase of the economic life of the islands, the sugar interests, in the very nature of things, would not afford to indulge in race-baiting or to erect race barriers. Unlike the plantation economy of other areas, for example, the Hawaiian plantation system had to endorse, at least in name, the doctrine of racial equality. This they were compelled to do in order to maintain an available labor supply. This they were also willing to do, since, by reason of their absolute monopoly of land and resources and their tightly knit system of interlocking controls, it was impossible for other racial groups to compete with them. "In the paternalistic system of the sugar plantations," writes William Carlson Smith, "the workers, mostly Orientals, have occupied a position so inferior to that of all white men, that there has been no competition between the two groups." [18] The planters were, moreover, able to maintain their policy of racial tolerance, since there were no "poor white" groups on the islands — who, had they existed, might have come into direct competition with non-white racial groups. "In a community like Hawaii," writes Galen Fisher, "which has an abnormal economic basis, there is no danger of serious friction so long as the immigrants are willing to stay in humble occupations."

Having said this much, however, it would be a mistake to conclude that the racial mores in Hawaii are utopian. Incidents in the recent past — as, for example, the celebrated Massie case in 1931 — clearly indicate that racial tensions exist beneath the surface. The violent labor history of the islands (almost unknown on the mainland) has, on more than one occasion, assumed a definitely racial character. Their labor problem is indeed, as *Fortune* has noted, a racial problem. "Status," writes Mr. Smith, "is inextricably intertwined with the plantation system and is not necessarily dependent upon race." If the sugarcane and pineapple workers had ever been successful in organizing, it might well have resulted, as *Fortune* says, in "the creation of a Pacific equivalent of the Czechoslovak Sudeten problem," with Japanese pitted against Filipino and Filipino pitted against Portuguese. These dormant tensions, inherent in the labor problem, are likely to come to the surface if and when the plantation workers are organized. To some extent, too, the war has disturbed race relations.

A race crisis, in fact, is rapidly developing, and for somewhat the same reasons that are responsible for increasing tension on the mainland. The roots of this developing crisis are to be found in the problem of the second generation. With an admirable educational system, it was inevitable that an educated second generation would come along which would be dissatisfied

[18] *Americans in Process*, p. 114.

with farm labor and yet be unable to find white-collar employment. It was this consideration which prompted Mr. Walter Dillingham, one of the island nabobs, to observe some years ago that "our troubles are ahead of us." As the younger Oriental groups come into keener competition with "whites" for the better paid jobs and professional opportunities, race feeling will come to the surface. This general situation has already been noted. "Superficially," writes Mr. Smith, "it would appear that the various races in Hawaii live in perfect harmony. Beneath the surface, however, there is considerable discrimination against the races of color in the occupational field. The Orientals are not promoted to the more responsible positions." This younger generation is just now reaching maturity, and but for the outbreak of the war it is altogether likely that the existing tensions would have found expression in a noticeable rise in race feeling. Fortunately the war has within it, so to speak, the dynamics which are capable of breaking up the plantation system and thereby creating a wider field of economic opportunity. The Armed Forces are known to be critical of the plantation system and its airtight monopoly of the economic life of the islands. This monopoly and the emphasis on a two-crop commercial agricultural economy are responsible for the fact that Hawaii is dependent upon the mainland for vital foodstuffs; also for the fact that food costs are 25 per cent above the mainland averages, electricity rates 10 per cent higher, and gas rates 15 per cent higher. The Army will not, and cannot, tolerate forever a system that ties up so much shipping in bringing sugar cane and pineapples to the mainland and foodstuffs to the islands. If the war is protracted, a portion of the rich farm lands of Hawaii are likely to be diverted to the production of foodstuffs for island consumption. There are those who already see in this developing situation the beginnings of the dissolution of the semifeudal plantation economy which, in turn, is responsible for the fact that the younger generation are so limited in their quest for economic advancement.

"When race relations," writes Mr. Smith, "in Hawaii are examined with care, a paradoxical situation becomes evident. It is a matter of tradition and principle that there is or should be no prejudice. That is a doctrine to which the leading spokesmen of the Territory subscribe, and practically all members of the community feel bound to maintain it. Race equality is visible on every hand — in the freedom of intermarriage, in the absence of legal segregation in school or in residential areas, and in the ease with which members of the different races mingle at various social functions.

"Beneath this apparently calm surface, however, are found inequality, discrimination, prejudice, cynicism, and bitterness. The plantation system, in spite of the doctrine of race equality, has manipulated the importation of laborers from the several sources so that a small group of white Americans are in control not only of the sugar industry but of all aspects of life in the Territory.

"Much is said about the educational opportunities in the islands, and the young people are urged to use them in order to become good Americans. They are told about the 'room at the top' that is open to all on an equal basis. The children go through the schools and even through the university looking forward to the days when they will play important roles in the further unfolding of the great American epic of which they have read so hopefully in their schoolbooks. Many, however, are awakened quite rudely from their dreams when, with diplomas in hand, they seek employment. Then they find barriers, some of them very subtle, to be sure, while their Caucasian classmates, protected by vested rights, move unopposed into the preferred positions.

"This disillusionment has brought mutation in the attitudes of many of the Hawaiian-born sons and daughters of Oriental ancestry, 'from one of unquestioning endorsement of the existing order to one of complete rejection of their former loyalties.'"

4. Towards the Future

There is no uncertainty whatever concerning the future of Hawaii's relations with America; any existing uncertainty was permanently dissipated by the attack on Pearl Harbor. Hawaii is and will remain an integral part of the United States. No one has suggested that the islands be given dominion or semi-autonomous status; no one has suggested that they should be "freed." The peoples of the islands and of the mainland have indicated a strong feeling that Hawaii should be admitted to the Union as a state. Sooner or later it will be admitted; of this fact there can be little doubt. And, in the long run, the admission of Hawaii, with its pattern of interracial mixture, is bound to have some effect upon our treatment of minorities on the mainland.

In the very nature of things, we cannot pursue one policy on the mainland with respect to Filipinos, Chinese, Koreans, and Japanese and still a different policy in Hawaii. When Hawaii has two Senators and a number of Representatives in Congress, some of whom are certain to be of Oriental ancestry, these spokesmen are likely to have something to say on the score of social equality, equality of economic opportunity, and discrimination of all types. Every discrimination aimed at resident minorities will find repercussions in the islands. The contrast between the treatment of Orientals in Hawaii and in California, for example, will then become glaringly inconsistent. Chinese youngsters, born in the islands, say that when they visit California they feel as though they were in a different world. In the future, we shall not be in a position to afford our indulgence in provincial prejudices.

In the world of the future, these Chinese Americans, Filipino Americans, and Japanese Americans need not be regarded as problem children; on the contrary, they should be regarded as potential population assets of the first value. Already Hawaiian-trained Chinese are at work in China as doctors, nurses, educators, and administrators. They can serve this country, in the future, in many and varied ways. Some of them, for example, would make ideal diplomatic and consular representatives in the Far East. We cannot, if we would, undo what has already been done in the islands. We cannot, for example, disenfranchise these new Americans of Oriental ancestry. They are American citizens, products of American training, experience, and education; the children of our institutions and our culture. We cannot prevent these Hawaiian-born youngsters from migrating to the United States; nor can we prevent a similar movement from the mainland to Hawaii. Also, if we are to preserve the racial *aloha* of the islands, we must sooner or later bring about a similar state of affairs on the mainland. In the nature of things, we can't kick Filipinos around in California and elect them to public office in Hawaii. Similarly, it is basically inconsistent to make the American Indian a ward of the government on the mainland and to deny any measure of special protection to the natives of Hawaii who also are in effect a conquered people. In the past, we have permitted affairs in the islands to take their own course — which is tantamount to saying that we have permitted the sugar interests to rule Hawaii, to people it as they saw fit, to establish whatever patterns of race relations they desired. Although this policy has worked with tolerable success in the past, there is every reason to believe that intervention will be necessary in the future. For Hawaii might well be the scene, in the future, of race disturbances that would seriously embarrass the nation. Mr. Smith poses the question in this way: "Will the *white* man in Hawaii be able to rub the sugar out of his eyes so that he can see things as they are? Will he be able to change a surface friendliness and show of equality into something which is real and genuine? Can the *white* man of America learn from the recent experiences of the white man in Burma and in India? There, to be sure, the white man did not even make a pretense toward equality. We are hopeful but not too confident." To this statement might be added another query: Given the present iron-clad control of Hawaii by the sugar interests, can these changes urged by Mr. Smith be adopted *without federal intervention?* The scene is obviously set in Hawaii for an extension of democracy, but can this extension be effected without focusing upon the problem the full force of American public opinion?

CHAPTER VI
The Puerto Ricans and Other Islanders

GUARDING the approaches to the Panama Canal, the key to the defense of the Caribbean area, Puerto Rico has great strategic value to the United States, as witness the $40,000,000 currently being spent for its fortification. This strategic importance it has always possessed, for Spain made San Juan its second strongest fortress in the new world. Puerto Rico, moreover, constitutes our one Latin-American possession (with the exception of the Canal Zone). "As such," writes Ruby Black in *PM*, "it is not merely our Gibraltar at the gateway to the Panama Canal, but it is the cultural and racial link between the U.S.A. and the republics of South and Central America."[1] Nazi propagandists, she points out, have been able with some truth and with a great deal of effectiveness to cite Puerto Rico as a place under the Stars and Stripes where there was little democracy. Long neglected by the United States — almost forgotten by the American people — Puerto Rico has been lifted out of the past by the dynamics the war and placed, perhaps for the first time, in the spotlight of national attention. It is today, in the words of Mr. Rex Tugwell, "one of the frontier places of democracy."

Our neglect of Puerto Rico prior to December 7, 1941, was largely intentional. The island was taken over from Spain after the Spanish-American War, "as a mere incident of guarding Cuba's independence." The expansionists of 1898, according to Mr. J. Fred Rippy, were interested in Puerto Rico almost solely by reason of its strategic importance. Since our interest was primarily strategic, we hesitated to define the status of the island. This hesitation crystallized in a policy characterized by *Fortune* as "almost journalistically whimsical." It was not until May 1,

[1] February 18, 1941.

1900, that we got around to establishing a civil government there.

Puerto Rico is neither a colony nor an incorporated territory; it is not a state nor does it have local autonomy. Still it is a part, a dependent and inferior part, of the United States. Its residents do not vote in Presidential elections; but they have a Resident Commissioner in Washington who, however, has no vote in Congress. The insular legislature has a measure of autonomy; but the Governor possesses an absolute veto power. The explanation of this curiously inconsistent and hesitant policy has long been noted but, for obvious reasons, has seldom been emphasized. The expansionists of 1898 hesitated about incorporating Puerto Rico as a territory, because, according to Mr. Rippy, "they recoiled from admitting alien races with divergent cultures to the privileges and responsibilities of American citizenship."[2] This hesitation was not shown in the case of Hawaii, but then Hawaii did not have a population which consisted, as did that of Puerto Rico, of a fairly large Negro element.

Just as the present war is forcing us to reconsider the status of Puerto Rico, so the first World War was responsible for an important change in our policy toward the island. For it was on the eve of World War I that Congress passed the Organic Act — the so-called Jones Act — which still governs our relations with Puerto Rico. The act was passed under circumstances which "savored strongly of a bid for Puerto Rican loyalty" during the conflict which then impended.[3] If such was the motive for the act, it seems to have been fully justified. Some 12,852 Puerto Ricans were called up for military service in the first World War and history records no complaints about their loyalty or that of the civilian population. Under the terms of this act of March 2, 1917, all Puerto Ricans were made citizens of the United States. Only a negligible number — 288 to be exact — relinquished the right to American citizenship and most of these have since been naturalized. Thus under the pressure of wartime considerations we hastily acquired 1,869,255 new citizens. It should also be

[2] *The Caribbean Danger Zone*, 1940, p. 242.
[3] See *Porto Rico: A Broken Pledge* by Bailey W. Diffie, 1931.

noted that all persons born in Puerto Rico since March 2, 1917, are likewise citizens of the United States. Neither at the time nor subsequently has the importance of this population acquisition been appraised in the light of our own domestic minority problem. For example, just who are these new American citizens?

1. The People

While not quite as variegated as the peoples of Hawaii, the Puerto Ricans are, nevertheless, a hopelessly "mixed" population. At the time of the discovery of the islands by Columbus, it is estimated that there were about 50,000 native Indian inhabitants. The rapidity of their subsequent decrease was almost unbelievable. Today there are no Indians left, but many of their cultural traits persist. Negro slaves from the West Indies were imported as early as 1513, and in later years came in large numbers. Since the color line was never drawn in Puerto Rico, Indians, Negroes, and Spanish (and also some Portuguese) freely intermarried. "As a result of this commingling of blood there lives in Puerto Rico today," writes Mr. Diffie, "a large section of the population which is not Spanish, Indian nor Negro, but so complete a fusion of all three that it is impossible to say in what proportions these various elements are represented." In the Deep South, by rule of law, a drop of Negro blood is sufficient to mark a person as "colored"; but in Puerto Rico the contrary rule prevails— namely, that a drop of "white" blood is sufficient to make a person "white." Consequently the census enumeration of "whites" and "non-whites" is notoriously inexact; the tabulation has, in fact, been characterized as no more than a "statistical guess." In the 1940 census, 23.5 per cent of the population was returned as non-white; but the percentage should unquestionably have been higher. Mr. Trumbull White, in 1938, estimated that at least 35 per cent of the population were of mixed white and colored blood. The percentage of non-whites has, however, steadily declined, from an estimated 87 per cent in 1531 to 27 per cent in 1930. The fact is that it is almost impossible to determine whether a person is white or slightly colored in the islands today.

The population is "extremely intermixed and there are not only two colors, but an infinity of shades," according to Mr. José C. Rosario. All that one needs to do in order to appreciate the degree of intermixture is to recall that for four hundred years Negroes, Indians, and Spaniards lived on the island in almost complete isolation with no barriers, legal or otherwise, against intermixture. Furthermore a study of the changes taking place in the intercensal period "indicates that intermixture is going on at a rapid rate and that within a comparatively short time the people of pure Negro blood will be practically nonexistent." [4]

Because of the high percentage of racial intermixture, it has been impossible to draw the color line in Puerto Rico, except among the upper classes, where the line is sharply drawn.[5] There has never been, for example, a miscegenation statute in the island. Throughout Puerto Rico, in contrast with the Deep South, the various racial groups stand in exact equality before the law. According to Mr. White, there is no segregation either by rule or by practice. No cognizance is taken of racial differences in shops, schools, theaters, hotels, or public carriers; nor is the line drawn in the professions or in public service. "Intelligent, educated, and forceful colored men and women," to quote from the Brookings Institute Survey of 1930, "are found in all walks of life, where they associate without apparent discrimination with whites. Negroes are numerous in the teaching profession, and colored pupils attend, on terms of equality, public schools and higher educational institutions." Aside from the fact that most of the "blacks" live in the coastal areas (having driven the "poor whites" or *jibaros* into the hills during the period of slavery, much as Negro slave labor drove the "poor whites" of this country into the southern Appalachians), there seems to be no geographical, or occupational, segregation.

The significance of the race mores of Puerto Rico, in terms of American policy, was carefully noted some years ago by Mr. Luis Munoz Marin. "Perhaps the island should be of interest

[4] *The Puerto Rican Migrant in New York City* by Lawrence R. Chenault, 1938.
[5] *The American Empire*, 1940, p. 62.

to the American people," wrote Mr. Marin, "chiefly as a laboratory experiment in racial ethics, as there you will find the nearest approach to social equality of this sort within the supposedly permanent territory of the United States. From the middle class down, the union of white women to brown or black men is not unusual enough to astonish or enrage anybody, and the union of black or brown women to white men is of course more frequent. Discreet instances of both varieties of intermarriage may be found in the highest social pinnacles . . . lynching and the humiliation of Negroes by statute are unthinkable. There are no segregated districts . . . Jim Crow cars would seem as freakish as a man with two thumbs on one hand and eight fingers on the other. . . . A good proportion of the school teachers are of Negro and mixed extraction and they give their services to black, brown, and white indiscriminately. White, Negro, and Mulatto lawyers, physicians, journalists, poets, politicians, philosophers, lead a common professional and spiritual life. One of the ablest and most respected leaders of the Republican Party was Dr. Barbosa, a Negro physician. A newspaper in Ponce employed Carrion Maduro, a well-known Negro writer, as editor, with a white staff under him. Our most expressive composer was Campos, a light Mulatto. Men of both races get along quite well with one another in all social strata." [6] This wholly admirable social democracy has, in fact, persisted to this day, despite an increasing American economic penetration. Where the color line has been drawn, we have drawn it. "The American authorities," adds Mr. Marin, "in so far as they may act without fear of raising a hullabaloo, introduce segregation, as in the National Guard." This interesting ethnic laboratory has, in fact, much to teach us on the score of race relations; nor is this experience irrelevant to conditions in the United States. There was, for example, an age-old pattern of slave relations in Puerto Rico; slavery, as such, was not abolished until 1872, a decade after the issuance of the Emancipation Proclamation. Despite a background of slave relations, however, Puerto Rico has always been able to maintain admirable relationships between the white and Negroid races.

[6] *Nation*, April 8, 1925.

Puerto Rico represents our first experience in dealing at first hand with the problems of acculturation in respect to which we, as a nation, have been and remain the crudest novices. We have, for example, never related our tragic experience with the American Indian to somewhat similar problems of cultural adaptation in Hawaii, the Philippines, New Mexico, and Puerto Rico. We never think of these problems as belonging essentially to the same category. It is in Puerto Rico, in particular, that the problem is brought sharply into focus. For, as Mr. Marin wrote some years ago, "the gods have made Puerto Rico the first colonial experiment of the United States. The slices taken from Mexico were empty or more American than Mexican (*sic*) in almost everything but political allegiance; the power exercised over the Philippines is explicitly temporary; Hawaii came as a motley of peoples dominated by an American business and planting group. In Puerto Rico, on the other hand, the Americans acquired for permanent use a rather well-rounded civilization — here for the first time the American people undertook to boss a foreign culture." What, then, was the nature of this culture which we undertook to "boss"; and how have we succeeded in the bossing?

2. *The Cultural Complex*

When we acquired this island outpost, we seem to have forgotten that its population was of a culture and background and concept of life sharply at variance with our own. Puerto Rico was at the time a melting pot which "seethed with a strong compound of Hispanic and African spiced with aboriginal blood." The cultural background of the island is, of course, Latin-American, with most of the people speaking a Spanish patois. Because of its insularity, the people had, in fact, tended to develop their own island culture. Failing to recognize that the general outlook of the people was Spanish, not Anglo-Saxon, and that the basic elements of their culture, history, and law were drawn from Spain and not from England, we crassly attempted to impose an alien culture upon them. The form that this attempted imposition took was a "haphazard cultural attack," compound of Rotary, American educational practices, and a ceremonial parliamentarianism. The net result has been, of course, that the change in sovereignty has made the Puerto Ricans Americans in name only. "They are still Latin, with a different point of view, different ideals, different manners and customs, and with a different temperament from that of continental Americans."[7] "I do not believe," wrote Mr. Marin in 1925, "that American overlordship is Americanizing us to an important degree."

The problem of cultural adjustment in Puerto Rico is, in fact, quite different from that, say, in Hawaii. "As a noncontiguous possession, somewhat distant from the continental land area, Puerto Rico has all the salient features of a fully developed and unified nationality. Its fast growing population is ethnically united. . . . In language, culture, and customs, Puerto Rico is a perfectly well-defined people, conscious of those elements of nationality that Ernest Renan indicated as indispensable to existence; unit of speech, purpose, and experience."[8] Since Puerto Rico has been overpopulated for years, "the American colony that has grown up is small and cannot expand in terms of settlers." Thus Puerto Rico's contacts with the United States have been not collective, but individual. It is this problem of cultural conflict which, as Mr. Pattee states, makes "adjustment of Puerto Rico to American rule difficult and fraught with pitfalls and dangers. Puerto Rico," as he says, "is a very different case from Hawaii with its numerous racial groups, the Canal Zone with its preponderantly military emphasis, or the Virgin Islands of limited population and possessed of few marked cultural characteristics. It is also interesting to observe that the situation of Puerto Rico bears little resemblance to that of the Spanish-speaking population of Arizona, New Mexico, or Texas, where isolation, cultural disintegration, and economic considerations have influenced the development of this racial element." There is, therefore, "a compact unit (in Puerto Rico) that is to be

[7] *The American Empire*, p. 57.

[8] "The Puerto Ricans" by Richard Pattee, *Annals of the American Academy*, September 1942, p. 49.

found in none of the other areas subject to American rule."

It would be a mistake to say that "our cultural mission" in Puerto Rico has been a failure, for in actual fact there is little in the record to indicate that we ever recognized the existence of a cultural problem. Likewise, our original intention seems to have been to hold the island for strategic reasons and to ignore its internal development. At the time we undertook the government of Puerto Rico we were, as a nation, inexperienced administrators. Certainly our preparation for such an assignment was negligible. Just a few years prior to 1898, we had concluded the last of our Indian wars (1890) and were still tragically blind to the problems of Indian administration. There is, therefore, much to be said in extenuation of the sorry mess that we have made of Puerto Rican affairs. The basic mistake has been our failure to recognize the existence of a cultural problem. This mistake we were probably predisposed to make, because we had traditionally thought of ourselves as one people and also because of the fact that, by and large, we had assimilated so-called white immigrants (many of whom came from a somewhat similar cultural background) with a large measure of success. What had worked, after a fashion, in the United States would, therefore, succeed in Puerto Rico.

We failed to recognize, in relation to Puerto Rico, the truth pointed out by Mr. Marin that "saving a culture, even an inferior one, from becoming the monkey of another, even a superior one, is a good in itself." This was nowhere more strikingly illustrated than in the field of educational practice and policy. We set about Americanizing the Puerto Ricans by attempting to make them all speak English (precisely the same mistake that we made in New Mexico in 1849). The result of mingling languages indiscriminately has been to make for emotional instability; or, as *Fortune* puts it, "illiteracy in two languages and a general negativism." Instead of first trying to understand the local culture and then seeking to preserve it, we have endeavored to superimpose an alien way of life upon the peoples of the island. As a result, we have manufactured so-called "marginal men" and "cultural hybrids." It has only been of recent years, comparatively speaking, that Spanish has been made the language of instruction in the lower grades. Today, according to a report issued in 1939, the policy in Puerto Rico is "to emphasize English and to retain Spanish," which represents at least a concession toward cultural autonomy. Trying to anticipate the cultural future of his people in 1929, Mr. Marin suggested that "perhaps we are destined to be neither Puerto Ricans nor Americans, but merely puppets of a mongrel state of mind, susceptible to American thinking and proud of Latin thought, subservient to American living and worshipful of the ancestral way of life." [9] This seems, in fact, to have pretty closely approximated the facts. For, according to Messrs. Pico and Haas, "Puerto Rico at present is not American; it is not Spanish; it is not pre-Spanish. It is a mixture, not a compound of all; it is new, yet still unamalgamated." [10] With this mongrelized cultural pattern in mind, it is small wonder that the "psychological problem" in the island should be of concern to our military experts (and this after forty-four years of American rule), and that many Puerto Ricans should have been on the "wrong side during the Spanish civil war." [11]

Ignoring the native culture and economy, in complete innocence of what might be called "the anthropological approach," we have poured millions of dollars into the island in an effort to lift the level of living to the American standard, in accordance with solemn promises made the natives in 1898. In a large-scale public-works program, we have spent millions on roads and buildings (with most of this money, somehow, drifting out of the island as soon as it was distributed). Despite these expenditures, however, two experts could state in 1940 that the island districts "seethe with misery." As late as 1931, it could be said with fairness that the natives only enjoyed about the same measure of independence that prevailed under the semi-autonomy which Spain had voluntarily granted in 1897.

[9] *American Mercury*, February 1929.
[10] *The American Empire*, p. 27.
[11] See the *New Republic*, "Puerto Rico Also Serves" by R. G. Tugwell, July 13, 1942.

In 1931, the death rate from tuberculosis was reported to be "higher than in any other civilized country of which we have accurate record." In 1934 the infant mortality rate was approximately twice that of the national average in this country; nearly 90 per cent of the rural population and about 40 per cent of the urban population are suffering from hookworm; diarrhea and enteritis were responsible, in 1934, for about 35 per cent of all infant deaths. In 1930 40 per cent of the population was reported as illiterate and 80 per cent as unable to speak English. Over a period of years, the mortality rate for tuberculosis per 100,000 population has been between five and six times that of the United States.[12] The density of population per square mile of *cultivated* land is about 1500 — almost exactly the same as Java. It has been said, in fact, that the *effective* density of population in Puerto Rico is perhaps the greatest in the world.[13] The natural increase of population is around 38,000 per year.

In 1927 the annual average per capita income of Puerto Rico was estimated to be $111, as compared with $738 for the United States.[14] In 1933, 92 per cent of the working population made less than 14 cents an hour and 63 per cent made less than 11 cents an hour. With 52 per cent of the population engaged in agriculture, 82 per cent of these are farm laborers. Land monopolization and absentee ownership have long prevailed and are only now being seriously attacked. Prior to the New Deal, it could be said that thirty-five years of American rule had witnessed only slight improvement in economic conditions. Even today a large part of the workers live in permanent jungles and shanty towns that have come to be acceptable as accustomed housing accommodations.[15] "Children of famine," Mr. Diffie called these islanders in 1931. Here, in "Uncle Sam's Sweatshop," the natives spend 94 per cent of their income for food; and 50,000 women and children work for wages of from one to four dollars a week. As late as 1928, malnutrition was reported to be a large contributing

[12] See Chenault, p. 40.
[13] See "The Dilemma of Puerto Rico" by Earl P. Hanson, *Science and Society*, Vol. I, No. 4, p. 501.
[14] Chenault, p. 44.
[15] *Nation*, March 30, 1940.

factor in a death rate from tuberculosis five times higher than that of the United States.[16]

These facts are reported, not for the purpose of calling attention to human misery, but to emphasize that we have failed in the island in part because we have not taken into account the culture of the area and based our whole program upon a sensible adjustment of the existing culture to the necessities of modern industrialized society. We have long taken the position that to grant cultural autonomy would somehow be at variance with our purposes in the island. Even present rehabilitation measures being undertaken by Mr. Tugwell are not likely to succeed, until the Puerto Rican people, as Mr. Hanson states, "liberate themselves from the present dilemma," and "succeed in breaking through to the consciousness of the American people in their pleas for independence and for their own right to help themselves out of an intolerable social-economic morass." "The spiritual problems," writes Mr. Pattee, "of self-definition, of a determination of destiny, and of the creation of a collective sentiment of purposefulness in the modern world, are not matters that can be dismissed as unrealistic. They strike at the very heart of the existence and reason for being of Puerto Rico." And these are primarily cultural problems. If we were chargeable merely with economic exploitation of Puerto Rico, then one would assume that, when Puerto Ricans escaped to the mainland, their condition would improve. But what are the facts?

3. The Migrants

In thinking about Puerto Rico, we seldom realize that immigration to the mainland from our dependencies has markedly increased since the first World War and that the greatest net gain has been from Puerto Rico (with Hawaii second and the Philippines third). Since 1920 the number of Puerto Ricans entering the United States has doubled and this fact has brought about a gradual realization that "although in a sense citizens of

---

[16] *New Republic*, April 15, 1940.

this country, the residents of our island possessions constitute a real racial problem." [17]

Given the economic plight of Puerto Rico, it is not surprising that emigration should be high. Some students have, in fact, strongly recommended heavy emigration as one solution to the problem of "overpopulation" in the island, and this despite the fact that "a wholesale migration of half or even a third of the people is not practicable and would not solve the problem permanently even were it feasible." [18] The opportunities of emigration are, moreover, limited. The more advanced South American countries have not shown any tendency to encourage emigration from Puerto Rico; quite the contrary. And on the neighboring islands in the Caribbean conditions are, if anything, worse than in Puerto Rico. Workers have been recruited on the island for agricultural employment on two occasions. In 1900, about 5000 were recruited for employment in Hawaii. An extremely heavy emigration to Hawaii would unquestionably have developed to meet the ever-expanding labor needs of the plantations had it not been for two factors: the absence, at the time, of a direct and regular method of transportation (the Panama Canal had not been built); and, also, the Puerto Rican's Negro blood was a matter of some concern to the plantation owners.[19] Although they have combed the world for plantation workers, even the sugar interests hesitated over injecting the Negro problem into the already complicated Hawaiian race situation. In 1926 some 1500 Puerto Ricans were imported to Arizona to work in the cotton fields.[20] With these possible avenues closed, the working classes of Puerto Rico began, according to the Brookings Institute Survey, "to look forward to a North American rather than to a European or a Latin-American future. The mainland represents high wages and other economic opportunities and relatively progressive labor policies. The ties of organized labor

[17] See *Races and Ethnic Groups in American Life* by T. J. Woofter, Jr.
[18] *The American Empire*, p. 63.
[19] See *The Filipino Immigrant in the United States* by Honorante Mariano, 1933.
[20] See *Ill Fares the Land*, pp. 79–80, for an account of this sorry fiasco.

are entirely with the states." Of all areas in the United States, Puerto Ricans have been primarily interested in New York City (50 per cent of all the Puerto Ricans in the United States live in Harlem). Nor is it difficult to account for this preference. Since most of the Puerto Ricans have a "color visibility," they have feared "racial discrimination which might be encountered" in many areas in the United States.[21]

With foreign immigration curtailed by the passage of the Immigration Act of 1924, the notorious "runaway" needle trades of New York began to look about for bigger and better sweatshops. During the twenties, an extensive trade was worked up in Puerto Rico, with needlework being "contracted out" to the natives. Designs were developed in New York and contracts for labor entered into with Puerto Rican contractors and subforemen on a "homework" basis. Simultaneously with this development, workers began to migrate to New York City. The actual beginnings of this migration date from 1919 when the insular legislature established an immigration bureau and arranged to send 130 Puerto Ricans to Brooklyn to work in a cordage factory. But it has been the needle-trades commerce which has been primarily responsible for the large-scale movement of the late twenties. From 1921 to 1930 it has been estimated that about 100,000 Puerto Ricans migrated to New York City.[22] *Fortune* fixes the number of Puerto Ricans in New York at around 150,000 and the 1940 census figures, while not clear, would seem to confirm the fact that the number in New York is between 125,000 and 150,000.

In connection with the migration of Puerto Rican workers, our basic failure to be concerned with population problems is strikingly revealed. Immigrants from our dependencies are not, in fact, regarded as immigrants; yet they encounter, particularly by reason of racial barriers, more difficult problems of adjustment than an immigrant from Europe. Being a newcomer to the labor market in New York, with little industrial skill or training, and suffering a language and color handicap, the

[21] Chenault, p. 55.
[22] Part I, Tolan Transcript, p. 116.

Puerto Rican has not fared well. Almost 25 per cent of the unsettled, or transient, relief load of New York City is made up of Puerto Ricans. Only a limited number have found jobs in private industry; the majority of them are employed as menials. In New York, of course, most of them live in Harlem. This "unamalgamated" Harlem colony is in size equal to the largest city in Puerto Rico. As to their problems, one Puerto Rican told the Tolan Committee: "We know that through language handicaps, through race, through cultural traditions, we are not an assimilable element, and we know that as conditions are today, we are distinctly a problem for the city and its welfare organizations. We know that in many cases we are looked down upon, we know that in many more cases we are not wanted." [23]

The same cultural handicaps which they face in Puerto Rico, they carry with them as immigrants, whether they go to Hawaii or Harlem. In Hawaii many of the 1901 and 1903 immigrants are supported by charity.[24] As Dr. Romanzo Adams has noted, "The Puerto Ricans are at a considerable disadvantage. The general social situation in Puerto Rico prior to their departure was bad. . . . They are few in number and widely scattered. Except for such organization as is created by the plantations they have been almost unorganized. In the city they seem to be less able than the members of any other immigrant group to work out a satisfactory economic adjustment. More than others they are found in prison and jails and in an exceptionally high degree they depend on the agencies of charity. More than thirty years have passed since the main body of Puerto Rican immigrants came to Hawaii, but even in Honolulu where more than a third of them reside they have made only a slight beginning toward the creation of an organized social life for themselves and they made little progress toward a satisfactory status in relation to the rest of the community." [25]

In 1940 I was surprised to find, in making a housing survey

[23] See also *Puerto Rico and Its People*, 1938, by Trumbull White.
[24] *The American Empire*, p. 289.
[25] *Interracial Marriage in Hawaii*, p. 290.

of Russell City — a shacktown in northern California — a large number of Puerto Rican families. Inquiry revealed that they or their parents had gone around the Horn from Puerto Rico to Hawaii in 1901 and, after some years in Hawaii, had moved on to California. Spanish-speaking as a group, they passed in California for Mexicans. They were living in shacks which they had built on the site of an abandoned salt mine within a few feet of the Bay — a sorry end to a tragic adventure. Coming as they do from the existing background of Puerto Rico, it is not at all surprising to find that neither in Hawaii nor in Harlem nor in California have Puerto Ricans succeeded as immigrants.

Puerto Rican migration to New York is made up almost exclusively of family groups. By and large, the ratio between "white" and "colored" groups among the immigrants is substantially the same as in the island, some 26 per cent of the immigrants being colored. Immigrants, for the most part, stem from the poorer classes — those with the least resources to assist in the adjustment. Over 70 per cent of the immigrants have settled in Harlem or in the neighborhood of the Brooklyn Navy Yard. In New York, the Puerto Rican becomes lost in a great confusion of people; ironically, he is of course "a citizen," and, as a consequence, is not classified separately for health, employment, or other social purposes. Working in such occupations as laundrymen, porters, domestics, and needleworkers, Puerto Ricans, considering the higher living costs, do not fare much better than they did in the island. They suffer, in the main, from the same diseases that in Puerto Rico have plagued the entire populace.[26] They also discover, rather to their amazement, that they are all classified as "Negroes"; and must, perforce, buck the color line. Regardless of their degree of color, however, all Puerto Ricans tend to live in the same section of Harlem, being held together more by the fact that they are Spanish-speaking than by any other single factor. They endeavor, by many devices, to distinguish themselves from the regular Negro community of which they are a part. Likewise, many American Negroes resent their competition; in fact, they

[26] See Chenault, p. 78.

do not regard immigrants from the West Indies with much favor. The degree of dependency among Puerto Rican immigrants, in general, is indicated by the fact that in 1937 there were some 32,000 persons in Puerto Rican families in Harlem on relief. "Migration of the Puerto Rican worker to New York is at best," notes Dr. Chenault, "only a partial solution to his problem." That they bring their health problems with them is an acknowledged fact. "They are heavily infected with parasites," according to Dr. F. W. O'Connor; the highest infant mortality rates are found in the neighborhoods in which they are concentrated; and the same may be said of the incidence of venereal diseases. In short, as Dr. Chenault observes, "the health of the Puerto Rican worker and his family in New York shows no great improvement over that in Puerto Rico." The absence of social adjustment is reflected in high crime and delinquency rates.[27] Despite the existence of these conditions, "there has been no organization created specifically" to deal with the problem. Puerto Ricans, because they are citizens, remain outside the scope of even immigrant-aid programs. Perhaps the "shock" of being placed in such a new environment will, in the long run, be beneficial to this immigrant. But, at present, Dr. Chenault believes that their position "may be even less secure than it was on a tropical island where the subsistence level is much lower." When these facts are measured against the estimate of Mr. Alvarado Hernandez that there were 400,000 people in Puerto Rico in 1929 who were planning to come to the United States, the magnitude of the potential migration problem can be appreciated. Prior to the war, an immigrant could come to New York from Puerto Rico for approximately forty dollars.

4. War Changes the Pattern

As a consequence of the Puerto Rican migration (seldom noted in the treatises on how to improve Latin-American relations), a new element has been added to the population of Harlem. "Nationalist campaigns for independence in Puerto Rico," writes Dr. Chenault, "have extended to the settlement

[27] See Chenault, p. 131.

in New York." During the trial of Albizu Campos, a Puerto Rican nationalist, some 10,000 Puerto Ricans and Negroes paraded in Harlem shouting "Free Puerto Rico!" and "Down with Yankee Imperialism!" Shortly afterwards Vito Marcantonio was dispatched by his constituents to make a first-hand inspection of conditions in Puerto Rico. Because Puerto Ricans in New York "often complain that their lands have been taken from them and refer bitterly to the causes which they say made them leave their native land," they have added further leaven to the ferment in Harlem. And, conversely, they have been disaffected by the current of ideas they have encountered in Harlem. This situation becomes the more interesting when we recall, as Mr. White has pointed out, that the United States remains "the only country to which our fellow-citizens of Puerto Rico have unrestricted access, by right of citizenship, to come and go at will," and without passports. While the depression curtailed migration, we have by no means heard the last of Puerto Rican immigration. With 100,000 Puerto Ricans feeling that they are social outcasts in New York, Puerto Rico itself becomes increasingly restless. Inevitably the disaffection of the Puerto Ricans in Harlem finds an echo in the island. This Harlem-Puerto Rican rapprochement is of added significance in view of the large Negro population throughout the West Indies, the Caribbean, and Central and South America.

The present war has, of course, greatly changed the political aspect of the Puerto Rican problem. The specter of Hitlerism has, for example, appreciably subdued the insular agitation for independence. Mr. Marin now contends, according to *Fortune*, that independence is no longer an issue. From a number of accounts that have appeared recently in the press,[28] it would seem that few Puerto Ricans today want complete independence. The war, in most instances, has drawn the outlying possessions into a closer relation with the mainland. Quite apart from the fact that the independence movement has subsided, it is altogether unlikely that this country will ever grant Puerto

[28] See, for example, a series of articles by Ruby Black in *PM* — February 18. 19, 20, and 21, 1941.

Rico unrestricted freedom. The war has taught us some lessons in hemispheric defense. Modern technology has completely altered strategic considerations. "Will freedom ever be possible," asks *Fortune*, "for a small island in a strategic area in the day of the airplane?" Industrially, Puerto Rico is completely within the orbit of American influence: 95 per cent of the total trade of the island was, even before the war, with the United States.

During the war neither Puerto Rico nor Hawaii can expect a change in status; both possessions are, in effect, under military rule for the duration. Whatever the future may hold, so far as these possessions are concerned, it is unlikely that either will be granted complete independence. On the contrary, it seems to be more likely that they will be admitted to the Union as states. If Puerto Rico should be admitted as a state, then a new point of view on racial questions will be heard in Congress. Sooner or later, we must settle the question of the political status of Puerto Rico and Hawaii. If Puerto Rico is to be admitted as a state, then it follows that the educational emphasis will be different than will be the case if it is to be granted complete autonomy. And whether it becomes a state or an independent republic, the problem of cultural adjustment will remain.

5. Other Islanders

To most Americans the outlying territories and possessions of this country have never seemed an integral part of the nation; much less have the peoples of these territories been thought of as fellow citizens. While this attitude has been understandable in the past, it cannot prevail in the future. The war has brought these possessions directly within the orbit of our day-to-day thinking. We must, therefore, take stock of our outlying "minority problem." In addition to Hawaii and Puerto Rico, there is Alaska with a population (1940) of 72,000, 50 per cent of which is made up of Eskimos and Indians. In the Virgin Islands are some 24,889 people, most of whom are colored. In the Panama Canal Zone may be found 51,827, with a large number of "mixed" and "colored" persons. In Guam, 21,000 out of 22,000 residents (1940) belong to the native Indonesian stock known as Chamorros. American Samoa has a population of 12,908 people, most of whom, aside from missionaries and government officials, are native Polynesians.

Small as these groups are numerically, they nevertheless seriously complicate the larger minority problem in this country. In our treatment of these various native peoples, we have adopted no general policy nor have we developed an adequate administrative apparatus to cope with the problem which they present. Furthermore, we have utterly failed to relate these people in our thinking, much less in our policy, to the colored minorities resident on the mainland. When we think of Negroes, we never include Puerto Ricans or Virgin Islanders; when we think of Indians, we never include Eskimos; when we think of Hawaiians, we seldom think of Chamorros or Samoans. Since we acquired most of these possessions for purely strategic reasons (Puerto Rico, Guam, American Samoa, the Virgin Islands), we have forgotten about their native populations. Their economic development (or rehabilitation) is intimately related to the problem of cultural adjustment, and it is precisely at this point that our administrative apparatus is most defective. The average American hates to think that we should have what are in effect, if not in name, "colonies." But this natural aversion should not obscure the fact that, whether we like it or not, we have assumed a definite responsibility to the residents of these possessions.

As indicating the weakness of our administrative apparatus, American Samoa may be used as a case in point. Samoa has an "indefinite political status": it is regarded as a territory; its natives owe allegiance to the flag of this nation; yet it is governed by the United States Navy. Here, on a small scale to be sure, the government faces the problem of adjusting an indigenous culture to Western ideas and institutions. By reason of the fact that the Navy has prohibited land alienation and has prevented the influx of "white" people, the problem has been minimized. Frankly discouraging white settlement and enterprise, the Navy has, at least for the present, deliberately retarded the process of acculturation. Had it not done so, as one observer pointed out, the natives "would have had gold in their teeth, but little or no land; trousers and shirts, but nothing to speak of in the way of chests." About all that can be said for Navy rule to date (and it is a good deal) is that remarkably little damage has been done to native custom and culture.

Under the pattern of native culture in American Samoa most of the land was communally owned. Mr. Felix M. Keesing, writing in 1934, pointed out that the Navy was sharply divided on the question of future land policy. One group would like to break up this communal system and supplant it with individual ownership; subsistence agriculture would give way to an intensive commercial agriculture. Another group, however, is fearful of "any move to disturb the Samoan economy unduly," and favors the preservation of the native system and its gradual adjustment to a higher level of efficiency. The same dilemma has arisen in connection with educational policies. The Navy has stressed the teaching of English in native instruction, from the lowest classes to the highest. That this policy has not been successful is indicated by the existence of a tendency toward "cultural pauperization" and the presence of many maladjusted individuals and disorganized families around such centers as Apia and Pango Pango. It is inevitable that American Samoa, like Guam and the Virgin Islands, must go through a process of great internal change. How is this change to be effected? On this score, Mr. Keesing makes an interesting suggestion: "There is need for detailed anthropological surveys of the Samoans and part-Samoans, not only regarding their old life but also their present position; that officials should be so trained as to be able to translate these into effective action; and that the personnel should be stabilized, and an adequate system of records kept." [29]

Faced with the problem of dealing with the natives, the Navy was forced to create the position of Secretary of Native Affairs. In a recent letter to me, dated October 27, 1942, Dr. Gordon

[29] See *Modern Samoa: Its Government and Changing Life* by Felix M. Keesing, 1934.

Brown, of Temple University, makes some interesting comments about this development: —

The work of the Secretary of Native Affairs is somewhat complicated by the fact that the holder of the office changes once every eighteen months. This means that a new man must make decisions upon quickly acquired knowledge. In the secretariat there are filed many reports and notes, but, in my opinion, it is not in such a form that it will give the Secretary the kind of background he needs to make decisions concerning social organization. Further, the office is relatively new. The office of Chief Justice was formerly combined with that of Secretary for Native Affairs, the division of functions being made about 1929. The Secretary of Native Affairs is, or was until very recently, also the Attorney-General.

In spite of many anomalies, the system works pretty well. There is a continuously functioning government structure, composed of native District Governors, County Chiefs, and Mayors. A stability is achieved which it would take an unusually stupid official to disturb. It also achieves a conservatism which is, on the whole, valuable, but which would be greatly threatened if some unexpected factor came upon the scene. Such a factor may be at work now. I assume that Samoa, as a naval base, will be fairly heavily garrisoned. Several thousand sailors and marines in contact with 10,000 or 12,000 natives will bring about many changes quickly.

Much the same situation has arisen under Navy rule in Guam. The problem there has been interestingly summarized by Dr. Laura Thompson: —

For three centuries in Guam a pattern of life based on absolute values has been imposed on the individual by the family, the Church and the state. In his moral standards, and to a considerable extent his social and political life, the individual has had little or no choice. Jesuits and Augustinians have been replaced by Capuchins, at least as reactionary, if not more so, than their predecessors, and Spanish imperialism has been supplanted by the strict military rule of the American naval government. After forty years of American rule, however, the ideas and ideals of American democracy, as taught in the schools, are beginning to disturb this traditional bulwark. Individuals are becoming self-conscious, and, as might be expected, serious conflicts in home life, religion, economics and politics are arising.

In the opinion of the writer, a considerable amount of conflict and misunderstanding in Guam arises from the lack of a definite colonial policy carried out consistently through all the administrative departments. At present there is a marked contrast between administrative theory and practice on the island.

We have seen that the present military rule limits the participation of the natives in social planning and social control. On the other hand, the American public school attempts systematically to inculcate the ideals of American democracy into the youth of Guam. Unless a consistent colonial policy is applied to both the political and the educational systems, an increase in personality maladjustment and social disorganization may be expected. On the other hand, a strategic program of native education leading to a definite goal consistent with administrative aims might resolve many of Guam's cultural conflicts and aid materially in the achievement of a new cultural integration on the island.[30]

The importance of the problem is merely emphasized by the fact that no one, I take it, advocates that we should grant independence to American Samoa or Guam.

[30] *Guam and Its People,* 1941, p. 236.

CHAPTER VII
The Little Brown Brothers

THE Philippine Islands have long constituted an important outpost of Western civilization — a bridgehead of democracy — in the Far East. "The early influences of the Asiatic continent, of Arabia and India; three centuries of Spanish domination; and the last forty years of American rule," writes Catherine Porter, "have produced in the Philippines a unique social and cultural pattern. An Oriental people, geographically and racially close to the great cultures of the East, has become westernized to a large degree through its familiarity with western language, law, custom, and religion." According to the census of 1939, 91 per cent of the 16,000,000 Filipinos were classified as Christians (27 per cent of the islanders understand English). Through years of Spanish and American rule, Filipinos developed an attitude toward Western civilization quite different from that prevailing generally in the Far East. This difference in attitude is reflected, for example, in such matters as the higher status enjoyed by Filipino women by comparison with the status of women generally in the Orient. The constitution adopted by the Filipinos provides for a democratic state; it contains a bill of rights; and it expressly stipulates that ultimate sovereignty resides in the people. In this island republic, the peoples of the Far East have witnessed the beginnings, rudimentary in form, of democratic rule.

Long before Pearl Harbor, we had come to appreciate the importance of the Philippines — if not the Filipinos — in the American scheme of things. "The position of the islands in the Western Pacific," wrote Dr. George Matthew Dutcher in 1925, "and in relation to eastern Asia constitutes an important strategic advantage to the United States commercially as well as politically." But the postwar significance of the islands looms even larger than its prewar strategic and commercial importance. For the seeds of democracy have been sown in the Philippines and a way of life initiated that, in time, will certainly have profound influence throughout the Orient. To the reconstitution of this faraway outpost we stand thoroughly committed. "I give to the people of the Philippines," said President Roosevelt on December 28, 1941, "my solemn pledge that their freedom will be redeemed and their independence established and protected. The entire resources, in men and material, of the United States stand behind that pledge."

That our future security, as a nation, lies in the direction of furthering the democratic cause throughout the world has been clearly demonstrated since December 7, 1941. When the Japanese invaded Burma, the natives did not lift a hand to aid the British; on the contrary, it has been reported that, in many areas, they shot Britishers whenever and wherever they had a chance. The natives of the Dutch East Indies seem to have shown a somewhat similar reluctance to rush to the defense of their rulers. But all observers agree that, in the Philippines, "the little brown brothers" fought with great courage and admirable spirit. "There has been nothing but praise," writes Miss Porter, "of the attitude of the people and particularly of the Filipino soldier." The Office of War Information has announced that Filipinos are still fighting the Japanese in the islands. The heroic delaying action fought at Bataan Peninsula, largely by Filipino soldiers, may well be regarded as a turning point in the war. Nor is this loyalty of the Filipino a matter of recent origin. During the first World War, Filipinos contributed over $500,-000 to the American Red Cross, purchased $20,000,000 in liberty bonds, and presented the destroyer *Rizal* as a gift to this country. Twenty-five thousand Filipinos served in our armed forces during the first World War. Instead of being rewarded for this demonstration of loyalty, however, they were snubbed by this country. Out of deference to British sensitivity on colonial issues, President Woodrow Wilson refused to receive a Filipino delegation or to permit them to attend the Versailles Peace Conference.

The loyalty of the Filipino is all the more remarkable in view of the fact that forty years of American rule have not been an unmixed blessing. That we have dominated the economic life of the islands since 1928 is an obvious fact: over 50 per cent of all capital investment in the Philippines represents American capital. "The favorable United States market," writes Mr. James S. Allen, "for agricultural products has tended to maintain and bolster the colonial agrarian economy which has made the Philippines a classic land of peonage. At the same time, the American monopoly of the Philippine market has effectively hindered the development of native industry." With 90 per cent of the Filipinos living in rural areas, they have acquired only a slight interest in such industry as exists and even retail trade in the islands has largely passed into Chinese hands. While the American government made notable public improvements, established schools (which, for the most part, were ill-adapted to the needs of the islands), and brought about important reforms in public health administration, nevertheless our trusteeship has been sadly deficient. At the end of 1939, of nearly 10,000,000 Filipinos thirteen years of age and over, 40 per cent were illiterate.

Part of our failure in the Philippines may be traced to our failure to recognize the existence of a problem of cultural adjustment. Prior to the arrival of the Spaniards in 1521, writes Mr. Carlos Bulosan, "a primitive but distinct culture was already in existence, and it took nourishment from the indistinct culture brought by the early traders who inhabited the neighboring islands." The long years of Spanish rule and the increasing dictation of secular affairs by the Church confused, unsettled, and disorganized the growth of this native culture. Confusion was compounded when, in 1898, we assumed control of the Philippines. "The linguistic homogeneity that had been incorporated in the Spanish language," writes Mr. Bulosan, "was uprooted by the English language, and the weaker dialects of the people succumbed one after the other without any favorable effects upon either invading or invaded culture." We were certainly not prepared, in 1898, to understand the problem of cultural adjustment involved; and, as a consequence, Filipinos tended to acquire the forms, but not the substance, of American culture. After 1898, as Mr. Salvador P. Lopez has said, "a generation was uprooted and transplanted into the hothouse of American civilization." The very absence of a deeply rooted culture or a settled mode of national life facilitated the adoption of non-Oriental forms and customs. Thus while Filipinos quickly adopted American ways, their curiously mixed culture failed to achieve a marked degree of integration. If we are to assist, therefore, in the postwar rehabilitation of the islands, we should be giving special consideration, now, to the problem of cultural adjustment presented in the Philippines. For the Filipinos are still a people who, while showing many evidences of American influence, speak some forty languages divided into eighty-seven dialects, "whose traditions and customs represent a selection and synthesis of primitive, native, Spanish, Chinese, and American cultures with minor influences besides."

Since the defense of Bataan Peninsula, Americans have begun to take a new interest in the Philippines and to regard Filipinos with marked favor. It is generally recognized today that, for better or worse, the destiny of this country is inextricably involved with that of the Philippine Islands. After the Japanese are driven from them, our obligations will not have ceased. Even assuming that the Philippines can be liberated before July 4, 1946 (when they gain their independence), we must continue to exercise a measure of influence in island affairs. We shall still continue to guarantee Philippine independence as a means of protecting our position in the Far East. The postwar period will probably see America devoting more, not less, attention to the Philippines. Before this rush of wartime enthusiasm for the Filipinos has spent itself, therefore, it might be well for us to consider the plight of some 100,000 Filipinos who reside in Hawaii and the United States. In any postwar settlement of American-Philippine interests, the economic, social, and legal status of these Filipinos must be considered. Until we have recaptured the Philippines, there is little that we can do for the natives of the islands (and recapture may be long de-

layed). But in the meantime we can and should concern ourselves with the thousands of Filipinos in our midst, for they
constitute an important link by which our influence in the
Philippines may be strengthened. We should also recognize that
the manner in which we treat resident Filipinos has a vital bearing upon our external relations, not only with the Philippines,
but with other nations in the Far East. "India, China, the
Philippines, and Malaya," writes Pearl Buck, "are waiting for us,
whether they tell us so or not, to make clear the stand of the
white peoples toward them." So far as the Philippines are concerned, we should make that stand clear now. For if our record
in the Philippines has not been entirely discreditable, our record
so far as the treatment of these resident Filipinos is concerned
has been extremely bad. This ugly chapter in American-Fili-
pino relations must be corrected now, by affirmative governmental action, without delay and before the war is over. A mere
recital of the facts is enough to indicate the necessity for action.

1. The Pinoy Arrive

The early American educators in the Philippine Islands felt
it their duty to implant, in the Filipino youth, a sense of American ideals, history, and tradition. Great emphasis was placed on
civics, politics, and oratory; and American ideals became, in the
process of transplantation, somewhat inflated. Young Filipinos
were given prizes for florid orations on Daniel Webster, Abra-
ham Lincoln, and George Washington. Liberty and freedom
were emphasized to the detriment of vocational training, agron-
omy, and economics. This practice of extolling everything
American had, as Dr. Bruno Lasker observed, an enormous
effect upon a naturally emotional people. A generation of
American-educated Filipinos came into existence, most of whom
aspired to become lawyers and orators. These same youngsters
also saw in the developing bureaucracy of the islands a chance
for advancement, particularly since most of the trade, industry,
and commercial agriculture was controlled by resident Americans. Using American textbooks and methods, insisting upon
instruction in English from the first grade on (Tagalog, a native

dialect, was not adopted in the schools until 1940), and using a frame of reference in instruction that was utterly meaningless to the natives of the islands, we succeeded in educating many of the young Filipinos away from the islands, so to speak, and toward the United States.

Virtually all of the Filipino immigrants to the United States prior to 1920 came here as students or "fountain-pen boys," as they were called. For the most part, they came here to study in the nonscientific arts and showed a marked preference for rhetoric and the law. By and large, they made a wholly favorable impression. Many of these initial immigrants came from the "better families" of the islands. They were bright, courteous, and charming. The Filipino "school boy" became something of a favorite on many an American university campus. He was not only liked as a student, but prized as a "house boy" in many faculty homes. Young, well-groomed, and cheerful, these youngsters made the rounds of the Y.M.C.A. and other religious "youth conferences" and worked at delightful summer resorts during their vacations. Naturally they wrote home rather glowing accounts of their romantic experiences in America. Since these initial immigrants constituted only a small group (there were only 5603 Filipinos in the United States in 1920), and since they were not concentrated in particular areas, they found it possible to obtain a wide variety of miscellaneous jobs. After they had finished their schooling, most of them stayed on, not as lawyers, however, but as menials. To this group should be added a fairly large number of "mess boys" who, after a period of enlistment in the United States Navy, took their discharge in American ports. Prior to 1920, however, there was no Filipino problem in this country. As a matter of fact, there are no articles on resident Filipinos listed in our periodical indexes prior to 1928. In May 1926, the *Survey Graphic* devoted an entire issue to the problem of Oriental immigration but did not once mention the Filipino.

The original immigration from the Philippines had been voluntary and, to some extent, selective. It was not long, however, before this immigration began to be artificially stimulated. Fearing that the Gentlemen's Agreement of 1907 would restrict their supply of Japanese field workers, the Hawaiian Sugar Planters Association, in that year, brought the first shipment of Filipinos to Hawaii: 188 men, 20 women, and 2 youngsters. From 1907 to 1926 the planters imported upwards of a 100,000 Filipinos to Hawaii. Filipinos became in fact the mainstay of their labor supply. Since there were no restrictions imposed against the importation of labor from the islands, offices were opened in the Philippines to facilitate the traffic. Special lecturers and motion pictures were used to induce the Filipinos to sign up for a period of three years as plantation workers in Hawaii. Steamship agents throughout the islands distributed handbills and placed advertisements in the newspapers which contained glowing accounts of the wonderful working conditions in Hawaii. Many of these ship brokers, as the steamship lines themselves admitted, were "crooks — they misrepresent facts; they overcharge emigrants; and often they are pimps."[1] Later this same type of ballyhoo was used to induce Filipinos to come directly to the mainland without stopping in Hawaii.[2] So successful was this type of advertising, supplemented by word-of-mouth rumor, that in 1926 the Hawaiian Sugar Planters Association was able to discontinue the prepayment of transportation expenses without reducing the flow of Filipino workers to Hawaii. When Japanese plantation workers went on strike in 1920, the sugar planters again stepped up the importation of Filipinos. And, after the passage of the Immigration Act of 1924 (which barred Japanese immigration to Hawaii or the mainland), another major effort was made to encourage Filipino immigration. Between 1925 and 1929, some 45,000 Filipinos arrived in Hawaii, most of whom, incidentally, paid their own transportation expenses.

After 1920, however, Filipinos began to move from Hawaii to the mainland; in fact, it might be more accurate to say that some of them "were moved" to the mainland. For in 1924 the

---

[1] See *Filipino Immigration* by Dr. Bruno Lasker, p. 217.
[2] See statement by Mr. Camilo Osias, Commissioner of the Philippine Islands, as reported in the *New York Times*, January 30, 1930.

Filipinos had conducted a sensational strike in Hawaii in the course of which five policemen and fifteen strikers lost their lives. After the strike, many of the "boys" were blacklisted in Hawaii and, perforce, had to move on. Other factors also served to attract them to the mainland. During the twenties the pending Box Bill and the Harris Bill threatened to cut off the supply of Mexican field labor in California. The pendency of these bills and the passage of the Immigration Act of 1924 brought about a situation in which California growers began to encourage Filipinos, not only in Hawaii but in the Philippines, to come to California. During the period 1923–1929, Filipinos arrived in California at the rate of 4177 a year. Virtually all of them were transported by the Dollar Steamship Company and the Los Angeles Steamship Company — the two lines that had secured a monopoly on the traffic. Of this great influx to the mainland in the late twenties, approximately 56 per cent came by way of Hawaii as a first stop, 35 per cent came directly from the Philippines, and 9 per cent came from Chinese and Japanese ports. As the decade advanced, more and more Filipinos came directly to California from the Philippines. By way of summarizing the entire movement: from 1907 to 1930 approximately 150,000 Filipinos left the islands either for Hawaii or for the mainland. While a sizable number of these immigrants eventually returned to the Philippines, most of them remained. In the Hawaiian Islands today there are 52,810 Filipinos (16,201 citizens, 36,609 aliens); while the census of 1940 showed 45,563 Filipino "aliens" in continental United States. There are, therefore, about 100,000 in Hawaii and on the mainland.

The Filipinos who came to the United States after 1920 were not students or "fountain-pen boys," but plantation workers in search of employment. As the traffic increased, newer areas were tapped in the Philippines. Over half of these latter-day immigrants came from the relatively backward *Iloco* provinces. Many of these boys were without formal education and spoke no English. Even those who had received some education were notably lacking in any type of vocational training. They had no special skills or trade experience. The initial student group had, over the years, become widely distributed; whereas the immigrants after 1920 were concentrated in agricultural employment in California. In California, unlike Hawaii, these latter-day immigrants encountered a sharp racial antagonism; in fact they inherited all of the accumulated anti-Oriental venom of the state. Culturally, linguistically, racially, they were definitely handicapped. And a number of factors, moreover, tended to restrict them to California; climatic considerations, for example, tended to prevent a wider geographical distribution.

It is doubtful, in fact, if any immigrant group has ever suffered more handicaps (in this country) than the Filipino. In the first place, he was the latest immigrant in point of time. As an immigrant, he came from the East, not the West; culturally he was not the equal of the typical European immigrant and he stemmed from an entirely different background. The Chinese and the Japanese, for example, came from societies that were complex and even modern by comparison with the society of the Ilocanos. The Filipino was not widely distributed in area, but concentrated on the West Coast, principally in California where anti-Oriental bias was traditional. Most of the Filipino immigrants were, moreover, quite young and they came alone, unaccompanied by parents, wives, or children. From 1920 to 1930, 1395 Filipino males entered California for every 100 Filipino females. The present ratio of men to women in the mainland Filipino population is 14 to 1, by comparison with a ratio of 1.1 to 1 in the general population. In 1930 it was estimated that there was an excess of 39,328 males over females. In many areas where Filipinos live in small numbers, such as Oregon and Washington, Chicago and New York, this discrepancy is even greater. Most of these boys were between sixteen and thirty years of age when they entered the United States; 84.3 per cent, for example, were under thirty. Being mostly of a uniform age level, they are today, on an average, around thirty-five or forty years of age and 77 per cent of them remain unmarried. These facts alone are sufficient to indicate the rough and rocky experience that the Filipinos have faced in California.

* * *

In light of the successful agitation against further Filipino immigration which has culminated in their exclusion, it is well to keep in mind one or two basic facts about immigration from the Philippines. As in the case of the Chinese and the Japanese, there was no initial disposition on the part of the Filipinos themselves to migrate. During the 333 years of Spanish rule, they had not been a migrating people; and during the first ten years of American rule they had shown no disposition to come to this country or Hawaii, except as students in limited numbers. It is undeniable that the movement of Filipinos to Hawaii and the mainland was brought about by the solicitation of American interests. By permitting Filipinos to be recruited under these circumstances, the government in effect placed its stamp of approval on the entire movement. There is, therefore, scarcely a Filipino in Hawaii or on the mainland who did not leave the islands as the result of a direct or indirect invitation to do so.

It should also be kept in mind that the Philippines are underpopulated. "A very conservative estimate of the number of people that can be comfortably accommodated in our country is 50,000,000," wrote Dr. Serafin E. Macaraig in 1938. The Philippines show an average of 147 persons per square mile, as compared with 488 per square mile in Japan and 822 in Java. With over half of the land in the islands being classified as potentially arable, only 27 per cent was in cultivation in 1938. At the time Filipinos began to migrate in large numbers, there was population congestion in a few areas in the Philippines, notably in Ilocos Sur and Cebu, but the pressure of population on resources in these few areas could have been easily relieved by making it possible for peasants to move into the better farming regions of the islands. It is altogether possible that our policy of excluding the Chinese from the Philippines, which has been in effect since 1902, has tended to retard economic development and thereby to restrict employment opportunities. Certainly our policy of treating the Philippines as a colonial area set apart as an exclusive market for American manufactured products has notably retarded the growth of industry. "There must be a quickening of Filipino economic life, a steady forward progress of Filipino industry, and a raising of the wage scale before we can stop emigration," editorialized the *Manila Times* on November 26, 1929. It was because of the dearth of industrial employment and low wages for agricultural employment that many Filipinos were willing and eager to sign the far-from-liberal three-year contracts of employment offered by the Hawaiian Sugar Planters Association. Attempts at a planned resettlement of farm population in the Philippines, both under American rule and subsequently, have been so limited in scope as to be almost wholly negligible. Our responsibility for the welfare of the 100,000 Filipinos in Hawaii and the mainland, therefore, rests upon much broader grounds than the mere fact that technically they are "wards" of this government. We are directly responsible for the fact that they left the Philippines in the first instance.

2. *California Whirligig*

If ever an immigrant was cut out to be a "sucker," that immigrant was the Filipino. He began to be imposed upon the moment his boat docked in San Francisco; in fact, the imposition really began with the glowing steamship advertisements back in the Philippines. One of my friends among the Filipinos in California is a young man who, today, works as a reporter on a Filipino newspaper. The story of his arrival in San Francisco is fairly typical. On his arrival in California, he carried an enormous suitcase and had sixty dollars sewed to his shirt. He was nineteen years old and knew not a single soul in California. An enterprising taxi driver grabbed his bag and hustled him into a cab before he knew what had happened. "I know a good hotel for you," said the taxi driver, and my friend, dazed by the impact of strange surroundings, said nothing. He was taken to an old rooming house where he was very hospitably greeted by a middle-aged, and rather bedraggled, blonde. Shown to a room, he was told that he could work in the hotel as a kind of janitor — dusting, cleaning, attending to the garbage. This seemed almost too good to be true and he went to work at once. It was not until about three weeks later that he discovered he was working in a house of prostitution. But he stayed on, since he at least had a room and a job. Anxious to go to school, he found that he lacked the necessary credentials and, furthermore, that his work interfered. But, undaunted, he read in a newspaper about the wonders of a correspondence course and promptly invested. While he was industriously reading his correspondence course lectures one day, the hotel was suddenly raided by the police and he was carted off to jail and given a thirty-day sentence. When he finally got out of jail, he found that the owner of the bagnio had disappeared and that his suitcase and the priceless correspondence course were nowhere to be found.

His story is by no means unique. For years fly-by-night taxis worked a lucrative racket in transporting newly arrived Filipinos from the Embarcadero in San Francisco to Stockton — one of the large Filipino settlements in California. These taxis would meet the Dollar Line boats and, if they saw a group of Filipinos, would approach them and ask if they were, by chance, going to Stockton. Most of them were, in fact. Without further explanation, four or five of them would be herded into the cab and off they would go for Stockton. The fare for such a group, in a taxicab, might be around $65 or $75; the regular train or bus fare would have been about $2 per person for the same trip. Taxi drivers, rooming-house operators, labor agents, and *took advantage of* Filipino contractors were all on the lookout for the innocent Pinoys as they arrived. Ironically, these boys were all "wards" of the government of the United States; "our little brown brothers" whose protection we had, by solemn treaty provision, eagerly assumed.

The Alien Registration Act of 1940 revealed that there were 32,338 Filipinos in California (with a total of 45,563 in the United States). Prior to the defense program, they were to be found in three general types of employment: domestic and personal service; fish canneries; and as agricultural field workers. In 1930, about 11,441 were working in West Coast cities, principally in California, as domestic and personal service employees — bellboys, bus boys, hall boys, janitors, kitchen helpers, pantrymen, and dishwashers. Another group, which in 1930 numbered

4210, worked in the Alaska salmon fisheries, on either the "long season" of about seven months commencing in April, or the "extra season" of about three months commencing in June. The balance of them were engaged in agricultural employment, particularly in the lettuce and asparagus crops, as members of fairly large crews under the direction of labor contractors and row bosses. Until 1937, around 4000 worked in the merchant marine; but in that year most of them were discharged as a result of a Congressional act providing that 90 per cent of the members of such crews must be American citizens. Out of a total of 45,563 in the United States, only 635 were, in 1930, engaged in general trade.

Those who have found urban employment, if only as domestics, have fared somewhat better than the rest. In Los Angeles, where a sizable colony reside, they are to be found living in the cheap rooming houses and hotels along Temple Street and on Bunker Hill. A few of the restaurants and hotels in the district carry a sign in the window reading: "This is a Filipino place." Both in the city and in the country, the Filipinos live together in groups. Overcrowding is dictated by economic necessity, but it also provides a measure of social protection. The "boys" have their own night clubs, their own pool halls, their own rackets. Group ownership of automobiles, clothes, and musical instruments is quite common among them. Hedged in by every conceivable social tabu and by numerous legal and extralegal restrictions, they lead a bizarre and fantastic existence. The intense prejudice against them is everywhere reflected in the most scathing denunciations. Judge Sylvain Lazarus of San Francisco has referred to them as "a race scarcely more than savages"; they are listed, when arrested in Seattle, as "headhunters"; while to Dr. George Clements of the Los Angeles Chamber of Commerce they are "the most worthless, unscrupulous, shiftless, diseased semi-barbarians that ever came to our shores."

Wherever they congregate, either seasonally or otherwise, a kind of tenderloin section has come into existence. Characterized as "an eager, ardent, social being," the Filipino is a natural prey for pimps and prostitutes. As a matter of fact, pimps are highly respected in the Filipino community. Wherever they foregather, the taxi-dance halls spring into existence and also the "Filipino Social Club" which is usually a blind for a gambling center. In 1933 there were six major taxi-dance halls in Los Angeles, employing 500 women, who catered exclusively to the Filipino trade. These dance halls represent, perhaps, the costliest entertainment of its kind to be found in California. In one of the largest dance halls in Stockton, Filipinos are charged ten cents a dance and the dance lasts exactly one minute. At these rates, an evening in a taxi-dance hall is far more expensive than an evening in the Mark Hopkins Hotel in San Francisco. Filipinos love all types of gambling and such sports as cockfighting and prize fighting. It has been estimated that half of the earnings of the Filipinos in California (the total earnings being somewhere in the neighborhood of $20,000,000 a year) are lost in one form or another of gambling.[3] In Stockton — "the Manila of the United States" — the "take" on Filipino gambling and prostitution has been estimated at $2,000,000 a year.[4] Their sexual experiences are, indeed, fantastic. Some years ago a Los Angeles newspaper carried a story about 22 Filipino boys who lived in an old house on Bunker Hill and kept a single blond prostitute — an arrangement which seems to have worked out quite satisfactorily for all concerned. Preyed upon by every variety of leech, kicked around as a matter of course by the police, the Filipinos have also been grossly imposed upon by members of their own race. The Filipino racketeer, urban and rural, is a stock figure. He takes bets on the races; arranges cockfights; sells the Pinoy everything from automobile insurance to mandolins; he sells them tickets to raffles, picnics, lotteries, and sweetheart contests; and initiates them, for a fee, into a bewildering variety of lodges, social clubs, and fraternal organizations (there are 103 Filipino organizations in Los Angeles alone). Not infre-

---

[3] See *The Filipino Immigrant in the United States* by Honorante Mariano, 1933.
[4] *Proceedings of the First Official Filipino National Convention in America*, 1938, p. 82.

quently elements in the Japanese and Chinese communities have made a business of catering to their vices. In Seattle, for example, more than two thirds of the Filipino arrests are made in or near the gambling resorts, dance halls, and poolrooms of Chinatown.[5] Spending their hard-earned dollars on clothes, entertainment, gambling, and prostitutes, they are chronically broke and habitually in debt. Endlessly bewitched by the bright lights of American life, many of them have become a sadly demoralized lot of boys-grown-old. Their own native cultural values have been cast aside, yet, at the same time, "an uncrossable chasm has existed between them and American life at its best." The longer they have resided in this country, the more cynical and hard-boiled they have become. Gradually they have "settled into a life which was far different from that which they had hoped to find." [6] Despite these highly unfavorable circumstances, crime rates among them, as a group, are low. The Wickersham Report, for example, demonstrated that, on the whole, they have a good record. Within the group are many fine and progressive spirits: poets, journalists, labor leaders, novelists. Any number of Filipinos, with Ph.D. degrees from leading West Coast universities, make their living as chauffeurs and mess boys.

"Unlike many of the minority groups in the United States," writes Dr. Kirk, "the Filipinos have not developed any great social stability." They have not, for example, created permanent settlements. Their "little Manila" districts are really just centers where they gather in periods between jobs or for purposes of entertainment. These districts are not tightly knit communities; on the contrary, they tend to be attached to an already existing Chinatown or Little Tokyo. Most of the enterprises patronized by Filipinos are operated by Chinese or Japanese; seldom, if ever, are they operated by Filipinos. The high degree of mobility among Filipinos, coupled with the fact that there is little settled family life among them, largely accounts for the obvious lack

[5] *American Journal of Sociology*, May 1938.
[6] See "The Filipinos" by Dr. Grayson Kirk, *Annals of the American Academy*, September 1942, p. 48.

of social organization. While there are no Filipino communities, as such, on the West Coast, there is a Filipino community. A strong feeling of nationalism among them has made for a kind of social cohesiveness. The existence of this feeling is attested by the large number of Filipino newspapers (at one time six or eight were published in Los Angeles alone). The mere fact that assimilation has been so slow and that they have been subject to so many external pressures has made for group feeling if not for social organization. The "community," vague as it is, is held together, not by family or kinship ties, but by nationalistic sentiments and tribal loyalties.

Not only has a highly abnormal sex ratio prevailed among them as a group, but they have been barred by miscegenation statutes in some ten states from marrying persons of the Caucasian race. Nevertheless of 7409 married male Filipinos in this country in 1930, 1775 were married to women of other races. Of late years, Filipinos have been marrying both Mexican and American girls, usually in New Mexico where such marriages may be performed. Any number of Filipino boys have married "Okie" girls. Through these strangely assorted mixed marriages, a second generation is coming into existence. This development of course is more pronounced in Hawaii (which does not have a miscegenation statute). In 1938 some 16,201 Filipinos in Hawaii were listed as American citizens. Most of these must, therefore, have been born in Hawaii. Because of these and other circumstances, Filipinos have been forced into a situation which, as Dr. Kirk has said, "is thoroughly undesirable in every respect, a situation which they themselves would scarcely elect under conditions of freer choice. Underpaid and without permanent employment, they have been exposed to little more than the most seamy side of American life."

Not only is a most complicated second-generation problem coming into existence, but the facts indicate that we shall face, in the not too distant future, an extremely serious Filipino old-age problem. Most resident Filipinos are today around thirty-five or forty years of age; and most of them remain unmarried. By and large, they have not accumulated savings and have made no provision for the future. They will soon find themselves physically incapable of carrying on the types of strenuous field work in which they are engaged — turning out at four o'clock in the morning, with miner's lanterns fixed on their caps, to work in lettuce, carrot, and asparagus fields. Nor are there many other types of work for which they are trained or into which they might fit. What will happen, therefore, ten, fifteen, or twenty years from now, when most of these "boys" will be fifty and sixty years old?

3. *"Legally Undesirable Heroes"*

The Filipinos had not been in California for more than a few years before they became involved in the backwash of the extremely ugly current of anti-Oriental feeling on the Coast. Representing "the third wave" of Oriental immigration, they caught the brunt of the accumulated anti-Japanese feeling of the twenties. Beginning in Yakima, Washington, September 19, 1928, a series of violent anti-Filipino race riots swept the West Coast. Riots were reported in Tulare, California, in October 1929; in Watsonville in January 1930; and in Stockton a mob bombed the Filipino clubhouse. Similar rioting was reported in Hood River and Banks, Oregon; and in Imperial Valley, California. When one group of Filipino field workers migrated from California to Florida to work in the vegetable crops, riots were reported there in July 1932.[7] Many of these were quite serious, resulting in loss of life and considerable destruction of property. Even after Filipino immigration was barred by statute, riots occurred. As late as June, 1939, anti-Filipino riots were reported in Lake County, California.[8] No reparations or indemnities were ever made for these repeated outrages; nor were the culprits ever punished. What has not, however, been generally noted about these disorders is that they provoked serious repercussions in the Philippines. When the body of Fermin Tobera, a Filipino killed in one of these riots, was shipped back to the Philippines, he was referred to as "a martyr of American intolerance";

[7] See *New York Times*, July 24, 1932.
[8] *San Francisco Chronicle*, June 19, 1939.

Manila designated a National Humiliation Day, and 10,000 peoples attended the public funeral that the government provided.[9]

These riots merely gave added impetus to the drive to exclude Filipino immigration and, if possible, to deport all resident Filipinos. As early as May, 1928, Congressman Welch of California introduced legislation designed to prohibit further immigration from the Philippines. But the difficulty with this and other measures of the same type, all of which were patterned after the Chinese Exclusion Act of 1882, was that the Philippines were, in effect, a part of the United States. As long as the American flag flew over the Philippines it seemed logically and constitutionally difficult to justify the exclusion of Filipino immigration. Consequently, it soon became apparent that the agitation for Filipino exclusion was strengthening the claims of the Philippines to immediate independence. This merger, so to speak, of the two movements became particularly marked after it had been determined that, under the existing law, Filipinos had a perfect legal right of entry into the United States and that they were not subject to deportation. About this time, therefore, as Dr. Kirk states, "labor leaders interested in exclusion reached the same conclusion as those who were determined to erect a tariff wall against Philippine commodity imports, i.e, that no satisfaction could be obtained until or unless an independence act could be driven through Congress."

Prior to the passage of the Philippines Independence Act, it had been ruled that natives of the islands had not become citizens of the United States by cession; and that none of the subsequent acts of Congress had conferred citizenship upon Filipinos. The possibility of citizenship by naturalization, however, still remained. Here the Filipino immediately encounterd the provision about "free white persons," and apparently, in view of the dictum in *Loyota* vs. *the United States,* 268 U. S. 402, and *Ozawa* vs. *the United States,* 260 U. S. 178, he was to be regarded in the same general position as the Chinese and Japanese; hence ineligible to naturalization. Some Filipinos, however, did

[9] See Mariano, *supra.*

in fact become American citizens by reason of service in the Navy.

The Philippines Independence Act of March 24, 1934, ended this deadlock and made possible the exclusion of Filipino immigration. Under the provisions of the act, citizens of the Philippine Islands who were not citizens of the United States were to be regarded as if they were aliens. But because the American flag still flew over the islands and Filipinos still owed allegiance to this country, they were not actually characterized as aliens but were merely regarded, for certain purposes, as though they were aliens. Prior to the passage of this act, Filipinos had a perfect legal right of entry; they were, and for many purposes still are, regarded as "wards" of this country. When, for example, they traveled abroad they carried a passport stamped "American citizen." The truth of the matter is, as Charles Beard has said, that the Filipino hangs between two worlds: he is not an alien, not a citizen, nor can he be a citizen. It was this anomalous situation which, after Pearl Harbor, prompted a newspaper to refer to Filipinos as "legally undesirable heroes." Under the terms of the Philippines Independence Act, Filipino immigration was placed upon a quota basis, but the quota was fixed at 50 a year. This is the lowest immigration quota provided by our statutes; in fact, it is tantamount to total exclusion and was regarded as such when it was established. Monaco, with a population of 2020, is allowed a quota of 100 immigrants a year; but the Philippines, under American rule for forty years, with a population of 16,000,000, are allowed a quota of merely 50 immigrants a year. But the exclusion of Filipino immigration had two additional features. In the first place, the exclusion was not made absolute in so far as the Hawaiian Islands were concerned. It still remains possible, with the approval of certain government officials, to lift the bars and permit further Filipino immigration to Hawaii. This inconsistent proviso was inserted, of course, at the behest of the plantation interests. At the same time, it became impossible for Filipinos legally resident in Hawaii to move to the mainland, except in limited circumstances. This regulation was also adopted at the request of the sugar interests in Hawaii to make it possible for them to hold the resident Filipino workers in the islands.

Even this legislation, however, failed to satisfy the demands of those in California who were seeking, not only exclusion, but deportation of all resident Filipinos. Obviously, the 45,000 Filipinos in the United States could not be compulsorily deported. But a strategem was worked out which, under the guise of repatriation, sought to accomplish exactly this purpose. On July 11, 1935, President Roosevelt signed HR 6464, the so-called Repatriation Act. This bill provided that the United States would pay the transportation expenses back to the Philippines of any resident Filipinos who desired to return. But it also provided that "no Filipino who receives the benefits of this Act shall be entitled to return to the continental United States." The thought behind the act was that Filipinos would respond to the bait of free transportation and leave and, if they did leave, they could not return. Here, again, a significant proviso was inserted to protect the interests of the Hawaiian Sugar Planters Association, for the bill was not to apply to those Filipinos resident in Hawaii. Many of these would unquestionably have taken advantage of the act; but by this proviso they were in effect trapped in Hawaii, where they have remained. As a matter of fact, the existing legislation trapped all resident Filipinos both in Hawaii and on the mainland, since, if they returned to the islands to visit their relatives, they could not return except under the quota.[10] At the present time, the repatriation act has expired; that is, no further Filipinos may "take advantage" of its provisions. In a letter from the Immigration and Naturalization Service dated July 27, 1942, I was advised that, prior to its expiration, a total of 2190 Filipinos had been repatriated.

The exact status of those Filipinos still resident in Hawaii and the United States remains, however, unsettled. When the Alien Registration Act of 1940 was passed, Attorney General Robert Jackson, in a curious opinion, ruled that, while not

---

[10] See my article in the *Nation*, September 4, 1935, which discusses the act in detail.

exactly aliens, nevertheless resident Filipinos must register as aliens under the act. Filipinos have been made subject to most of the state and federal statutes which bar aliens from public-works projects; they have been discriminated against as applicants for relief; and they are denied, in most states, the right to practise the various professions. They are not eligible to citizenship nor can they hold public office nor can they vote. Nevertheless, they are subject to the draft and, since most of them are of draft age and have no dependents, several thousand have been conscripted. On January 2, 1941, President Roosevelt announced that they were eligible for enlistment in the armed forces. Many Filipinos have, of course, served for years in the Navy, but only as mess boys. Just what these various inconsistent rulings and opinions imply as to the present status of a resident Filipino is anyone's guess. For years the Filipinos themselves have contended that they should be made eligible for citizenship. Legislation along these lines has, in fact, been introduced in Congress. Since most of the Filipinos probably intend to remain in this country, those actually resident here should be extended the privilege of naturalization. As Dr. Kirk points out, the number is so small that "it is doubtful if there are many valid reasons for opposing this simple solution to a situation which since the outbreak of war has become even more complicated and embarrassing."

To see the problem in its entirety, the reverse aspects of the matter should be considered. The naturalization laws of the Philippine Islands are subject to control by American authorities, at least for the time being. American citizens can enter the Philippines in any number, without restriction, and without being subject to any special penalties or discriminations. In 1939, some 8639 Americans were living in the Philippines, most of whom had business or professional interests there. Americans have invested about $258,000,000 in private industries in the islands and own some 63,000,000 acres of land. In other words, the record stands as follows: we induced upwards of 100,000 Filipinos to come to Hawaii and the mainland, forced them into a rigid caste system, and refused to grant them even the rights accorded nationals of other countries. At the same time, as a nation we insist upon the privilege of unlimited and unrestricted emigration to the Philippines and our citizens there must be accorded the fullest protection and given unlimited rights to engage in trade and industry. No Filipino resident here can become an American citizen; but an American in the Philippines may become a citizen of the Philippines (I am speaking, of course, of the pre-Pearl Harbor situation). How long we can continue to insist upon this sort of one-sided relationship, enjoying privileges which we deny to others, remains to be seen. Certainly in a general postwar settlement some consideration should be given to the problem of these 100,000 Filipinos in Hawaii and the United States. They have, I believe, an unanswerable case. They have served this nation well, both in Hawaii and in California. The very interests which, a few years ago, clamored for their deportation now beseech the federal government to release them from the Army so that they may work in the fields. They have fought for their and our interests in the Philippines; and they will also fight for us in Europe. The Associated Press of August 23, 1942, reported that Filipino troops were among our forces who, on that date, landed in Eire.

4. Since Pearl Harbor

Since Pearl Harbor many changes have occurred in the attitude of resident Filipinos. With some 16,000 Filipinos registered in the first draft, it was decided to form an all-Filipino unit. The unit, at first, was to be limited to a battalion; now it has become a regiment (the first Filipino Regiment commanded by Colonel Robert H. Offley); and there is even talk of making it into a Division.[11] The fact that military service opens the gate to United States citizenship (enlistees become eligible for naturalization within three months) has served to stimulate recruitment. In this manner, several thousands of Filipinos will unquestionably acquire American citizenship. Having granted citizenship to this group, it will become increasingly difficult to

[11] *Asia*, October 1942, p. 562.

deny it to the others. Once Filipinos acquire American citizenship they will be able to return to the Philippines, perhaps acquire a wife, and then come back to the mainland. This should do much toward making for social stability and the growth of a more normal life.

"In the United States," writes Mr. Fernando A. Taggaoa, "the war is doing wonders for the resident Filipinos. Many are employed in defense jobs. The majority employed in the agricultural industries are receiving higher wages and better treatment than ever before. A few are operating truck gardens in California. Some are joining the navy as mess boys. Many more are in the army." In all the years, writes Doroteo V. Vite, "I was here before the United States went into the war, I felt that I did not belong. I was a stranger among a people who did not understand and had no good reason to understand me and my people. It was a pretty difficult business to be a Filipino in the United States preceding Pearl Harbor. Now I am an American citizen." "Oh Emancipating War!" rejoices Mr. Taggaoa. "Gone will be the thousands of Filipinos, particularly in California, relieved of the brunt of prejudice and injustice. No more shall the illiterate workers be oppressed, exploited and made to live in shacks and hovels, for they will have gone to fight and die for their freedom. And when I go, as I surely will, and other Filipinos are left behind in the great United States, please remind them that their Islands are waiting for them. By their hands will arise a New Philippines consecrated in the blood of Americans and Filipinos alike."

While enthusiasm runs high among Filipinos, Dr. Kirk observes that "it is questionable if the sudden manifestation of public interest will be sufficient to produce remedial legislation." Just because this enthusiasm, this new-found Filipino-American solidarity, is likely to abate after the war, there is all the more reason to press for remedial legislation now. Obviously the uncertain status of these Filipino residents cannot be continued much longer; some decision will have to be made one way or the other. It is quite possible that many will return to the Philippines after the war, for there are likely to be more opportunities there in the future than there have been in the past. But most of the resident Filipinos will prefer to remain here and, as Dr. Kirk states, "those who do plan to return wish to do so at their own expense with pride unimpaired." If the government were to sponsor a sensible educational program, designed to give these Filipinos specialized training in skills needed in the islands, it is quite possible that many more would decide to return. Many that I have talked with have expressed a strong disinclination to return to the islands "without something to show" for their years in America. Having allowed their hopes to be stirred anew in this manner, we should not disappoint them again. For they are entitled to salvage something out of their years in this country. "The Filipinos in America," states Julius B. Ruiz of Seattle, "are loyal to the United States and the democratic system of government, but they are tired of so much dishwashing."

Viewing their experiences in retrospect, several Filipinos have expressed feelings which, I am sure, are shared by many others. What they have to say should be of interest to every American. "Where is the heart of America?" asks Manual Buaken. "I am one of many thousands of young men, born under the American flag, raised as loyal, idealistic Americans under your promises of equality for all, and enticed by glowing tales of educational opportunities. Once here we are met by exploiters, shunted into slums, greeted only by gamblers and prostitutes, taught only the worst in your civilization. America came to us with bright-winged promises of liberty, equality, fraternity. What has become of them?" [12] Scores of Filipinos have raised this same question and they are entitled to an answer. Because of its eloquence and restraint, I cannot refrain from quoting in full a short piece by Carlos Bulosan which appeared in the *Cannery Field Workers News* of August 24, 1942: —

Now that we are on the threshold of a great catastrophe, I should like to go back to the beginning of the years. I have been in the United States too long to be foolish enough to misunderstand why we are here. I still recall how, when I first landed in the United

States, I felt that I would become a part of America. Now after fifteen years I know that I have become a part of another America — the America that died some two hundred years ago — when the spirit of true democracy was growing up, now crushed by the commercialism of a fast growing industrialism. However, I feel sure now, because of the war and what it will bring to the world, that this America that was stifled by a materialistic age will grow again. It will grow again to its former name and give every man his former dignity to walk upon the earth.

I have tried everything like any Filipino immigrant to be a part of America. I have tried to find what part of America is my own — is our own — but the America which I thought is ours was hidden away a long time ago by the enemies of freedom and free-loving people. Now with the war and its vast implications in the struggle of the people for more rights and privileges, that part of America which is ours is at last appearing for every man to see and give it a name. I am a part of America. When I say this, I say it because I don't mean names and places, but a conviction deeply felt and fully integrated in my thinking and living. Becoming a part of America is not merely living in its streets, but it is becoming a growing part of its social, spiritual, cultural and political life. It seems to me that the democratic institutions of America will never die. So long as there are men who don't cry to suffer for liberty, so long will America live and triumph with its democratic institutions which were founded upon revolutionary principles.

I have come again from Alaska. I have worked there for the last few years; first as a common laborer, then as a representative of the union. I have seen other kinds of people there — the Indians who are truly American. In my experience and dealings with them, I understood that they, too, love America as much as any true American. And they love America more because they live far away and their perspective is keener. Those who were born in the United States take its history for granted. They take America for granted. They have seen too much democracy, too much wealth, and too much exploitation and brutality, that they take everything for granted in America. America has very little meaning to them. To them it is a wide stretch of land with an enormous wealth. To them it is New York, Hollywood; it is baseball, movies; pulp magazines and books. But to the Indians in Alaska, to the foreign born, America is a living force — a great institution that changes with society —

something that begins to live when it begins to die. The Indians feel this way about America.

Now the foreign born is another matter. Coming here as an immigrant, I had a difficult time. Yet immigrants made America. Back down there in the beginning of the country were brave immigrants who worked hard and sacrificed so that America might live. I came with this same feeling for America. I wanted to give something to it, to make it grow again as it should, and after fifteen years I know that they can't destroy the America that grew in me. When I die then it will die with me, America. But the process will go on forever, because America will go on immortally.

Now at the beginning of a terrible war, which will probably end a great many of our prejudices and misconceptions and false ideals and racial theories, I feel confident that our people will participate with America. They will stand by and fight like their brothers who stood and fought with the American soldiers in the Philippines. And like the founders of this nation, they will fight without conceiving any false illusions as to the rewards of the future. They will fight because they want America to live again.

I have attended the universities and colleges because I wanted to know what is America. I am glad I did: in the colleges is something of the spirit that started the United States. However, I know that I found more in the lives of simple people — those who did not go to colleges and have to suffer in the building of a better America. In the fields of California, in the canneries in Alaska, in the colleges and churches — I found America. But it was only after several years that I was able to integrate my experiences — that I came to my own understanding of America. Now I know that to be a part of America I must contribute something toward its protection and growth. I will never understand America if I demand something from her. It is only in the giving the best I have that I may be able to become a living and growing part of America.

The years came and went. The war came, but it will go away. But institutions and millions of men and women will die with it. Generations will be born, and they will write a pattern of history for the years to come. This war they will understand better than we did: they will create a society whereby a man is no longer ashamed to walk in the street because he is poor, where a colored man is no longer afraid to walk in the street because of his race. I know this society will come. Otherwise we have suffered in vain in these last few centuries of starvation and rootlessness.

5. *Afterthoughts*

Anti-Filipino agitation in California followed precisely the same pattern of the earlier agitation against the Chinese and Japanese: first, the argument of economic competition; and second, the argument of racial unassimilability. Neither of these arguments will stand up under careful analysis. But, as with the Chinese and the Japanese, California had a case, not necessarily against the Filipino, but against the manner of his importation and the lack of any affirmative federal policy. California rightly resented the fact that special-interest groups were artificially stimulating Filipino immigration without regard to the welfare of the community. California also had a case against the federal government, since it knowingly acquiesced in this unscrupulous traffic and, at the same time, ignored the local problems which it created.

Exclusion, however, was not the remedy; exclusion, in fact, only intensified the problem in the United States. For it cannot be too often repeated, as noted by Dr. Macaraig, that "national policies of exclusion of non-assimilable races by powerful nations have been very influential in intensifying race conflicts." Such laws intensify race conflicts in two ways. The proposal to exclude Filipinos, for example, provoked intense resentment in the Philippines. On April 12, 1930, Manuel Roxas voiced the unanimous protest of both major political parties in the Philippines against the exclusion bill. "It is unthinkable," said the *Manila Times*, "that the American flag should fly over the Philippines while the citizens who look to it for defense and support are barred from entering the United States." There is no doubt that the subsequent passage of the exclusion bill would have aroused the bitterest opposition had it not been for the fact that exclusion had become interlocked in the issue of Philippine independence. Because they wanted independence, the Philippines acquiesced in exclusion. But exclusionary laws also intensify local race prejudice, since they set the resident

Oriental apart from the rest of the community, thereby inviting all manner of race baiting, exploitation, and abuse. Furthermore, the exclusion of Filipino immigration was extremely shortsighted in terms of our national interests. Speaking before a Congressional committee in 1930, the Secretary of War said: "To spurn the allegiance of the Filipino after it has been nurtured for thirty years, for the sake of a minor domestic difficulty in one part of the United States, requires careful consideration." But, in the absence of an affirmative federal policy, the "minor domestic difficulty" assumed such proportions that it dwarfed the larger national interest.

The correct approach to the Filipino problem was noted years ago. "There are those," wrote Dr. Bruno Lasker, "who consider the chief cause of Filipino maladjustment, and the chief cause of the agitation against his presence, to lie in the failure of American institutions to facilitate his adaptation to American conditions. They prefer administrative and voluntary methods to legislative ones, and feel that the judgment of the value of Filipino immigration is premature until steps have been taken to protect it against avoidable causes of social and economic difficulty." Other observers have made exactly the same point. Dr. Emory Bogardus, who has devoted more attention to the Filipino than any other American sociologist, suggested the wisdom of creating "a special Federal commission with adequate representation given to the Filipinos" as a first step toward a solution of the problem. It should be remembered that our immigration service functions in a purely mechanical manner: it is primarily a police agency. We never have had an administrative apparatus which could assist in the adjustment of such groups as the Filipinos to our society and culture. Thus our failure to recognize a problem of cultural adjustment in the Philippines was part and parcel of our failure to recognize a similar problem with respect to Filipino immigrants.

One reason that we so signally failed to develop an adequate administrative apparatus for dealing with immigration is that we have tended to measure the importance of resident minorities in terms of the actual numbers here. But a small group in the

United States may represent a vast section of the world's population; consequently the treatment of this negligible minority may have world-wide implications. Such, for example, is the case with the Hindu. The number of East Indians in the United States has probably never been in excess of 6000. Today only 2405 Hindus reside in the United States and the number seems to be steadily decreasing (there were 3130 in 1930). But even so small a group can have considerable international significance.

The Hindu, like the Filipino, is a relatively recent immigrant. Most of them came to this country from 1900 to 1910 – the overwhelming majority from the province of Punjab. Like the Filipinos, most of them were single men. Feeling against them as Asiatics rapidly developed, following the pattern already indicated for the Chinese and Filipinos. Hindus were attacked in Bellingham, Washington, in September 1907; at Live Oak, California, in 1908; and in St. Johns, Oregon, in 1910. In the latter year, the immigration authorities began, by a strict construction of existing statutes, to exclude Hindus; and on February 5, 1917, the "barred zone provision" of the Immigration Act stopped further immigration. (Previously, in 1909, Canada had raised the bars against further Hindu immigration.) Since 1930, only a few Hindus have entered the country.

Most of them came to California by way of British Columbia. They worked in the state, first in the lumber mills, then on the railroads, and finally in agriculture. In the course of a few years, many of them became successful farm operators. In 1919 some 1000 Hindu farmers were cultivating nearly 45,000 acres of rice, 35,000 acres in vegetables, 20,000 acres in cotton, and 3000 acres in fruit. The heavy investments which they made in the war years proved, in fact, to be their undoing. "Huge investments were wiped out and many farmers were reduced to paupers." [13] Despite the fact that a few Hindus had previously been naturalized, the Supreme Court ruled in March 1923 that they were ineligible to citizenship. This decision brought them clearly within the provisions of the Alien Land Act of Cali-

[13] Unpublished report of Kharaiti Ram Samras, January 25, 1940.

fornia; and as a consequence they ceased to be of major importance in agriculture. The decision of the Supreme Court was "denounced as totally unjustifiable in the Punjab, where the people speak an Aryan language and claim to be of the white race." [14]

No single immigrant group in this country has remained so completely isolated from American social life as these Hindu farm workers in California. "The Hindu culture traits," writes Mr. Hedin, "which most clearly measured the social distance between the two peoples were the very ones which these men from India prized most highly" — as, for example, long hair, beards, and turbans. Encountering sharp hostility and being numerically insufficient to establish a self-contained economy, they became increasingly embittered, developed violent quarrels within their own group, and showed marked evidence of both social and individual disorganization.[15] In a few areas, such as Imperial Valley, Hindu farm workers have become small-scale farmers. There they have married Mexican women and the children of these marriages tend to follow the cultural pattern of the mother's race. These small Hindu-Mexican communities are, in fact, organized on a matriarchal basis.

Small as the Hindu minority is in this country, nevertheless it has made itself felt. Dhan Gopal Mukerji (who worked as a field laborer in California), Kedar Nath Das Gupta, Taraknath Das (who also worked in the fields in California), and a few others have become very articulate spokesmen for India in the United States. The *India News*, which carries on an effective campaign for India's independence, is published in Los Angeles by R. Lal Singh. The fact that such leadership exists among the resident Indians (some of whom are citizens) truly entitles America to the claim of being "a nation of nations." India's fight for independence has aroused many of these individuals and organizations to new activity. Although there are only about 1200 East Indians in British Columbia, they have begun to clamor for recognition since the war. Recently they peti-

[14] *Our Racial and National Minorities*, New York, 1937, p. 453.
[15] See *Factories in the Field*, pp. 143–144.

tioned the Canadian government to be granted the privilege of citizenship, in default of which they have decided to oppose the draft.[16] Like the Filipinos, the Hindus have been at a disadvantage in that they have had no consular representation or protection. British consuls, not wishing to antagonize the Dominion of Canada, have had little to say on behalf of East Indians, either in the United States or in Canada. While it has been possible in the past to build up an unyielding prejudice against these "ragheads," unquestionably a free India will have something to say about them in the future. In any case, it will become incumbent on us in the future to give some consideration to the highly specialized problems of these small isolated minorities. In many cases, members of these small minority groups have been made extremely race-conscious by reason of their experiences in America. "In the final analysis," writes Taraknath Das, "the hidden cause of Anti-Asianism in the West is not based upon economic rivalry alone, but something more fundamental — a psychological and deep-rooted aversion to something foreign and unwanted. There should be a single standard for naturalization of aliens, based not upon the color of the skin, but on a definite and high standard of personal attainment and spirit to serve the cause of humanity. Unless this standard is adopted and discriminatory measures against the Orientals discarded, there will be continued bitterness. It is not that all Orientals wish to give up their nationality, but they do not like to be objects of legalized discrimination because of their race and color." [17]

[16] *Christian Science Monitor*, October 19, 1942.
[17] *Christian Science Monitor*, October 16, 1942.

CHAPTER VIII
The Negro Problem: A Case History

No other social problem in the United States has received so much attention as the Negro problem. In addition to the antebellum literature on the subject, an enormous body of material has been accumulated since the Civil War. While undoubtedly there is a great deal more to be learned about the Negro, relatively he has been overstudied.[1] In point of fact there is actually something rather unwholesome about the accumulation of such a bulky literature on a particular problem when that writing is so barren, as it happens to be in the case of the Negro, of definite suggestions for social action.

On the other hand, if one regards the development of the Negro problem — how our conception of the problem has changed — then I believe that the lack of constructive social suggestions can be partially explained and the problem itself placed in a workable frame of reference. For while the Negro has been with us time out of mind, the Negro problem itself has not remained the same. In this chapter, therefore, I have not attempted, as in previous chapters, to summarize some of the data about a particular colored minority, but rather to provide a natural history of the Negro problem. Not only would such a summary be impossible in a single chapter, but the present status of Negroes has been so minutely investigated and so thoroughly documented as to dispense with the necessity for it.

1. A Forgotten Episode

Prior to the Civil War, it was the institution of slavery, rather than the problem of the Negro, that engaged the at-

[1] See comments by Dr. Edgar T. Thompson, *Race Relations and the Race Problem*, 1939, p. IX.

tention of the nation. There was, in fact, no general recognition of the existence of *a* Negro problem. "Where distinctions based on class, caste, and race," writes Dr. Robert E. Park, "are part of the established social order, as they invariably are in a static society, each caste and class lives within the limitations of its own world and accepts the definition imposed upon it as if it were a part of the order of nature." Something like this state of affairs prevailed in the South prior to the Civil War. "A race problem developed for the first time," according to Charles S. Johnson, "when the fixed social position of the Negro slave was changed by his emancipation." An initial recognition of this fact is of extreme importance, since, if there is more racial conflict in America than in other democracies, it is in part owing to the fact, as pointed out by Dr. Park, that there is "more change, more progress. The Negro is rising in America and the measure of the antagonism he encounters is, in some very real sense, the measure of his progress."

As a matter of fact, "it was only with the advance of the invading armies farther and farther into Southern fields that the significance of the Negro as an element in the contest became more exactly defined and more generally apparent." [2] As the Union armies advanced, hundreds and later thousands of Negroes came to the federal camps for support and protection. Here, for the first time, the North began to encounter the realities, and the true dimensions, of the Negro problem. At first the care of the Negroes who swarmed around the federal camps was left to the judgment of the individual army commanders. Later various "freedmen's associations," made up of individuals who realized that the destruction of slavery as an institution did not imply that the Negro problem had been solved, were formed throughout the country. As a result of the acute problem faced by the military commanders and the agitation of the freedmen's associations, Congress was finally forced to take cognizance of the Negro.

Various ways and means of dealing with the problem were

[2] See *The Freedmen's Bureau*, by Dr. Paul Skeels Peirce, 1904, from which monograph much of the following information has been obtained.

proposed in Congress during 1863 and 1864. It is interesting to note that one Congressman thought that the care of the Negroes should be vested in the Department of Interior in "a bureau similar to the Bureau of Indian Affairs." To indicate the naïveté of the Northern leaders, suffice it to say that Lincoln himself was initially impressed with the desirability of colonization. Schemes for colonizing Negroes in Africa, South America, Central America, the West Indies, Mexico, and Texas were, in fact, seriously discussed, as witness an appropriation by Congress of $10,692.15 in 1864 to study such proposals. After the issuance of the Emancipation Proclamation, however, it became apparent that some affirmative federal program would have to be adopted in lieu of colonization proposals.

When a bill was finally drafted looking toward the establishment of a Freedmen's Bureau, it was opposed chiefly on the ground that it would "retard the development of independence and self-reliance in the freedmen"; and defended on the ground that it contemplated "not control, but aid and assistance." No one knew, in fact, just what should be done with the liberated Negroes since, previously, it had been slavery rather than the Negro which had concerned the nation. As one person observed: the Negro presented more than a task — he presented a problem. Hence it was only after *two years* of Congressional debate that the bill creating the Freedmen's Bureau in the War Department was finally passed on March 3, 1865. One reason for Congressional uncertainty was that the nation had assumed, without realizing it, an utterly unprecedented responsibility. No nation in the world had ever faced just such a problem; and surely there was little in our previous experience upon which we could have drawn for guidance. There was, to be sure, our experience with the American Indian, but neither then nor later could anyone see a connection between the two problems.

Despite all the thunderous agitation over slavery, here was the nation suddenly and unexpectedly confronted with the problem of adjusting some 4,100,000 Negroes (92.2 per cent of all those in the United States) to a new way of life. Slavery had been abolished, but how were these uprooted, uneducated, and confused Negroes to be initiated into the essentially bewildering rites of freedom? Of these, nearly 1,700,000 were of school age. Not only were the adults largely illiterate, but the problem of providing schools for the children, in areas where no such schools had previously existed, presented an enormous task. It was not so much a matter of adapting existing institutions to new needs as of improvising an entirely new set of institutions, on the spur of the moment, to meet an unprecedented emergency. In creating the Freedmen's Bureau, Congress gave only vague and general directives and neglected to provide an initial appropriation. To head the new agency, President Johnson, following a suggestion by Lincoln, appointed General Oliver O. Howard. Without funds, without precedents, and with no clearly formulated policy, General Howard set about the task of dealing with the liberated Negroes. Systematically libeled in the works of reconstruction historians, the Freedmen's Bureau has been pointed to as the ultimate proof of the folly of governmental interference in race matters; as conclusively evidencing the corrupting propensities of all paternalism; and as a miserable failure. At the present time, it is particularly important to revalue the work of the bureau, since it represents the *first*, and to date the *last*, attempt made by the national government to deal affirmatively and specifically with the Negro problem. In making such an appraisal, it is necessary to keep in mind that the bureau was only in existence from March 3, 1865, to June 30, 1872; that it was uniformly opposed in the South and only halfheartedly supported in the North; and that it became a central issue in reconstruction politics. When these factors are kept in mind, then, in retrospect, the work of the bureau is deeply impressive.

While it failed to meet the educational problem (some 500,000 children were not provided with the slightest schooling), nevertheless the bureau had under its supervision, when it was abolished, some 2677 day and night schools, with 3000 teachers and 149,581 pupils. In setting up secondary schools, it seems to have been rather impractical and to have emphasized Greek and Latin rather than vocational training; but in doing so it merely followed the educational bias of the times. Its schools, in any case, were extremely popular with the Negroes, who clamored for more and similar facilities. The bureau was also directly responsible for the establishment of Howard and Fisk Universities — institutions which are, of course, still in existence. It also gave important and valuable aid to, and assisted in the establishment of, many other institutions of higher learning for Negroes.[3] It trained 1871 teachers in 1869 alone, over half of whom were Negroes. And in many areas it laid the foundation for what later became a system of tax-supported public schools. These achievements were effected in the teeth of the most violent opposition. In many Southern communities, mobs of irate Southerners dispossessed Negroes of their schools, teachers were not allowed to enter upon their duties, and churches and school buildings (built by the bureau) were burned to the ground. Nevertheless such bureau-sponsored institutions as Fisk, Hampton Institute, St. Augustine Normal School, and Howard University inaugurated, as Dr. Peirce states, "a system of professional, normal and industrial training which is doing much to solve the Negro problem today."

The bureau also provided institutions for the care of the sick and the infirm, the insane and the crippled, the aged and the deaf-and-dumb. During its brief existence it established an excellent medical-aid program for Negroes; founded hospitals; provided direct medical treatment; and built asylums. Dr. Peirce estimates that at least 1,000,000 Negroes received medical care from or through the bureau. It also aided in the care of orphans and provided for the destitute. Later an effort was made to induce some of the Southern states to take over the hospitals and other institutions established by the bureau; but in most cases the requests were refused and these sorely needed institutions simply passed out of existence.

In an effort to relocate Negroes who had drifted away from their homes, the bureau provided transportation for some 30,000 freedmen. It arranged to have public lands in Mississippi, Missouri, Arkansas, and Florida thrown open for settlement and

[3] See page 78 of Dr. Peirce's monograph for a list of these colleges.

actually located some 4000 Negro families in these areas, and this despite the fact that it lacked funds to provide operating loans. It also sought, in an intelligent way, to adjust the Negro to a free labor system. It intervened between the former slave and the plantation owner for the purpose of negotiating an equitable labor contract. Not less than 50,000 such contracts were prepared under the supervision of the bureau — contracts that at least stipulated for food, fuel, shelter, and the payment of a stated money wage. And, of still greater importance, the bureau served as a legal-aid clinic, advising the Negro in personal, property, and other legal matters. In many cases, its agents appeared in court on behalf of Negro litigants. Moreover it established its own courts to pass on certain types of disputes in which freedmen were involved. In Maryland and Virginia, agents of the bureau forced the release of hundreds of Negro children who had been "farmed out" to employers under an outrageous apprentice system. Case after case may be noted in the bureau records where its agents successfully prosecuted those who had violated the civil rights of Negroes. To the Negro, the agents "imparted a conception — inadequate and distorted though it may have been — of his civil rights as a freedman." The bureau was, as Dr. Peirce states, important as "a temporary adjustment, a plank in the *bridge* from slavery to freedom." It advised the Negro to vote, probably told him how to vote, and saw to it that he did vote. "In general," states Dr. Peirce, "it was to protect him [the Negro] against violence and outrage, to protect him from any permanent, temporary, or partial system of slavery, to defend his right to hold property, to secure the enforcement of his contracts, to see that he had a fair trial, that his testimony was received in court, and that his family relations were respected."

In response to the Congressional mandate of providing every freedman with "forty acres and a mule," the bureau set about the task of distributing the abandoned and confiscated lands of which it had also been given jurisdiction. But by the time Congress had awarded the bureau jurisdiction over these lands it had begun to grant wholesale amnesties to former rebels and to reinvest them with title to confiscated properties. In all the bureau had only 800,000 acres at its disposal and the Treasury Department had already leased most of this acreage. Only two tenths of 1 per cent of the land in the insurrectionary states was ever held by the bureau; consequently it would have been impossible to have given one acre to every freedman. Such, in general, is the record of the bureau. Before it was abolished, however, it had become a football of reconstruction politics and, through the corruption of some (but only a few) of its agents, had become generally discredited. It was damned, however, not on its record — which was admirable — but as a matter of policy, as part of the reconciliation strategy.

It was not until years later, in fact, that belated justice was done the bureau in Dr. Peirce's important monograph of 1904. Even to this day, few Americans have ever heard of the bureau or realize that, for a few brief years, the national government did take official cognizance of the Negro problem with important, and beneficial, results. Involved in the discreditment of the bureau was the failure, in 1874, of the Freedmen's Savings and Trust Company, "morally and practically a part of the Freedmen's Bureau, although it had no legal connection." When the bank and trust company failed, as a consequence of the panic of 1873, Negroes lost $3,000,000 in savings, but the public forgot that the bureau had been responsible, in the main, for the fact that Negroes had accumulated any savings whatever.

"The accomplishments of the bureau," write Messrs. Abram Harris and Sterling Spero, "were undeniable. It set going a system of free labor and small holdings among the freedmen by aiding them in the purchase of public lands made available by the Act of Congress of June, 1866; by supervising the terms under which Negroes were employed on land leased to former planters and northern whites; by allotting small parcels of land to Negroes and later by leasing lands for management and cultivation; and by organizing destitute and vagrant freedmen into self-supporting colonies, for which purpose lands ranging from one to 10,000 acres were used in each state. Moreover, it secured the recognition of the black man before courts of law and opened the free public schools to him and to the south generally." Referring to the opposition which the Bureau faced, Dr. W. E. B. Du Bois has written: "Even under such conditions, the Freedmen's Bureau in its short hectic life accomplished a great task. Carl Schurz, in 1865, felt warranted in saying that 'not half of the labor that has been done in the south this year, or will be done there next year, would have been or would be done but for the existence of the Freedmen's Bureau. . . . No other agency *except one placed there by the government could have wielded that moral power* whose interposition was so necessary to prevent southern society from falling at once into the chaos of a general collision between its different elements.' " (Italics mine.)

In retrospect, a striking fact about the bureau should be noted — namely, that the one time when the federal government did attempt to deal, not negatively, but affirmatively, with the Negro problem, marked and permanent improvement resulted. During the time the bureau was in existence, General Howard on one occasion attempted to curtail some of its functions. His bservations about what happened at the time foreshadow, clearly enough, precisely what happened on a larger scale when the bureau was abolished. "A reaction," he stated, "against the interests of the freedmen immediately followed. . . . The practical effect of discharging the officers and agents has been to close up the schools; to intimidate union men and colored people; and, in fact, to paralyze almost completely the work of education." Considering the status of the Negroes at the time, it is today perfectly apparent to any thinking person that some such agency was a vital necessity, in constituting *a bridge* across which Negroes might have passed rapidly from a feudal to a free-labor system, *had the bridge been permanent*. But to have expected that such a transition could be effected in *seven years* was incredibly naïve.

2. A Deal Is Made

If an exception be made of the Freedmen's Bureau, then it can be said that little progress was made during the reconstruction period to clarify the nature of "the Negro problem." What was called "the Negro problem" during these years was merely the political issue over the nature of reconstruction which was fought on strictly sectional lines. The issue was finally decided in favor of the South in the great betrayal of 1876. It is impossible, here, to summarize the full sequence of events leading up to the so-called "compromise of 1876"; but the main facts are well known. Following the adoption of the Black Codes in the South, the Republicans enacted a radical reconstruction program in 1867. When confronted with this eminently realistic strategy, the South realized that, if the war were not to be resumed, a change in tactics was imperative. Thereafter, as Dr. Paul Buck has said, "'Reconciliation by acceptance' became the future basis of action. In the political parlance of the day this change of front was styled the 'New Departure' of the Democratic Party." Capitalizing upon the war weariness of the nation, the campaign of reconciliation rapidly gained adherents in the North, as witness the defection of the liberal Republicans in 1872. The drive for reconciliation, moreover, was aided by the fact that Northern industrialists were eager to resume trade with the South and to exploit the Southern market. "Social peace was needed," writes Mr. James S. Allen, "to obtain the full benefits of the new plantation production and the tremendous internal market. . . . If peace could be obtained at the price of the hard-won rights of the Negroes, this was but a slight concession to ask of the bourgeoisie."

The signal of the new orientation in national affairs was the passage of the Amnesty Act of 1872, despite Sumner's warning that the nation should be just to the Negro before it became generous with the rebel. Taking advantage of the split in the Northern alignment, the South pressed hard for the restoration of white supremacy. The bargain of reconciliation was actually sealed in 1876 when the deadlock between Hayes and Tilden was finally broken. There can be but slight doubt today that the basis of the deal whereby Hayes was elected was the surrender of the Negro to the South. "The bargain consisted," writes Dr. Du Bois, "in allowing the southern whites to disenfranchise the Negroes by any means which they wished to employ, including force and fraud, but which somehow was to be reduced to a semblance of legality in time. And then that the south hereafter would stand with the north in its main industrial policies and all the more certainly so, because northern capital would develop an industrial oligarchy in the south." It is not necessary to imply such an intention in the bargain of 1876, for the chief actors have themselves left records clearly indicating that such was the understanding.[4] "Hayes was tacitly committed," writes Dr. Buck, "to the restoration of white rule in the south, and southerners seemed perfectly satisfied with their share of the spoils." Henceforth, as the *Nation* observed in its issue of April 5, 1877, "the nation as a nation will have nothing more to do with the Negro."

The complete story of how this reconciliation was achieved is admirably told in Dr. Buck's volume *The Road to Reunion* (1937). So thoroughly was the propaganda of reconciliation disseminated that, thirty years after the war, Thomas Wentworth Higginson — ardent abolitionist, commander of a Negro regiment in the war — is pictured by Dr. Buck with a copy of *Marse Chan* on his lap, actually shedding tears over the death of a slave owner. Even the most progressive elements in the North came to accept, at face value, the South's theory of what was called "the Negro problem." For decades subsequent to 1876, as Dr. Charles A. Beard has written, "agitation of the Negro question became bad form in the north." How great was the South's ideological triumph is indicated by the almost universal acceptance in the North of the dogma that "the South will solve its own problem." To indicate how thoroughly this dogma came to be accepted in the North, Dr. Buck has prepared an interesting summation of contemporary views: —

1. The mass of Negroes are unfit for suffrage. — R. W. Gilder, A. D. Mayo, and James Bryce
2. The only hope for good government in the South rests upon the assured political supremacy of the white race. — Edward Atkinson, E. L. Godkin, Carl Schurz, Charles Eliot Norton, C. D. Warner

[4] See *Reconstruction: The Battle for Democracy* by James S. Allen, p. 205.

3. The Negroes are the American peasantry. — N. S. Shaler, J. B. Harrison, H. M. Field
4. One race or the other must rule; the true interests of both races require that control should be in the hands of the whites. — Hugh McCulloch, A. K. McClure, G. F. Hoar
5. If there is a race problem, time and education can alone supply its solution. — R. C. Winthrop, A. W. Tourgee, C. F. Adams
6. The Negro is better off in Southern hands. — A. D. Mayo, T. W. Higginson, R. W. Gilder
7. The history of the Negro in Africa and America leads to the belief that he will remain inferior in race stamina and race achievement. — A. B. Hart

So far as official attitudes were concerned, there was no Negro problem after 1876. The problem had been "solved" by surrendering the Negro to the tender mercies of his former master. This change in Northern sentiment and thinking is the real explanation of much that subsequently happened.

In order to safeguard the rights established by the Civil War, the radical Republicans had forced the adoption of the Thirteenth, Fourteenth, and Fifteenth Amendments to the Constitution. "The fourteenth amendment was not intended to confer new rights," points out Mr. Louis B. Boudin, "but to furnish a means of protecting old ones." [5] The amendment was adopted for the express purpose of making it abundantly clear that Congress had power to legislate for the protection and the enforcement of civil liberties — the civil liberties defined in the Bill of Rights to the Constitution. The Thirteenth, Fourteenth, and Fifteenth Amendments provide that Congress has power to enforce the amendment by appropriate legislation. That Congress intended to enforce the amendments is indicated by its adoption of the so-called Enforcement Acts and the Civil Rights Act. What happened to this legislation? But, first, what happened to the Fourteenth Amendment?

In the famous Slaughterhouse Case in 1872, the Supreme Court, with an eye on the new strategy of reconciliation, held

[5] "Truth and Fiction About the Fourteenth Amendment," *New York University Law Review*, November 1938.

that the Fourteenth Amendment, despite its clear wording, despite the unmistakable contemporary evidence of Congressional intention, did *not* accomplish the purpose for which it was adopted. Essentially such was the holding, for the court said that the "privileges and immunities" referred to in the amendment only had reference to those rights which existed solely by reason of national sovereignty, such as the right to travel from state to state. Later, in its celebrated decision in the Civil Rights Cases (1883), the court went further and struck down as unconstitutional the very measures which had been enacted pursuant to the clear authorization of the Fourteenth Amendment. And this was done despite the fact that Mr. Justice Miller, speaking for the majority in the Slaughterhouse Case, had stated that the Fourteenth Amendment was enacted specifically, if not solely, for the benefit of the Negro race, as to which there could not, in fact, be much doubt. In the Civil Rights Cases, Mr. Justice Harlan, in a famous dissent, asked the question: "Were the states against whose protest the institution [of slavery] was destroyed, to be left free, so far as national interference was concerned, to make or allow discriminations against that race, as such, in the enjoyment of those fundamental rights which by universal concession, inhere in a state of freedom?" The answer, of course, was that the decision *to do just that* had already been made; it had been made in 1876.[6]

In the Cruikshank Case (1876), in the Harris Case (1889), and in the Civil Rights Cases (1883), the Supreme Court had, in effect, put the federal bill of rights outside the protection of the Fourteenth Amendment. Presumably these rights were to be vindicated, if at all, by "resort to the laws of the state." This outrageous amputation of the Fourteenth Amendment was not effected by any inherently plausible or inescapably sound legal reasoning. On the contrary, the decisions by which the amendment was robbed of its original intent were actually "bad law"; a perversion of legal reasoning. These decisions, in fact, can only be explained, as Mr. Boudin has stated, "as part of that general

[6] See also "The Supreme Court and Civil Rights" by Louis B. Boudin, *Science and Society*, Vol. I, No. 3.

movement which a recent writer has called 'The Road to Re-union.' The south and the Democratic Party had fought bitterly the war amendments and particularly the Fourteenth Amendment; and they never really became reconciled to them. The 'road to reunion' had to be paved with the sacrifice of the rights granted by these amendments and every device had to be resorted to to destroy or at least minimize the protection offered by these amendments to the Negro race, and incidentally to other individuals and minorities. The Supreme Court decided that the sacrifice should be made, and it acted on that decision in interpreting these amendments." The real decision was, therefore, based upon purely political, not legal, considerations.

The importance of the highly artificial and strained construction which the court placed on the Fourteenth Amendment can scarcely be overemphasized. The decision in the Civil Rights Cases, for example, was a "green light" to the South. It resulted in the passage by practically every Southern state of Jim Crow laws enforcing the segregation which the Civil Rights statute had prohibited. Henceforth, as Messrs. Harris and Spero have said, the South "was free to handle Negro political aspirations according to its own standards." At first through terror and later by a pretense of legality, the South proceeded to rob the Negro of his constitutional rights in a systematic and thorough-going fashion. Discrimination was not limited to the right of suffrage; but, quickly and efficiently, other types of discrimination were devised: residential segregation; discrimination in public conveyances, in public institutions, in schools, in employment, in places of amusement. So much, of course, is generally known. But the holding of the Supreme Court had other and even graver consequences, for it effectively denationalized the sphere of civil-liberties legislation. It not only opened the door to the South to establish a system of white supremacy, but it effectively tied the hands of Congress. And, lastly, it made for the existence of a mood of futility in so far as the Negro problem was concerned. If the *nation* could not act, if it was powerless to protect the Negro, just what in fact could be done, except to pray with the Southerner? (Which is about all that the nation has done in relation to the Negro problem since 1876.)

Had there been no Supreme Court decisions, however, it is doubtful if Congress would have acted; in fact, Congress itself would probably have repealed the Civil Rights statute. For the decision to get rid of it was, as I have said, essentially based upon political considerations. The consequences, however, have been continuing in character. "Congress," writes Mr. Charles S. Mangum, Jr., "has remained discreetly silent since the days of the Civil Rights Act, and hence the problem and its control have been left in the hands of the individual carriers (referring to public conveyances). The railways in various sections of the country have therefore been permitted to handle the problem in any way they saw fit. Southern carriers have thereupon adopted a Jim Crow policy. It has been said that *congressional inaction* is equivalent to a declaration that railways and other interstate carriers may make such regulations." [7] Thus even with respect to one phase of the problem concerning which Congress could still have acted despite the Civil Rights Cases (the regulation of interstate commerce), it has not acted. Congress, therefore, as well as the Supreme Court, adhered to the bargain of 1876.

As a consequence of the national decision to vest control of the Negro problem in the South, a fixed dogma developed in this country — namely, that the Negro problem was essentially insoluble. "The race question," wrote Mr. John Moffatt Mecklin in 1914, "belongs to this class of essentially insoluble problems." "Relations between American Negroes and American whites," wrote Mr. Scott Nearing in 1929, "occupy a frontier of conflict which is beyond the pale of organized society." "I have been forcibly impressed," wrote Mr. William P. Pickett in 1909, "by the constant repetition of the thought that the problem is in its essential character insoluble." "No matter which way we turn in the north or the south," wrote Mr. André Siegfried in 1927, "there seems to be no solution. The colour problem is an abyss into which we can look only with terror." "In spite of growing race consciousness and the development of a 'New Negro,'"

[7] *The Legal Status of the Negro*, 1940.

wrote Dr. Everett V. Stonequist in 1929, "the problem of creating a race-wide program of action remains unsolved." Similar quotations, covering the period from 1876 to date, might be endlessly multiplied.

How could anyone propose a program of remedial legislation under the circumstances? Congress had been stripped of authority to legislate for the protection of civil rights by the Supreme Court; and the South was firmly in the grip of the whites. Only by recognizing this impasse is it possible to account for the sense of political frustration, reflected in the myth of the insolubility of the Negro problem, which prevailed after 1876. This sense of political frustration has had important psychological implications. It has made for uneasiness, unrest, bad consciences, a studied attempt to shy away from the Negro problem, an over-emphasis upon education as a solution, and the propagation of numerous crackpot theories. The frustration of the political will of the nation only increased when, at a later date, the Supreme Court proceeded to place its stamp of approval upon the Jim Crow legislation which sprang into existence after it had nullified the Civil Rights statute. Just ponder this hypocritical statement by Mr. Justice Brown in *Plessy* vs. *Ferguson* (1890): "The object of the fourteenth amendment was undoubtedly to enforce the absolute equality of the races before the law, but in the nature of things it could not have intended to abolish distinctions based upon color, or to enforce social, as distinguished from political, equality, or the commingling of the two races upon terms unsatisfactory to either." Or, again, "If one be inferior to the other socially, the constitution of the United States cannot put them upon the same plane."

Presidents of the United States have also acquiesced in the emasculation of the Fourteenth Amendment. The second section of the amendment (which it is hoped that the majority of Americans will get around to reading one of these days) provides for a reduction of the number of Representatives in Congress where qualified voters have been prevented from participating in elections. I cannot find an instance where the President has called this provision to the attention of Congress. Harrison,

Cleveland, McKinley, Roosevelt, Taft, and Wilson, points out Dr. Kelly Miller, all deplored lynchings, "but declared their impotence to deal with the evil." President Theodore Roosevelt, for all his expressions of sympathy for the Negro, "never made the slightest suggestion of an effective remedy through federal agency." It is this systematic perversion of a clearly expressed constitutional amendment, rather than any inherent obstacle, which is accountable for our national frustration over the Negro problem. "The evil," wrote Dr. Miller, "is indeed national. So must the remedy be. It is but hollow mockery of the Negro, when he is beaten and bruised and burned, in all parts of the nation, and flees to the national government for asylum, to be denied relief on the ground of doubtful jurisdiction. The black man asks for justice and is given a theory of government."

The year 1876, wrote Mr. George S. Merriam, "marked the disappearance of the Negro problem as the central feature of national politics." [8] For all practical purposes, it also marked the disappearance of the Negro in so far as Congressional attention was concerned. Somewhat shocked by the violence with which the South suppressed the Negro after 1876, Senator Henry Cabot Lodge, in 1890, proposed a bill in the Senate which provided that federal supervisors representing both parties should be appointed in any election district where five hundred voters petitioned the federal authorities. These supervisors were to have power to pass on the qualifications of voters in federal elections and to receive ballots. The bill was not pushed very energetically and was finally defeated in 1891. With the exception of this bill, and a measure proposed by Senator Blair of New Hampshire to grant federal subsidies for educational purposes in the South, no "important federal legislation directed specially at the south," on the Negro problem, was proposed from 1876 to 1906. [9]

The absence of any type of social action, with respect to the Negro problem, from 1876 onward was, indeed, most striking. "Since the discontinuance of the Freedmen's Bureau," wrote

[8] *The Negro and the Nation,* 1906.
[9] *Ibid.*

Mr. Harry Earl Montgomery, "the United States has shirked its duty by ceasing to provide the means whereby the Negro might learn to properly exercise his privileges of suffrage."[10] In the absence of national assistance or effective state action, private individuals and organizations made a feeble attempt to meet the obvious educational needs. The Peabody Fund was established in 1867, the Slater Fund in 1882, the Hand Fund in 1888, the Jeanes Fund in 1907. While these and other foundations did do important demonstrational work, nevertheless Northern philanthropy quickly became, as Messrs. Harris and Spero have said, "a powerful instrument for fortifying white supremacy." By setting up separate Negro schools and churches, they laid the foundations for what later became the "dual educational and welfare systems characteristic of the southern states." This development was almost inescapable, in the absence of a national policy against discrimination, since the foundations had to conciliate the whites before they could even function in the South. After it became apparent that the foundations intended to respect the existing social structure, then "the new South," so called, welcomed their activities. The work of the foundations, however, clearly indicated the necessity for some type of action and, in default of federal or state action, at least a beginning was made. It was not, however, until the turn of the century that public opinion would permit a full development of even privately sponsored programs based upon a philosophy of improving race relations.[11] From 1870 to 1900, the outside assistance furnished by the Northern foundations and the Northern missionary societies, according to Mr. Johnson, constituted "the sole constructive influence from without a south that was itself poor, disorganized, and reactionary."

3. The New Aggression

Despite the earlier pretense that the Negro problem had been "solved," it began to be abundantly apparent after 1900 that such was not the case. To be sure Negroes, from 1865 to 1900,

[10] *Vital American Problems*, 1908.
[11] See *A Preface to Racial Understanding* by Charles S. Johnson, 1936.

had made some important gains; they had been, as one of them stated, "inchin' along." The northward migration had commenced, but on a small scale, and might have developed rapidly had it not been for the reaction of Northern trade-unionists. Between 1880 and 1890, some fifty strikes were reported in the North against the employment of Negroes. The attitude of the trade-union movement had, in fact, "increased the Negro's dependence upon agriculture and domestic service." Even later, in 1910, 2,881,454 Negroes were engaged in agriculture; and the number in branches of industry other than cotton production constituted less than 0.5 per cent. Under the leadership of Booker T. Washington, they had nevertheless made some important gains in the South. New industries were developing in the region and, by 1900, most of the losses of the war period had been regained. As the South began to be partially industrialized, the Negro assumed increasing importance. For since it had been largely unaffected by European immigration, the South remained dependent upon a Negro labor supply. Labor became scarce; wages tended to rise; and the Negroes began to leave the plantations. After the Civil War, the South had restored its ancient edifice, but not completely or satisfactorily. "There *had* been a revolution," wrote Mr. Ray Stannard Baker; "society *had* been overturned." In the process, unexpected opportunities had been created for the Negro, on a limited scale, and he had not hesitated to seize them. As Negroes began to accumulate property and to get a foothold in wage employment, they became less dependent and more self-assertive. Many observers, noticing these tendencies, concluded that a "new day" had dawned in "the new South" for the Negro.

But just to the degree that the Negro made progress, social tensions increased. "The more progressive and ambitious the Negro becomes," observed Dr. Kelly Miller, "the less tolerable he seems to be to his white lord and master." For as the feudal structure of Southern society began to disintegrate, the poor whites (of whom there were 5,250,000 in 1860) began to be affected by the same social forces that had resulted in a measure of improvement for the Negro. As class antagonisms developed within the white group, both "poor white" and "Southern aristocrat" began to manipulate the Negro question to political advantage. While he had ceased to be a national political issue, the Negro had become an issue in intra-Southern politics. Beginning about 1890, the "poor whites" began to revolt against the dominance of Southern politics by the post-bellum aristocracy. Under the leadership of such men as Tillman, Jeff Davis, Hoke Smith, Vardaman, and Tom Watson, the poor whites commenced to assert themselves. "Wherever the whites divided as Democrats and Populists," writes Dr. Buck, "the rival factions courted the colored vote and some of the turbulence of Reconstruction came back again." Tillman discovered, for example, that the old-line Bourbon Democrats were voting the Negroes of the Black Belt against him. "In 1895," said Senator Tillman, "we changed our constitution and disenfranchised every Negro we could." This development, and fear of the passage of Senator Lodge's so-called Force Bill, compelled the South to place the disenfranchisement of the Negro upon a pseudo-constitutional basis, rather than to rely upon the extralegal and illegal methods employed during the reconstruction period. Also by 1895 most of the remaining enforcement legislation had been repealed by Congress. Commencing therefore in Mississippi, in 1890, the South began systematically to disenfranchise the Negro by "constitutional enactment": through grandfather clauses, literacy tests, poll taxes, and other devices. Similarly Jim Crowism was placed upon an official basis, as every Southern state (with the exception of Missouri) enacted, between 1881 and 1907, statutes requiring that white and colored persons be furnished separate accommodations in public conveyances, in schools, and in almost every phase of social life. As the poor whites came increasingly into competition with the Negroes, and as their demagogic leaders began to realize the vast possibilities of Negro baiting (which they seemed able to exploit more effectively than their opponents), the informal Jim Crowism of the postwar period crystallized into a rigid system of constitutional and legislative discrimination.

The new system was not merely a formal enactment of

already existing discriminatory practices: it went much further and actually multiplied and expanded Jim Crowism in general. There developed, as Mr. George S. Merriam noted, "a new or a newly apparent aggression upon the weaker race." Official Jim Crowism has, in fact, assumed increasingly insane proportions since 1890, with new and stricter prohibitions being added almost every year right down to the present time. A new aggression was also apparent after 1890 in unofficial manifestations of Jim Crowism. Once it had been the proud boast of the South that, at least in that area, every Negro could work if he wanted to do so. But the poor whites, by so-called legal and extralegal means, have sharply curtailed the range of Negro employment opportunities. "Negroes," writes Mr. Edwin R. Embree, "have been losing ground steadily in many of their historic occupations in the south. Hotels are replacing Negroes by Europeans as waiters, cooks, bellboys, in all branches of service. Where Negroes formerly controlled teaming, trucking, and horse-drawn vehicles generally, they have not carried over in large numbers into taxi-driving, garbage work, and other aspects of auto transport. As barbers and in other forms of personal service, and even in such menial and heavy tasks as street cleaning and road making, Negroes in the south are being shoved out by whites." [12] The new aggression, which began to be manifest in the South after 1890, soon challenged Mr. Booker T. Washington's famous theory that the Negro's best opportunity was in the South and that he could most readily utilize this opportunity by learning a trade.

Over a period of years the alienation of the races, which had begun during the years of reconstruction, gradually widened. The Jim Crow codes tended to deepen the breach and to extend the separation to all walks of life. "The tendency has been," wrote Mr. Merriam in 1906, "to a wider separation. Once the inmates of mansion and cabin knew each other's way. Now they are almost unacquainted." To keep the races separate and apart meant, in actual practice, to keep the Negro at a lower level. Not only is this the inevitable effect of separatism, but it also

[12] *American Negroes*, 1942, p. 47.

implies that the separate facilities provided for the Negro were, in each instance, inferior to those provided for whites. "A slow but widespread process of race separation in all parts of the country," wrote Mr. Mecklin in 1914, "is gradually divorcing the Negro from the white man's world. . . . The masses of the Negroes are today farther away from the white man's world than they were during slavery." This tendency was only evidenced by the increasing severity and complexity of the Jim Crow codes which became constantly more rigorous. In the course of time, the Negro came to have an almost distinct social and cultural heritage. "The Negro population," wrote Charles S. Johnson, "had its own social heritage which, in a relatively complete isolation, has had little chance for modification from within or without." Separatism or biracialism, far from minimizing, actually intensified race friction. Education for the Negro, within the framework of a biracial system, did not relieve these tensions; on the contrary, it probably increased them and created entirely new ones. The effect of the biracial system, noted Mr. Baker, was to make for "a silent, dogged, sanguinary struggle" in which the "combatants never rest upon their arms." In many areas, educational facilities for the Negro, such as they were, were actually reduced. "Every man," said Tillman, "who can look before his nose can see that with Negroes constantly going to school, the increasing number of people who can read and write among the colored race . . . will in time encroach upon our white men." Increased work opportunities for the Negro, as a result of better training facilities, also tended to aggravate, not minimize, existing tensions.

The Negro was compelled, in effect, to go along with this new development. Once Northern support for his ambitions to rise in status had been removed, he was forced to seek some basis of accommodation or adjustment with his white neighbors. "One of the natural and inevitable results," wrote Mr. Baker, "of the effort of the white man to set the Negro off, as a race, by himself, is to awaken in him a new consciousness — a sort of racial consciousness. It drives the Negroes together for defense and offense." The essence of Mr. Washington's philosophy was to accept the principle of separatism and to seek to turn it to the Negro's advantage. Since Negroes were refused service in many businesses and could not obtain adequate professional attention from whites, they tended to create their own businesses and to patronize their own professional class. Every force, noted Mr. Baker, seemed to be working in the direction of building up a "more or less independent Negro community life within the greater white civilization." "Negro businesses," write Messrs. Harris and Spero, "are chiefly the product of segregation: they are defensive enterprises." Since the whites controlled the basic industries, the raw materials, and, above all, finance, it was impossible for the Negroes to develop a broad enough base to sustain a real middle class. Nevertheless within a narrow range, Negro businesses rapidly developed and, as they developed, Negroes became increasingly race-conscious.

Shortly after the turn of the century, a number of events served to call the nation's attention to the fact that the South had not solved the Negro problem. For one thing, lynchings had increased. Between 1890 and 1900 there had been, on an average, 166 lynchings annually. The practice of lynching, as Mr. Johnson noted, took on a new impetus: it became "a hybrid of sport-vengeance." But no one event served so rudely to shatter the notion that the South had its own peculiar problem well in hand as did the savage race riots which took place in Atlanta in September 1906. After these riots, groups both North and South began to realize that it would no longer do to say that the Negro problem was insoluble, and that some type of action was imperative.

A new attitude began to find expression in such books as Ray Stannard Baker's *Following the Color Line* (1908) — one of the most readable books ever written on the Negro problem — and in such rationalizations of biracialism as Edgar Gardiner Murphy's *The Present South* (1904) and *The Basis of Ascendancy* (1909). In these and other volumes the existence of a social problem, as distinguished from a political issue, was definitely recognized. It was generally indicated, however, that the approach to the problem was by way of prayer, interracial education, and the application of the Golden Rule (within the framework, of course, of a definitely biracial system). It is interesting to note that Mr. Baker, while clearly recognizing that the Negro had become a national problem,[13] never so much as hinted at federal action. Later, in 1913, he wrote that "there is now no disposition anywhere in the north to interfere in the internal affairs of the south — not even with the force of public opinion." Many intelligent Southerners, after the turn of the century, also began to have a change of heart. They came to recognize the essential inconsistency of their position: by increasing the severity of Jim Crow regulations, they were driving the Negro from the South. This, assuredly, would never do. The creation of the Commission on Southern Race Questions, in May 1912, indicated a growing awareness that "something had to be done." The commission agreed, at one of its early meetings, that there was in the South "a realization of the pervasiveness of the problem; that in reality it is not an isolated situation out of touch with the affairs of the south at large, but an intimate, ever-present problem touching the life of the south at every turn, and involving the hygienic, economic, and moral well-being of every citizen of the south." At various religious meetings and conferences, Southerners, with a feeling of almost unspeakable self-righteousness, began to forgather with Negroes and to "discuss the problem." The dogma became pretty thoroughly established, judging by practice, that the Negro problem might be solved by "discussion" and the "spread of enlightenment." This development was, in turn, paralleled by the formation of race-conscious Negro organizations in the North: the National Association for the Advancement of Colored People (1909) and the Urban League (1910). "We refuse to allow the impression to remain," said Dr. Du Bois at the Niagara conference, "that the Negro-American assents to inferiority, is submissive under oppression and apologetic before insults." The Negro problem had thus been recognized by two widely divergent groups: a small minority of enlightened Southerners and a fairly large group of militant Negroes.

[13] See page 233 of *Following the Color Line.*

A number of Northern whites also began to realize that, with the passing of the old order in the South, the Negro problem had increased in magnitude and importance. "With the passing of the generation of whose life it [slavery] was an accepted fact, both black and white, the relations which it slowly evolved," wrote Dr. A. H. Stone in 1907, "are passing also. A new basis of contact is presented — that of unconditional equality." The existence of this changed situation did not imply more peaceful relations; on the contrary, it clearly indicated that there would be more, not less, friction. "Not only will there be race friction," wrote Dr. Stone, "but it will increase as the weaker race increases its demands for the equality which it is denied." About this time, a Captain H. A. Wilson of the English Army, traveling in Africa, noted that the natives, even in the most remote areas, had heard some vague report that somewhere, in the unknown, outside world, a yellow nation had defeated a white nation in war. "There can be no doubt," wrote Dr. Stone, "in the minds of any man who carefully reads American Negro journals that their rejoicing over the Japanese victory sounded a very different note from that of the White America. . . . It was a clear cry of exultation over the defeat of a white race by a dark one."

4. The First World War

The first World War measurably changed the proportions of the Negro problem in the public mind. To fight a war a democracy must have a measure of internal unity; war naturally serves, therefore, to emphasize basic faults in the social structure. Aroused by the stirring slogans of 1918, Negroes were soon made to realize that they were second-class citizens. Appealed to in the name of democracy, they were constantly discriminated against in the armed forces. While their enemies in the South cast aspersions on their fighting ability, they seemed quite willing to let the Negro be drafted. From Mississippi, 24,066 colored men, by comparison with 21,182 white men, joined the colors; in South Carolina the figures were 25,789 colored, 19,909 white; in Florida, 12,904 colored, 12,769 white.

According to a former special assistant to the Secretary of War, the Negroes contributed many more to the armed forces than their quota. Draft boards in numerous localities conscripted Negro married men "in defiance of both the spirit and the letter of the draft law." The first report of the Provost Marshal General indicated that of every 100 colored citizens called, 36 were certified; but of every 100 white men called, only 25 were certified. Negroes had "practically no representation upon the draft boards which passed upon their appeals." [14] Once in the service, Negroes were segregated, assigned to disagreeable and degrading tasks, and socially discriminated against. The South was horrified at the friendly attitude shown by the French people to the Negro troops. Major J. E. Spingarn of the American Expeditionary Forces publicly accused Southern officers of treason, "in that they preferred white ascendancy in the army to the measures necessary for efficiency and for victory." [15] This friction in the armed services naturally had its echoes in civilian life.

During the years 1917, 1918, and 1919, an estimated 500,000 Negroes moved from Southern rural areas to Northern industrial centers. In large measure, this migration was stimulated by the fact that, with the outbreak of war in Europe in 1914, immigration had sharply decreased. At a later date, between 1921 and 1924 (when the exclusionary Immigration Act was passed), an additional 500,000 migrated North to seek employment in the booming industrial areas. This movement made for increased tension North and South. "Whole sections of the south," writes Mr. Embree, "were depleted of labor. Southern planters who for decades had railed against the Negro masses suddenly were in panic at the threat of losing them. By edicts, by offers of better conditions, by force and threat, southerners tried to stem the flood." In the North, the use of Negro labor, particularly as strike breakers, made for sharp conflicts, as witness the frightful riots in East St. Louis in 1917, when 6000 Negroes were driven from their homes and 39 were killed. "Both in the north and in the south," wrote Mr. Seligmann, "each increase in prosperity

[14] *The American Negro in the World War* by Emmett J. Scott.
[15] *The Negro Faces America* by Herbert J. Seligmann, 1920, p. 136.

for the Negro made feeling about race relations correspondingly tense." Noting this tendency, many people began to wonder whether the emphasis placed upon finding industrial opportunities for the Negro was, after all, likely to make for improved social relations. "A disenfranchised working class in modern industrial civilization," said Dr. Du Bois, "is worse than helpless. It is a menace not simply to itself but to every other group in the community. It will be diseased; it will be criminal; it will be ignorant; it will be the plaything of mobs, and it will be insulted by caste restrictions." Even many Negroes began to wonder, in the postwar years, if their position was not worse than it had been before the war. It should be noted, however, that few of them showed any tendency to return to the South. For in moving North they had at least been subjected to what Mr. Johnson calls "the galvanizing shocks of change."

The real crisis developed, however, not with our entrance into the war, but immediately afterwards. This fact should be of particular significance to Americans at the present time. "A week before the Armistice, November 11, 1918," to quote from a publication of the Interracial Commission, "a traveler in the south would have been struck by the apparent solidarity of the population, white and Negro. In support of the war they were united as never before. Two hundred thousand Negro men were fighting in France and many more were preparing to go over. The millions of Negroes at home were responding heartily to every wartime appeal and, in proportion to their means, quite as generously as any other groups. A week after the Armistice one might have observed a subtle but ominous change. Distrust was awakening. What would be the attitude of the Negro troops when they returned from France? Rumors filled the air and . . . fear had taken a deep hold upon both races."

The public did not have long to wait in order to discover what would happen. In June 1919, bloody riots occurred at Longview, Texas; in July 1919, the disastrous riots occurred in Chicago; in Omaha a Negro was lynched, the courthouse was burned, and riots swept the city as Major General Leonard Wood, in charge of a detachment of federal troops, was sent in to restore order; riots occurred in Knoxville; in Charleston; in Elaine, Arkansas; in Washington. In all some 26 riots were reported in 1919. In 1920, riots were reported in Duluth; in Independence, Kansas; and in Ocoee, Florida. In 1921, riots were reported in Springfield, Ohio; in Rosewood, Florida; in Chester, Coatesville (where a Negro had been burned alive a few years previously[16]), and Johnstown, Pennsylvania. In Phillips County, Arkansas, riots had occurred in 1919 in which five white men and an estimated twenty-five Negroes were killed. It is worth noting that, in several cases, order was only restored when federal troops were sent into the areas of unrest.

Mr. Seligmann, who has graphically described these riots, notes that the war had not so much improved the position of the Negro as it had increased his strategic importance; and as his strategic position improved, tension gradually mounted. Far from tending to harmonize the two races, the war created a situation where the problem of the two living together in the same society "was made immensely more urgent *and more menacing*" (italics mine). The accuracy of the observation is established, not merely by the postwar race riots, but by the subsequent rise of the Ku Klux Klan. The rise of the Klan was, in turn, stimulated by highly provocative stories in the press throughout 1919 and 1920 about the alleged susceptibility of the Negro to radical propaganda. For a time the Negro became associated with the Bolsheviks — in the public mind — and this despite the fact that not a single Negro was arrested for subversive activities.

The postwar riots merely indicated, as Mr. Seligmann has observed, that the "south's color psychosis became extended, during the war, throughout the nation." Migration of the Negro merely spread the pattern of segregation to other areas, and segregation in the North tended to retard advancement as much as outright disenfranchisement. For segregation means unequal facilities, conditions, and opportunities. Lynchings in Delaware, Pennsylvania, Ohio, Indiana, Illinois, Colorado, and Kansas certainly indicated that the South did not have a monopoly on race

[16] See John Jay Chapman's famous Coatesville address, *Memories and Milestones*, 1915.

prejudice. Even Jim Crow legislation began to appear in the North, particularly in the form, after 1910, of devices aimed at residential segregation. The most urgent issue faced by the NAACP, after 1915, was that of residential segregation, mostly in Northern areas.

As a matter of fact no better or more convincing demonstration of the *national* character of the Negro problem could have been imagined than the race riots themselves. Faced with these riots many people were forced to a realization of the fact that some type of affirmative program was essential. If the states refused to act, if the federal government was powerless to act, then private individuals would act. The creation of the Commission on Interracial Co-operation in 1919 definitely indicated the existence of such a realization. Even with the stimulation of such organizations, however, the growth of local co-operation remained extremely slow. And toward the end of the decade 1920–1930, when, to quote from one of its reports, "the doves of peace and tranquility seemed to have settled over the south," the interracial commission began to shift its emphasis from field work to that of "research and study of college curricula."

Fortunately the significance of the 1919 riots was not altogether missed. In 1919 and 1920 two resolutions were introduced in Congress calling for an investigation of the shockingly high number of lynchings. The mere fact that such resolutions were introduced indicated that Congress had been forced to take cognizance of the problem. Even one or two states were moved to create commissions of inquiry. It is significant that, in reviewing the situation in 1920, Mr. Seligmann should have observed that he was tempted "to urge as an immediate step the creation of a federal department of race relations, with a cabinet officer responsible not only for investigating maladjustments where they show themselves, but of initiating campaigns of information and education of which the body of United States citizens are sorely in need." He pointed out that, given the state of the press in the United States, it was necessary that the government assume the responsibility of impartial investigation and an honest reporting of the facts. "The first step in an approach to the problems of race relations," he wrote, "will be a demand upon the part of United States citizens for information, exact information not only of the anthropologist, but with regard to the treatment of colored men and women by white men and women in the United States."

Once the necessity for such information was recognized, others were quick to observe that the federal government was the only agency which could undertake such a task. "The Negro problem," wrote Herman Feldman in 1931, "is much too wide in scope and national in character for research of a merely local or unco-ordinated kind. The United States government itself, through one or more of its agencies, should study the problem for the benefit of the country at large. The same recommendation could, of course, be made concerning other races and groups. Thus, while the U. S. Census supplies information about Negro population, the bare fact of residence does not give sufficient data on which to base conclusions as to the nature of migration, its volume from year to year in relation to industrial demand, the adjustments between migrating types, and the specific labor needs of different regions." [17]

It is interesting to note that, recognizing just such a need, the government had established in 1918 a Division of Negro Economics in the federal Department of Labor. This division was of great service during and immediately after the war, not only in disseminating information but in securing co-operation between white and colored citizens and in the placement and adjustment of Negro workers. "Opposition," states Mr. Feldman, "to the maintenance of the Division soon arose on the part of certain congressmen from the south, and the life of the Division was short. On April 26th, 1921, the Secretary of Labor issued a statement which was supposed to be an explanation of the reason for doing away with this agency. It is shallow and obvious word-shuffling." Certain attitudes which may be read between the lines of this announcement are illustrated by the first two paragraphs:

The so-called Division of Negro Economics has been abolished

[17] *Racial Factors in American Industry.*

by the Secretary of Labor largely because there is no such thing as segregating the "economics" of Negro wage-earners from those of any other race. It is fundamentally un-American to create classes or to recognize classes. Our laws do not distinguish between white men and Negroes or any other class or classes.

It is recognized that there is a race distinction and sometimes it is very convenient to have the assistance of a representative of a race in dealing with the members of that race. So far as labor matters are concerned the race distinction becomes more pronounced in the field of collective bargaining when troubles between employers and employees threaten. For that reason a member of the Negro race has been appointed a commissioner of conciliation, who has been detailed to service wherever the Secretary may feel the need of race representation and to advise the secretary.

It will be noted: first, that Mr. Feldman does not accept the explanation offered; and, second, that the explanation does not square with the fact that objection to the Division stemmed initially from Southern Congressmen. The division was only in existence from May 1918 to April 26, 1921. Under the direction of Dr. George E. Haynes, the Division had a staff of about forty members, thirty of whom were distributed in the eleven states where the Division had a paid personnel operating. Representatives of the Division in turn organized voluntary state and county committees, on which, at one time, some 1000 citizens were serving.

Being somewhat curious concerning the work of this Division, I wrote to Dr. George E. Haynes, its first and only director. In a letter to me under date of October 9, 1942, Dr. Haynes makes the following observations: —

At the close of the war and the reconstruction period we made an effort to get through congress an amendment to the Organic Act under which the Department of Labor operates to make the work permanent. Politics defeated the effort. The experiment, however, along with that of a similar advisory to the Secretary of War, set a pattern that has been continued and expanded in the Federal government service since that time. This has been greatly expanded during the present administration so that practically all of the principal departments and commissions of the national government have some outstanding race relations advisor or aide. The step, however, of having Negroes as administrative officers with administrative authority which would have been the case if the special service in the Department of Labor had been made a permanent bureau as was the Women's Division, has not to date been made.

Three other things have happened as a sequel to that war experience: in Ohio, Michigan and Pennsylvania, special services to Negro populations or services to deal with the problems of Negro labor and their relations to white employers and fellow employees have continued and some form of service started in several other states, notably: Missouri, New Jersey, New York, and Illinois. Most, if not all of these can be traced directly to the relationships the United States Department of Labor established with the states through our field representatives in those states during the first world war.

The effort to gather and make available special studies of experience with Negroes in industry was pioneered by the Department of Labor.

Finally, in the development of the United States Employment Service, special personnel or policies to deal with race relations in the industrial field have been included. The present setup to deal with Negro workers under the Manpower Commission has utilized the experience in handling Negro labor during the period 1918–1921, and some of the present policies stem from that experience.[18]

In a somewhat similar way, the establishment in 1922 of a Department of Race Relations, by the Federal Council of Churches of Christ in America, was an indication of a growing recognition of the necessity for affirmative action. The basis of such a recognition was clearly indicated by Dr. Kelly Miller in 1913 when he said that "broadly speaking, the Negro is hardly governed at all by the state, but merely coerced and beaten into obedience. He is not encouraged to have any comprehensive understanding of or participating hand in the beneficent aims and objects of government."

[18] See, in addition, *The Negro at Work During the World War and During Reconstruction*, 1921, Department of Labor.

5. Postwar Period

Down the years from 1900 one can detect a growing recognition of the national character of the Negro problem. For one thing, the expanding scope of governmental activity in the war and postwar years necessarily brought the government into closer contact with the Negro. "Race relations," writes Mr. T. J. Woofter, Jr., "have become more national and less sectional because, in its expansion, the federal government has come into contact with the Negro in new ways. The use of Negro troops, aid to the Negro farmer, application of the various funds appropriated for education and public health, the relation of the Negro to the labor problems of the nation, and the influence of the presence of large numbers of Negroes on the immigration policy are all concrete instances of the growth, altogether apart from party politics, of a national attitude to replace the old sectional view of race contacts." [19]

Even in the field of national party politics, however, it came to be recognized that the Negro was, in many ways, an enormously influential factor. With the Republican Party in the South becoming as "lily white" as the Democratic, the two-party system ceased to function. "Politics in the south," writes Dr. Buck, "became a game for professionals, and in every state where constitutional disenfranchisement occurred the number of white voters diminished in alarming proportions." Thus in South Carolina in 1902 an average of about 4600 voters cast their ballots in the election of each Congressman, while in New York over 40,000 votes were cast in Congressional elections. The South began to have a wholly lopsided representation in Congress, which, in turn, was reflected in the whole course of national legislation and national policy. "This rejected black man," wrote Mr. Baker, "whom the south has attempted to eliminate utterly from politics, has been for years changing and warping the entire government of this nation in the most fundamental ways." Southern race attitudes fusing with Northern industrial ambitions served to delay the granting of autonomy to the Philippines; and also

[19] *The Basis of Racial Adjustment*, 1925.

embarrassed the nation in other ways. For example, in the early years of the century the Turkish Ambassador became *persona non grata* when, in replying to a sharp note from this country to Turkey on the mistreatment of Armenians, he pointedly called attention to our treatment of the Negro. Obsessed with the Negro problem, the South could not give expression to new and vital issues in American democracy. It could ill afford to espouse measures for progressive change, notes Dr. Buck, until those measures had been conservatively adjusted to the biracial nature of its population. Thus a vicious circle existed: the South contended that the Negro should not vote because he was illiterate; and at the same time Dr. Du Bois contended, very plausibly, that the Negro's schools were bad because he could not vote. The strain of attempting to support two sets of institutions — schools, colleges, hospitals, reformatories, insane asylums, jails and prisons, and so on — imposed an insupportable burden on the South. Services for the Negroes were bad; but the services for whites were not good either. As a consequence many people came to see that some outside intervention was necessary in order to break the deadlock.

Also, with the passage of time, the Jim Crow system became increasingly unworkable. A glance at Mr. Gilbert Stephenson's *Race Distinctions in American Law* (1910) is sufficient to demonstrate the point. Litigation over Jim Crow regulations became, as it still is, one of the main props to any Southern law practice. Legal distinctions multiplied as life became more complex. Enough litigation developed over common carriers alone to fill a dozen volumes. To what extent are Southern Jim Crow regulations applicable to interstate carriers? What are equal accommodations? How should separate waiting rooms be designated? Should Jim Crow regulations be applied to Negro nurses attending white passengers? Who is a Negro anyway? Do these regulations apply to steamboats and, if so, to what extent? Do Jim Crow regulations apply to colored postal employees working on Southern trains? These and other equally horrendous issues have been engaging the attention of Southern appellate courts for the last fifty years and in an ever-increasing volume.

In general these cases constitute the richest field of unmined Americana in our entire national life. The average American would not believe that educated, adult persons could subject their minds to the ignominious task of spinning out, endlessly and minutely, these crazy distinctions.

"While prior to the World War," writes Messrs. Harris and Spero, "Negroes constituted an industrial reserve upon which employers could draw in times of labor shortage, or strikes, they had become by 1929 an integral part of the labor force in practically every important industry." In 1930 they constituted 22.7 per cent of the building laborers; 16.2 per cent of the unskilled workers in steel; and 25 per cent of the unskilled workers in the meat-packing industry. The growth of Negro settlements in urban areas was accompanied by the establishment of more Negro newspapers, the development of more Negro businesses, and the expansion of Negroes in the professions. The appearance of Mr. Alain Locke's anthology of Negro writing, *The New Negro,* in 1925, called the attention of the nation to the outstanding achievements of a small but growing group of Negro intellectuals. The rising tide of race consciousness among Negroes was indicated by the spectacular career of Marcus Garvey in the early twenties. With every insistence by the white world upon race separatism as the instrument for maintaining white supremacy, the Negro group became increasingly unified and more militantly race-conscious. After 1917 Negroes appeared in the legislatures of such states as Michigan, Illinois, Missouri, New Jersey, California, New York, Pennsylvania, Kansas, Ohio, and West Virginia; they also appeared as city councilmen, as public officials, and as judges. The Negro vote began to be of increasing significance in many states and, in one or two, it became of crucial importance.

Two events in the early thirties served to dramatize the growing strength of the Negro minority: first, the fight which the Negro organizations effectively waged against the confirmation of Judge Parker as a Supreme Court Justice in 1930; and, second, the militant manner in which Negroes rallied to the defense of the Scottsboro boys. The Supreme Court, always preoccupied with political currents, was quick to note this change. Over a long period of years, the Court began to reconsider its interpretation of the Fourteenth Amendment. By a strained and historically inaccurate construction of the "due process clause" of that amendment, it began, slowly and cautiously, to reinvest the amendment with the meaning which its sponsors had intended it should have in 1868. In *Moore* vs. *Dempsey* (1923) the Court suddenly discovered that it could, if it desired, guarantee a Negro a fair trial. Mr. Mangum, commenting upon the decision, suggests that perhaps it was due to "the shifting of the social outlook of some of the justices." In 1936, in *Brown* vs. *Mississippi*, the Court said that Southern courts might regulate their own procedure, but not in a manner to offend "some principle of justice so rooted in the traditions and conscience of our people as to be ranked as fundamental."

In the last decade, Negroes have won increasingly important victories in the Supreme Court. They have established, for example, the rights of Negroes in states having separate schools to every type of training available to any other citizen; they have established the right of Negro teachers in segregated schools to equal pay for equal training and work; and they have established, in the Mitchell case, the right to equal accommodations on common carriers. Two important observations should be noted about these and the other victories which Negroes have won in the Supreme Court: first, the victories have been important primarily in establishing *rights*, not in implementing rights; and second, most of these decisions have failed to arouse sharp antagonism in the South.[20] What needs to be done at the present time, therefore, is to implement by federal action rights firmly secured in theory for Negroes by the Supreme Court. For the Court no longer believes — any more than the nation believes — that the South should be allowed to deal with Negroes as it wishes.

As the Negro became increasingly enmeshed in the processes of national life, important changes occurred in the concept of

[20] See "The Color Line Cracks a Little" by Dr. Will Alexander, *New Republic*, September 22, 1941.

the Negro problem. For some years after 1900 a number of strange theories about the Negro continued to receive serious public attention. Some of the stock "solutions" of the problem that kept recurring were: biological extinction; colonization (or deportation); segregation (or biracialism); and autonomy. In retrospect, the crudity of some of these proposals is most striking; but it can be demonstrated that their sponsors were driven to the adoption of an extreme point of view by the assumed impossibility of federal action. The extinction theory, advanced by Dr. Willcox in 1900, was, of course, quickly proved to be fallacious: Negroes, as Negroes, will be with us for a long time to come despite racial mixture. Colonization, strongly urged by Mr. Pickett in 1909, became increasingly unfeasible and, for all practical purposes, collapsed with the Garvey movement. The idea that a separate economy could ever be established for Negroes is, today, no longer credible. In 1936 Mr. James S. Allen suggested that a separate Negro republic be formed of the counties in the Black Belt having a Negro majority. "Only by the complete realization of the right of self-determination," he wrote, "is it possible to overcome the age-old national enmities and prejudices." Quite apart from the obvious impracticality of such a proposal (given the present dispersal of Negroes all over the United States), is it not apparent that it does have a measure of validity *if* it be assumed that the national government, as such, is powerless to protect the Negro? (A similar proposal was advanced by John Temple Graves in 1900; and by Professor J. W. Gregory in 1924.) Even complete racial separatism has a measure of validity, if the same assumption is made. For if the government cannot protect Negroes, then they should seek, as a matter of self-protection, to minimize all contacts with the white world. Even colonization proposals have some validity, assuming that the national government cannot even assure the Negro free access to public institutions.

American thinking on the Negro problem was also strongly influenced, until recently, by the widespread acceptance of such pronouncements as W. G. Sumner's that, in so far as folkways are concerned, "it is not possible to change them by any artifice or device, to a great extent, or suddenly, or in any essential element. It is possible to modify them by slow and long continued effort, if the ritual is changed by minute variation." While no one would quarrel with this statement as a general proposition, nevertheless the prevalence of such thinking in the social sciences tended to support a counsel of despair. With people intellectually reconciled to the fact that only over centuries could any change be effected in race attitudes and that nothing could be done to accelerate the process, then the doctrine of the insolubility of the Negro problem found new adherents. Other doctrines having much the same effect were also widely accepted: the Negro problem, for example, was a "race" problem; "race" was essentially a biological fact; "race antipathy" was an instinct; the interbreeding of widely different types was generally believed to result in "weak, inferior offspring." Thousands of intelligent and well-disposed Americans were actually intimidated, in their thinking, by these pseudoscientific pronouncements. Volumes were devoted to stupid "cranial measurements," alleged intelligence tests, and supposedly scientific verdicts on inborn racial traits and tendencies. Above all people inclined to the belief that racial prejudice was a "natural antipathy"; and therefore that it was not subject to any type of regulation or control. An uncritical reliance upon, and possibly a misinterpretation of, these and other doctrines led to the rash of "race doctrine" books after 1914, in particular those of Madison Grant, Lothrop Stoddard, Henry Fairfield Osborn, and Dr. C. C. Josey. Later it was interesting to note, as Dr. Kelly Miller has said, "how these philosophers of Negro subordination have been compelled to shift from one discredited theory to another, like a frightened bird that flutters and flits from twig to twig, as they bend and break beneath its tremulous weight."

With the general improvement of techniques and methods in the social sciences, many of these limiting assumptions came to be rapidly discarded. This development is most strikingly illustrated by a comparison of the volume devoted to the Negro problem by the American Academy of Political and Social

Science in 1913, with a later volume on the subject in 1928. "Much has happened since 1913," stated the editor of the 1928 volume, "to make it desirable that another volume be devoted to the relations between the colored and white races in the United States. In fact, since that time students of race as well as laymen have had to discard or even reverse many of their theories concerning 'trends' and 'solutions' of Negro development and 'problems.'" It is interesting to compare, for example, the meager report on Negro criminality in the 1913 volume with the searching report on the same subject in 1928. The author of the 1928 report on criminality clearly recognized that the race question went to the very heart of our institutions and that Negro criminality could not be studied except in relation to the functioning of these same institutions. He was quick to note, for example, that Negroes were more commonly arrested than white persons; that they were more frequently convicted; that they received proportionately heavier sentences and fewer pardons and commutations. All along the line, Negro studies became increasingly more penetrating: they developed, so to speak, in scope and in depth. An author in the earlier volume had noted that the Negro problem, so-called, was "human and economic. . . . Insufficient food, housing conditions incompatible with health or decency, a childhood spent unprotected in the streets, — these things produce, not in this race or that, but in humanity, certain definite results: ill-nourished bodies, vacant and vicious minds, a craving for stimulants, lack of energy, weak wills, unreliability in every relation of life."

Noting the prevalence of crime, poverty, ill health, and delinquency among immigrants, many Americans had jumped to the conclusion that these groups were somehow racially inferior. But careful studies (for the most part after 1920) quickly refuted the assumption. Much this same sort of demonstration had to be made with reference to the Negro before the public could see the possibility of some workable solution to the problem. As more emphasis was placed upon specific problems of Negro health, housing, and education, the purely "racial" aspect of the question began to assume less importance. "Social science," wrote Mr. Woofter, "has made its contribution to the lessening of prejudice by greatly increased research in Negro problems. Prejudice in the past has rested on popular misconceptions as to the health, morality and mentality of the Negro, and the discovery and dissemination of the truth has ameliorated prejudice among well read people." [21] *Among well read people*, but whose task was it to see that these newer findings, this latter-day research, actually got to the masses of the people?

As these recent studies became more widely known, many people realized that there were Negroes and Negroes in the United States and that it was stupid to think of them as though they constituted a single homogeneous group of 12,000,000 people. Scientific research was necessary, however, before the "problem" could be removed from the domain of opinion and fixed in the realm of fact. As Mr. Robert L. Sutherland has pointed out in his report to the American Youth Commission: "For years the Negro has been a problem in Sunday school quarterlies, text books, and public addresses, but an understanding of the full and exact nature of the problem has seldom been attempted. Typically, these approaches have lumped all twelve million Negroes — black, brown, and light yellow, rich and poor, good and bad — together as a homogeneous group deserving the white man's sympathy, contempt, or assistance." Even the research specialist, obsessed with statistics on health, employment, and dependency, frequently failed to see the problem in its overall proportions and failed conspicuously to relate it to the problems of other colored minorities in the United States.

Further progress in the direction of a realistic grasp of the problem developed during the depression. The notion of a self-sufficient Negro economy received its death blow in 1929. "Last hired, first fired," became the order of the day, as Negro dependency mounted in all areas of the nation. It became quite obvious that Negroes were suffering proportionately greater hardships than whites. With the advent of the New Deal, people began to regain some degree of political confidence and to use the powers of government for many novel purposes. While Negroes were discriminated against in relief and work projects,

[21] *Recent Social Trends*, 1933, p. 592.

the mere fact that the government had acted to relieve distress helped to improve their position. Symptoms of marked unrest, however, were not lacking. On March 19, 1935, the Harlem riot occurred, during which Negroes invaded the business sections of Harlem by the thousand and destroyed upwards of two million dollars' worth of property — a riot which was later characterized by an official investigation as a "spontaneous and an incoherent protest."

As research into the Negro problem improved, the pertinence of this research to larger questions became apparent. The Negro, said Dr. Edward Reuter, offers one of the best and one of the most neglected opportunities for scientific study of any group in the modern world. In the Negro group the various stages of cultural development and adjustment can be traced; the development of personality can be studied from many new points of view; and the functioning of social institutions can be newly evaluated by studying their relation to Negroes. "The United States thus becomes," said Dr. Miller, "the world's most interesting laboratory for working out the intricate issues of race adjustment." As the Negro began to be studied from the point of view of cultural adjustment, the scope of the problem rapidly assumed, not merely national, but world-wide, implications. With the appearance of such volumes as *The Negro Around the World* by Willard Price (1925) and *The Negro in the Americas* edited by Charles H. Wesley (1940), an entirely new perspective was injected into considerations of our favorite "social problems." "In a world composed for the most part of colored races," wrote Mr. Seligmann, "fully embarked on new adventures toward autonomy, Americans had to be reminded not only by a great northward migration of colored people during the war, but by race riots, that new movements and aspirations were stirring on their own continent." The mere fact that the Negro problem can today be seen as part of a larger — a world — issue has already shifted the basis of our thinking on the subject. At the same time it has made imperative the formulation of an affirmative national policy.

CHAPTER IX
Outline for Action

AN utterly unique conjunction of events has presented America with a magnificent opportunity, at this moment, to go forward with the unfinished business of democracy. "Rarely has history provided," states *PM*, "such a happy confluence of a great ideal — the extension of democratic rights — and a great practical necessity — the winning of the world's greatest war." If we fail to measure up to the potentialities of this unprecedented opportunity, our failure will be so great as to defy measurement or appraisal. Now, assuredly, the time has come.

Historically, the time is most opportune. After the Civil War, America probably lacked the strength, as it certainly lacked the will, to go forward and consolidate the democratic gains which had been won at such a terrific price. It is also arguable that the masses of the Negro people were, at the time, not prepared to accept the responsibilities of full citizenship. Furthermore it may have been wise politically to have first given the South an opportunity to deal with the problem, despite the suffering and turmoil which the decision involved. The nation now possesses, however, the will and the physical unity and the power to achieve what it should have achieved fifty years ago — total democracy in the United States.

Scientific, as well as historical, developments now make possible a consolidation of democratic gains and the implementation of previously ceded theoretical rights. Until it could be scientifically demonstrated that there was no basis for the notion of "superior" and "inferior" races, there remained a preserve within which it was difficult to extend the democratic process. Democracy was compelled to rest its major premises on partial and extremely insecure foundations, until scientific research into race problems had reached a degree of maturity. In going forward with the extension of democracy today, we do so with the assured feeling that we are not acting quixotically but upon scientifically sound assumptions. A cultural lag existed, in this field, which had to be overcome. Today, for example, it is generally agreed that "the Negro problem is a race problem not in the sense that a purity of Negroid traits has given the American colored person a unique biological nature which makes him behave differently from white people, but rather in that being all or any part Negroid in appearance (the biological fact) has given him a condition of 'high visibility' which enables others to identify him and place him in a special position in society (the sociological fact)." [1]

It is not only in research into the concept of race that science has made marked progress of recent years. The general problems of cultural adjustment and of personality development have been thoroughly investigated and well-recognized techniques of demonstrated soundness exist today for dealing with cultural conflict. What are termed "race problems" are not essentially biological problems; they are not insoluble; they are "susceptible to social invention and intelligent manipulation." We must accept, as Dr. Ruth Benedict has said, "all the implications of our human inheritance, one of the most important of which is the small scope of biologically transmitted behavior and the enormous role of the cultural process in the transmission of tradition." Culture, as she points out, is not a biologically transmitted complex: "not one item of man's social organization, of his language, of his local religion, is carried in his germ-cell."

Also it has become possible to allay the fear of white people that they might be engulfed by some dark and alien strain in the population. Regardless of who its carriers may be at the moment, there is no doubt, writes Dr. Benedict, "about the cultural continuity of civilization." The best assurance against this once widely publicized bogy of engulfment is to spread democracy throughout the world and to extend democracy at home. People need no longer fear that the encroachment of

[1] *Color, Class and Personality*, 1942, p. xv.

colored peoples threatens their society and its institutions. "The desire of Negro youth," writes Robert Sutherland, "is not for admission to white society, but for a chance to support a way of living which would mark anyone, white or colored, as belonging to a culturally superior group."

Just as subject peoples throughout the world are coming into the possession of the technics of modern civilization, so colored minority groups within the United States are coming into possession of the rapidly developed wealth of anthropological, sociological, and psychological research of the last fifty years. As they acquire this knowledge, it no longer becomes even politically feasible to continue a system of wholesale discrimination. "The so-called racial explanation of differences in human performance and achievement," writes Mr. A. J. Toynbee, "is either an ineptitude or a fraud." In the face of this mounting wealth of scientific evidence, it is simply no longer tenable to pretend that "backward races" cannot acquire the fundamentals of civilized life. For the same forces, as Alain Locke has said, "which have all but annihilated longitude and latitude also have foreshortened cultural and social distance, and have telescoped their traditional but imaginary dividing lines." The increasing interdependency of all groups, not only in the nation but in the world, occasioned by the progress of civilization has laid the foundation for what Dr. Benedict calls a vast extension of "in-group mutual dependency and mutual support." We know, today, that "a nation can be administered without creating victims."

From a practical point of view, we are driven to precisely the same conclusion. "Since internal unity and co-operation," writes Mr. Sutherland, "are as much a part of national defense as are battleships and fortifications, the importance of allowing no large minority to feel arbitrarily excluded is obvious." And, if we consider world totals, all our minorities are large. Furthermore, as Mr. Lester B. Granger has demonstrated, there are not enough available workers in the United States to fill the needs of war industry and match the vast slave resources of the Axis powers. The training and full utilization of some 6,000,000

Negro employables is, therefore, an inescapable practical necessity.

The engineering of a program to end racial discrimination in America is, today, a practical political possibility. The war has released throughout the world (despite momentary manifestations to the contrary) a great upsurge of democratic sentiment. It is now possible to mobilize the political strength necessary to effectuate those controls and procedures essential to a real job of social engineering on race problems. One can sense the political feasibility of executing such a program; the problem, as Mr. Sutherland states, is "in the air." Today it is possible to count upon a progressive concern with democratic ideals which, as Alain Locke states, is "rising now almost to a ground swell of popular feeling and conviction," in endeavoring to pull "reactionary democracy out of the narrows and set us heading for new democratic goals." The reluctance of the rest of the nation to interfere in the South has noticeably abated in the last two decades. Thousands of people realize today that, as *PM* has stated, "the south needs help." Southerners such as Jonathan Daniels concede that "the south has not done anything approaching greatness in what may be called a self-reconstruction to give the Negro all that we wish all Americans to have." There are progressive elements throughout the South that would actually relish national intervention.

All of America is coming to a general realization of the fact that the South's attempted solution of the race problem — namely, a system of biracialism — is an obvious failure. Racial segregation, like slavery itself, is a malignant growth in a democracy.[2] Biracialism is stultifying, costly, stupid, and self-perpetuating. It is essentially impossible and impractical; it tends to spread throughout the nation; and it creates as Mr. Carter states, "a spiritual hiatus between the races, fostering in one a feeling of inferiority, and in the other an equally insidious superiority complex. It breeds resentment, suspicion and humiliation, and undermines the Negro's faith in democratic govern-

[2] See "Shadows of the Slave Tradition" by Elmer Anderson Carter, *Survey Graphic*, November 1942.

ment itself." It robs the Negro, and other minorities, of their rightful cultural and historical inheritance. The attempted enforcement of such a system during the last forty years has proved to be a dismal failure. By the 1920's biracialism had become, as Mr. Carter states, a dead end.

Now is not only the opportune time to liquidate the last vestiges of this system in America, but we *must* proceed to do so if the critical tensions already developing are not to explode, with disastrous consequences, either in the immediate future or during the postwar period. We face, as Jonathan Daniels has said, "a crisis about color." Increasing tensions in the South since 1940 demonstrate, as Mr. Daniels states, "the wearing thin of the relationships which for the most part southern white men have made." These tensions are certain to increase with the progress of the war itself; hence we must establish *now* those controls and safeguards which are essential to prevent a repetition of the postwar race riots of 1919–1921. Perhaps the most ominous sign on the horizon is the impending collapse of the plantation economy of the Deep South. During the past ten years, as Charles S. Johnson has pointed out, Negroes have been virtually forced out of agriculture. With the rapid expansion of mechanization in agriculture, the entire structure of the plantation system will be transformed. Ways and means must, therefore, be devised now by which Negroes may be absorbed into nonagricultural types of employment.

Industrial developments alone dictate the abolition of the biracial system. Segregation is not compatible with industrial efficiency; it is at fatal variance with the *modus operandi* of industrialism. "Modern industry," as Mr. Johnson states, "changes too rapidly and is too complex for a caste system." The Criminal Code of South Carolina provides today (Article 1272) that it is unlawful for any concern engaged in cotton textile manufacture to employ Negroes and whites to work in the same room, or to use the same doors of entrance or exit at the same time, or to use the same pay ticket windows or the same stairways or windows, or to use the same lavatories, toilets, drinking water buckets or glasses. Such a statute in an area where Negroes constitute the bulk of the available labor supply is an unwarranted and utterly indefensible shackle upon industry itself. Those who point to the South as our "Economic Problem No. 1" state that it must have more industrial development. But the greatest barrier to the industrial development of the South is Jim Crowism itself. Hence the bulk of war contracts are going to non-Southern areas (the South has received only about 6.3 per cent of these contracts to date). Actually, as Mr. Mark Ethridge has said, "The setup of industry incident to the war effort has retarded, rather than accelerated, the effort of the south to improve its position as an industrial section in relation to the rest of the nation." [3] The wartime development of industry, therefore, will not of itself be of much assistance to the South. The war does create, however, not only the necessity for industrial expansion, but the opportunity to use wartime emergency controls to develop a new pattern of relationships. While the use of these controls would unquestionably be upheld during the war, they might not be upheld afterwards. All the more reason, therefore, to use them *now*.

The metaphysics of this strange war also lead to much the same conclusions. Ideologically we have been driven to the necessity of making a world-wide declaration of human rights — the Four Freedoms — thereby laying the foundation for an international democracy. The outlines of such a new international order already exist, as Alain Locke has said, within the phalanx of the United Nations which "unites an unprecedented assemblage of the races, cultures and peoples of the world." This New World setting has, as he states, "altered the geography of our lives." We cannot retreat to the prewar relationship of races and cultures even if we desired to do so. For part of this development, we are indebted to the Axis. Once Germany and Japan had raised the issue of ethnic nationalism, racism became, as Dr. Locke states, "an avowed principle of state policy." We were forced to meet the issue. I say "we" advisedly, for it is America that has taken, and must continue to take, the initiative. The more we counter the Axis race propaganda, "the more

[3] *Louisville Courier-Journal*, June 21, 1942.

paradoxical our race attitudes and traditions will become in contrast." If we fail to recognize this dynamic now, then we are doomed to Fascism: we will, in effect, become Fascist. Thus the war has, as Dr. Locke says, brought the Negro question "around from a back-yard domestic issue to a front-porch exposure"; what was once "a minority disability becomes a general weakness." And what is true of the Negro is also true of all other colored minority groups in this country. For "these silent and waiting multitudes (the colored peoples of the world)," writes Frederick L. Schuman, "will conclude, wrongly no doubt but nonetheless irrevocably, that Western white men offer them only fair words and foul deeds, that the darker peoples have no stake in a war between rival oppressors, and that Axis arrogance may be more tolerable than democratic hypocrisy," unless we act *now*.

1. Toward an Affirmative Policy

In mapping out a program of social action on race problems the first consideration to be recognized is that, as Max Lerner has said, "the conditions under which a negative state was able to function — no longer apply. They have been destroyed by a world revolution. And yet the same revolution gives us the tools for *an affirmative state*." We should not fear the exercise of the power of the state for democratic objectives. The mere fact, for example, that government has not acted in a particular field does not constitute a reason why it should not act now, if the necessity is apparent. It is also necessary to recognize that, while we have moved far away from *laissez faire* doctrines in economics, we still anachronistically pursue *laissez faire* theories in population matters. At the outset of democratic development, it was perhaps sufficient merely to define human rights. In a world of open resources and expanding industrial opportunities, it was sufficient to define the right and to remove the shackle. But in this kind of world it becomes imperative that the right be implemented and that the vague declaration be enforced.

Our first assignment, therefore, is to establish the principle that, *as a matter of national policy*, there shall be no discrimination against individuals because of race, color, creed, or country of national origin. Such a statement seems innocuous; but it is the crux of the matter. For once such a national policy has been proclaimed (and we have already attempted to do so), then it can be implemented in a limitless variety of ways. It can be made applicable to every concern from which the government purchases so much as a single lead pencil. To implement such a policy is merely to enforce the declarations in the constitution. In making grants and subsidies to states and local communities, such a declaration of policy can be written into every grant as a condition to the appropriation (a precedent established in the second Morrill Act of 1890). If we adopt a national policy against discrimination, it can be implemented by appropriate directives to every national planning agency. It can be carried into effect, for example, in planning postwar urban redevelopment programs. Governments today license a vast number of enterprises which, by their nature, are invested with a public interest. Into each and every permit issued, a condition of nondiscrimination can be written. In default of compliance, the license can be revoked. In fact, such a policy, if it is firmly and conclusively established, can be implemented in an endless variety of ways which do not involve direct compulsion.

To assist in the development of such a policy, a Congressional committee of inquiry should be created to investigate the whole problem of colored minorities in the United States. The scope of the inquiry should be broad and all-inclusive; it should not be limited to any one group or to any particular area. It should embrace conditions in our outlying territories and possessions as well as on the mainland. Nor should the committee be limited in its objectives: it should look at the world situation as well as the national scene. It should, for example, visit South America and observe, at first hand, how Brazil treats its Negroes. Committees of inquiry are invaluable devices for the development of two types of opinion: Congressional opinion and general lay opinion. The report of a Congressional committee goes directly to Congress. It focuses the attention of Congress and of the nation upon a particular subject. It cannot be ignored as easily, for example, as the report of a lay organization or, for that matter, of a government agency. The hearings of such committees, by dramatizing situations, are priceless opinion-developers: they are news. That Congress had moved in this direction would do much to demonstrate immediately to the world, and to minorities throughout the world, that America had acted. Out of such a hearing would come, I am convinced, a series of concrete recommendations.

These recommendations would be based upon a recognition of the inadequacy of existing legislation. The weakness of the federal government has always been its failure to enforce rights guaranteed by the Constitution.[4] By 1894 the Supreme Court had held unconstitutional, or Congress itself had repealed, virtually all of the Civil War enforcement legislation. On the federal statute books today remain the following civil rights provisions: a statute on the disqualification of jurors; a provision of the Hatch Act about the intimidation of the beneficiaries of federal aid; a provision of the same act about intimidation in federal elections; a statute on slavery and peonage; a statute on searches and seizures; a statute on the intimidation of federal witnesses; and two general laws defining conspiracies to deprive citizens of the free exercise of "a right or privilege secured to him by the constitution or laws of the United States."[5] That these statutes are inadequate has been frequently acknowledged. In creating the Civil Liberties Unit of the Department of Justice, the Attorney General (Frank Murphy) stated: "It must be borne in mind that the authority of the Federal Government in this field is somewhat limited by the fact that many of the constitutional guarantees are guarantees against abuses by the Federal Government itself, or by the State Governments, and are not guarantees against infringement by individuals or groups of individuals."[6] In considering what additional legislation is necessary, it is well to keep in mind that, as a former Chief

[4] See "The Supreme Court and Civil Rights" by Louis B. Boudin, *Science and Society*, Vol. I, No. 33, pp. 300–309; also *The Legal Status of the Indian in the United States* by Felix S. Cohen, 1940, p. 3.

[5] See *Bill of Rights Review*, Vol. I, No. 3, p. 206.

[6] *Bill of Rights Review*, Vol. II, No. 4, p. 252.

Justice of the Supreme Court once said, "the Constitution is what the judges say it is." The American people should not be limited, therefore, by what the Court may have said about a miscegenation statute in 1882. Based on these premises, then, just what additional legislation is necessary?

2. Enforce the Bill of Rights

The first step which Congress should take is to enforce — to implement — the rights guaranteed by the Constitution. This action should take the form of re-enacting a new federal civil-rights statute. To be sure, the Court held the original act unconstitutional; but precedents have been reversed and, in view of the way in which the Court has changed its own theory of the Fourteenth Amendment, it is altogether likely that such an act would be upheld today. The necessity for the immediate adoption of such a statute may be quickly demonstrated.

In the first place, we need such a federal statute to protect the rights of racial and national minorities in this country. In earlier chapters, I have shown how the national government, on many occasions, has been embarrassed by its inability to protect rights secured by treaty provisions. Unless we want to make it possible for a single state to determine the international policy of this country, then such a statute is imperative. Its necessity on this score has been recognized by Theodore Roosevelt, William Howard Taft, Grover Cleveland, and Woodrow Wilson.

In the second place, only eighteen states have adopted civil rights statutes. Since a majority of the states have failed to provide adequate enforcement of civil rights, the federal government should act.

In the third place, the nation has, through the progress of civilization, become a single unit in a sense that was certainly not true in 1876. Not only do citizens of the United States travel more frequently (at least prior to the war), but they travel greater distances. In order to travel in the United States today, American Negroes annually purchase 15,000 copies of *The Negro Motorist Green Book* so that they may know where they can get a room in which to sleep, where they can find a restaurant to get a meal, and where they can find a barbershop in which to get a haircut.[7] The only way to cope with this situation is by federal legislation. Furthermore, Congress should outlaw Jim Crowism on all types of interstate carriers. The past failure of Congress to act in this respect has actually encouraged the states to adopt Jim Crow regulations, which constitute an unwarranted burden on interstate commerce.

To appreciate the necessity for federal legislation, it should be kept in mind that local Jim Crow regulations have been constantly increasing — not decreasing — in severity. In Virginia, for example, a Negro was formerly defined as a person who had one fourth or more Negro blood. In 1910 this definition was changed to one sixteenth and in 1930 it was changed to apply to any person in whom there is *any ascertainable quantum* of Negro blood. Coupled with this new definition, Virginia also passed in 1930 a race registration act. Most other Southern states have followed the same trend.[8]

With Jim Crow regulations multiplying in the South year after year, it has become perfectly apparent that the whole bi-racial system is falling apart, and that the entire system has become unworkable and unenforceable. In Arkansas, for example, "a person in whom there is a visible and distinct admixture of African blood" cannot ride in the white section of a bus. But with so many cases of mixed blood, how in the name of all that is sane and sensible can a conductor apply this test in practice? That many persons of non-Negroid blood are frequently caught in these absurd regulations is clearly indicated by the increasing number of libel and slander actions that have been successfully prosecuted in Southern courts. As the percentage of persons of pure Negro extraction decreases (as it is doing), the classification upon which Jim Crow statutes are based becomes increasingly unreasonable. Many statutes are, for this reason alone, clearly unconstitutional. A Louisiana appellate court recently held invalid a marriage between a white man and a woman whose great-great-grandmother was a Negress. How can such

---

[7] *PM*, October 22, 1941.
[8] See *The Legal Status of the Negro* by Charles S. Mangum, Jr., 1940, p. 13.

a classification be upheld as reasonable? A few years ago a woman in Arizona, who was part Negro and part white, challenged the constitutionality of a miscegenation statute on the ground that, the way it was worded, she could not contract a legal marriage with either a Negro or a white man. With understandable vehemence, she contended that the restriction was slightly unreasonable.

In most Southern states today the races are separated, by legislative enactment, in telephone directories, in places of employment, in schools. Statutes provide for separate toilets; separate pool halls; separate buses and bus drivers; separate teachers and separate schools; separate playgrounds and separate libraries; and separate hospitals, asylums, reformatories, prisons, and orphanages. Even separate Bibles are provided in court, for each race must swear to the same God on a separate copy of the identical text. In the South, the races cannot play pool together, or box with each other, or wrestle with each other. Railroads have been held liable in damages because a conductor, in making the call for dinner, inadvertently called a white person at a time when Negroes were about to be served. Railroads must provide separate waiting rooms, separate toilets in waiting rooms, separate accommodations on trains, and even, if you please, *separate boxes* on which passengers step in entering trains; likewise, separate entrances and exits. The expense occasioned by these regulations clearly constitutes a tax on the entire traveling public in the form of increased passenger rates. In Florida, Kentucky, Oklahoma, and Tennessee it is a crime for anyone to allow students of the two races to commingle even in a private institution; and the teachers themselves are liable. In Kentucky, if free schoolbooks have been used by one race, they cannot thereafter be used by the other. In Louisiana, apartment-house owners cannot rent an apartment to a person of a different race from the existing occupants. Furthermore, separate means completely separate. A school building divided into two sections is not sufficient: the buildings must be wholly separate in space.

It should also be noted that these statutes not only make the provision of separate facilities mandatory, but they make all persons punishable who, in any way, have failed to observe the prohibition. Thus in Florida it is a criminal offense for a member of one race to instruct the children of the other. In some cases, ministers are prohibited from performing a marriage ceremony for persons of another race. In all of these situations, the proprietor and the patron are punishable for nonobservance of the ritual. For example, if I were to enter a Negro pool hall and attempt to play pool, I could be prosecuted even if I were there because I wanted to play pool with Negroes. These same statutes apply, in most cases to *all* colored people. In Mississippi the Supreme Court held that a young Chinese girl could not attend a white school and the decision was upheld by the United States Supreme Court.

Back in 1882 the Supreme Court held, in *Pace* vs. *Alabama*, that the "privileges and immunities" guaranteed by the Fourteenth Amendment did not include the right to marry outside one's own race. This decision is not predicated upon sound legal reasoning: it is pure Jim Crowism — a mere rationalization of attitudes existing at the time. Since then marriages between Negroes and whites have been prohibited in all Southern states, in most Western states, and in Indiana, Iowa, and Minnesota. Marriages between Mongolians and whites are prohibited in fifteen states; marriages between whites and Malays in ten states; and in five states marriages between whites and Indians have been prohibited. Quite apart from the fact that these statutes represent an unconstitutional invasion of personal right, they encourage rather than prevent interracial sexual intercourse. While courts can order support for the children of such alliances, nevertheless alimony cannot be ordered since the marriage is void. Therefore, by removing a measure of responsibility, the statutes would seem actually to encourage such relationships. That such is the case is indicated by the fact that many Southern communities, some years ago, formed Anti-Miscegenation Leagues which sought *to persuade* white men from forming such alliances. The only inference to be drawn is that, despite the statute, colored and white persons were cohabiting.

In Texas an ordinance makes it illegal for white men to visit

Negro women at their residences, unless it appears that the visitor is a doctor, a collector, or a delivery man (thereby making a favored class, some will say, of doctors, milkmen, and bill collectors). In Florida and North Dakota, persons of opposite race cannot occupy the same hotel room *at night* (presumably they may do so between sunup and sundown). In one Texas city, Negroes and whites are prohibited from having sexual intercourse *within the city limits*. In Virginia, the State Children's Home Society attempted to take two minor children away from their white mother because she had remarried a man who was less than one-fourth Negro. In Mississippi it is a crime to publish, print, or circulate any literature or writing which urges interracial marriage or which advocates social equality. In New Orleans, white and Negro prostitutes must operate in separate bagnios.

The unofficial rituals are even more complex. In some Southern communities, curfew regulations are enforced against Negroes who appear in white residential areas. Negroes find it dangerous, in many areas of the South, to own automobiles, or to wear good clothes, or to smoke cigars. In some restaurants, a Negro may buy a sandwich if he will eat it on the street; in other cases, he must go to the back door for the sandwich. In one Florida community the ritual dictates that a Negro may enter a telegraph station to send a wire but he must wait outside, hat in hand, to receive the reply. In fact, a special code of behavior is required wherever the races meet, except in the case where they meet as white merchant and colored customer.[9]

To end this despotism of bigotry, an all-inclusive federal civil-rights statute should be adopted. It should, moreover, be termed, not a civil-rights statute, but a Fair Racial Practice Act. In method and procedure, it should follow the pattern of the National Labor Relations Act; and its enforcement should be delegated to a similar administrative agency. The difficulty with most civil rights statutes is that their enforcement is left up to the individual. Most of the state statutes provide that the individual aggrieved may bring an action in the state courts for the

---

[9] *Race Relations and the Race Problem*, 1939, Ch. VII.

recovery of a penalty. The recovery of the penalty may assuage the feelings of the injured party, but it does not prevent the unfair racial practice. All too frequently the injured party lacks the funds, or the spirit, to bring the action. The statute which I propose should provide for administrative enforcement as a matter of public policy, rather than for individual enforcement as a matter of personal privilege. The individual may not feel injured by the discrimination; but society may well feel that its stability is being undermined by the practice.

One illustration will serve to demonstrate the point. Joe Doakes runs a lunch counter. Joe is a good guy; he has no race prejudice whatever. Personally he has no objection to serving Negroes, or Indians, or Chinese; as a matter of fact, he wants their patronage. But perhaps his white customers object. By refusing to patronize Joe, they can force him to deny service to colored people. Also Joe may have a competitor down the street who denies service to Negroes; to meet this competition Joe may be forced to operate an "All-White" restaurant. Society should protect the decent impulses of Joe Doakes and discourage the prejudices of his white customers. It should throw its protection around him, in the form of a fair racial practice act, which would permit him to do what he probably would like to do — namely, serve all alike without discrimination.

Similarly if I want to associate with Negroes, or Chinese, or Japanese, or Filipinos, I should not have to do so in a furtive and clandestine manner. If I want to take a Negro to lunch, I should be at liberty to do so without fear of embarrassment to my guest. A fair racial practice act would, therefore, enlarge my rights while protecting those of the Negro. In the absence of such a code, society penalizes the decent impulses of its citizens, and makes the expression of liberal attitudes unnecessarily difficult and complex. Society not only should establish the policy of no discrimination: it should enforce the practice.

By the issuance of cease-and-desist orders, after the pattern of the Wagner Act, these unfair racial practices can be largely eliminated. To be sure there would be opposition (there was violent opposition to the Wagner Act); and doubtless it would take a long time to secure compliance. But that compliance can be obtained through the use of these methods I am firmly convinced. I knew employers who hated union organizers more than they disliked Negroes. Thanks to the work of the National Labor Relations Board, however, the principle of collective bargaining is firmly established today. This does not mean that anti-union prejudice has been eliminated; but its expression, in certain forms, has been checked. An unfair racial practice act would not eliminate race prejudice, but it would check discrimination. "Any society," writes Dr. Ruth Benedict, "selects some segment of the arc of possible human behavior, and insofar as it achieves integration, its institutions tend to further the expression of its selected segment and to inhibit opposite expressions." It is sheer nonsense to say that society cannot develop the expression of one type of behavior and inhibit its opposite manifestation, if it wants to do so. Institutions play a far more important part than we realize in conditioning human behavior.

What I am suggesting is not, perhaps, as novel as it may seem. In an awkward and clumsy manner, we have already moved in this direction. The creation of a Civil Liberties Unit within the Department of Justice is in itself a recognition for specialized skills in the enforcement of civil rights. The Civil Liberties Unit, however, is not an administrative agency, and it is the administrative approach that is most effective. If the enforcement of the Wagner Act had been entrusted to local United States District Attorneys, it would have remained a dead letter. One of the objections to state civil rights statutes, in fact, is that they must be enforced by actions in state courts. Only federal courts, according to Mr. Thurgood Marshall (national counsel for the NAACP), can be counted upon to do justice in civil rights cases;[10] and their role should be restricted to passing upon the validity of administrative orders made pursuant to an unfair racial practice code.

There is clear constitutional warrant for such legislation. It could be justified both under the Fourteenth Amendment and under the interstate commerce clause. That unfair racial prac-

[10] *PM*, July 19, 1942.

tices clearly constitute a burden on interstate commerce is a proposition which could be readily documented. Negroes have organized effective boycotts of stores which do not employ Negro labor. They have conducted strikes to implement the declared boycott; [11] and their right to do so has been upheld by the Supreme Court. Such strikes can have precisely the same effect on interstate commerce as a strike called in a labor dispute. Given the present interpretation of the commerce clause, a wide segment of American life could be embraced by an unfair racial practice act. Besides, the power of Congress to enforce civil rights by appropriate legislation is authorized by the Fourteenth Amendment.

3. Additional Measures

To be effective federal intervention must take place on several different levels. One of the most serious handicaps which colored minorities face today is that of residential segregation. Segregation by ordinance has been held unconstitutional; but segregation by restrictive clauses in grant deeds has been upheld. Construed as restraints on use and occupation, rather than as restraints upon alienation, these clauses do not offend against the existing laws of real property. In a recent decision (*Hansberry* vs. *Lee*), the Supreme Court refused to pass on the question of whether or not such clauses violate the Fourteenth Amendment.

Eighty per cent of the city of Chicago is covered by restrictive clauses of this character. While the clauses tend to break down as Negroes infiltrate marginal areas, nevertheless the area of expansion is carefully restricted. The existence of such natural barriers as parks, rivers, and railroad embankments serves to buttress the policy of restriction. Within the black ghetto, buildings deteriorate and fall down and it becomes cheaper to remove them (and save taxes) than to repair them. Ninety-five per cent of the buildings tenanted by Negroes in Chicago are absentee-owned. "Absentee owners," it has been noted, "have no incentive to rebuild and rehabilitate as long as the demand

[11] See *New Negro Alliance* vs. *Sanitary Grocery Company*, 303 U. S. 552, decided in 1938.

exceeds the supply, indeed they have an incentive to keep the demand in excess of supply." The city government, moreover, is reluctant to secure compliance with existing health and building ordinances lest property owners tear down their buildings, thereby depriving the city of improved property taxes. This is an almost universal pattern and, by its nature, it tends to be self-perpetuating.[12] By refusing loans to Negroes who desire to purchase houses, except in areas where Negroes constitute more than 50 per cent of the residents, the FHA merely assists in perpetuating the existing pattern of segregation.

There are ways, however, to break such a pattern. Local planning commissions may provide, as they have in some cases,[13] that new subdivisions will not be approved if it is proposed to restrict the use or occupation of lots on a racial basis. Urban redevelopment projects can follow a similar policy; in fact, the policy can be enforced, since most of such projects will be federally financed. Furthermore, the United States Housing Authority can be utilized to break the existing deadlock and provide decent housing without racial segregation. Also, if necessary, local communities with federal aid can purchase or condemn land and thereby remove the obnoxious restrictions. With public housing being boomed as an essential postwar industry, the possibilities for improvement along these lines are immeasurably greater than they were a few years ago. In the exercise of its wartime powers, the federal government can unquestionably disregard these restrictive clauses or even suspend their enforcement for the duration if it so desires. Wartime rent-control measures can be used in a similar fashion.

Congress should also outlaw the poll tax in federal elections. The states themselves cannot be expected to take the initiative, since, in most cases, repeal of the tax would involve approval by state legislatures made up of legislators who have been elected by voters who have paid their poll taxes.[14] An estimated 10,-500,000 American citizens are prevented from voting by the

[12] See "The Trouble They've Seen" by Milton Mayer, *PM,* September 18, 1940.
[13] Mangum, p. 179.
[14] See the *Nation,* July 26, 1941, p. 74.

existence of the poll tax in eight Southern states. The tax dis-
enfranchises white as well as colored citizens; it makes for
political corruption; and it is destructive of the democratic process.[15] Not only is the tax opposed by a large number of Southern newspapers, but the Gallup poll indicates that 63 per cent
of the nation's voters would like to see it eliminated. The adoption of the Soldiers' and Sailors' Voting Act indicates that the
poll tax will be eventually outlawed by the federal government
by the passage of some such measure as the Geyer-Pepper
Act. Congress also has the power to force the states not only
to eliminate the poll tax in local elections, but to drop every
device which Southern ingenuity has invented to disenfranchise
the Negro. Section 2 of the Fourteenth Amendment clearly provides that if any state restricts the right of its citizens to vote
on account of "race, color, or previous condition," its representatives in Congress shall be reduced accordingly. In June 1929,
Representative Tinkham of Massachusetts attempted to enforce
this section and, to the surprise of the nation, he nearly succeeded.[16] Congress can, if necessary, supervise federal elections.
The approach to the problem must be, therefore, by *affirmative
Congressional action*. The Supreme Court, in a series of notable
decisions, has upheld the Negro's right to vote by striking down
most of the devices used to disenfranchise him. But, as history indicates, the Southern states can devise new schemes of
disenfranchisement as fast as the Court can hand down decisions.
In large measure, therefore, it is a waste of time and money to
bring new test cases. The courts can define rights but only Congress can effectively enforce them; also, while we are at it, we
should pass a federal anti-lynching statute.

In June 1940, the National Defense Advisory Committee announced that henceforth there should be no discrimination in
defense employment on the ground of age, sex, race, or color.
A short time later, the Commission of Education announced
that "in the expenditure of Federal funds for vocational train-

[15] See series of articles by Jennings Perry in *PM*, March 20, 21, 23, and 24, 1941.
[16] See *The Negro in American Civilization* by Charles S. Johnson, p. 342.

ing for defense there should be no discrimination." When these measures failed to stop discrimination, the Negro March on Washington was organized. Almost immediately thereafter President Roosevelt issued, on June 25, 1941, his famous Executive Order No. 8802. For the purpose of effectuating the previously announced policy against discrimination, the order provided: —

1. That all government agencies concerned with training programs should take measures designed to prevent discrimination.
2. That all government contracting agencies should include in defense contracts a provision obligating the contractor not to discriminate against any worker because of race, color, or country of national origin.
3. That there should be established a Committee on Fair Employment Practices to investigate complaints of discrimination and to take appropriate steps to redress valid grievances.

Later the President instructed all government agencies to examine their personnel policies in an effort to eliminate Jim Crowism in government service.

The creation of the FEPC unquestionably constitutes an extremely important precedent. This committee, as Dr. Malcolm S. MacLean has said, did more in the first eighty weeks of its existence to bring the Bill of Rights closer to reality than anything accomplished in the past eighty years. Negro employment increased in commercial shipyards from 6952 to 12,820; in navy shipyards from 6000 to 14,000; and in aircraft from 0 to 5000. This improvement has been accomplished, moreover, despite the fact that the FECP has no legislative sanction; that it has no real powers of enforcement; and that not a single government order has been canceled since the committee was created. Violently opposed in the South, the committee has not been firmly supported, in all cases, by those whom the President appointed as its members. Speaking in Birmingham, Mr. Mark Ethridge, a member of the committee, said that "no power in the world — not even in all the mechanized armies of the earth, Allied and Axis — could force the Southern white people to the abandonment of the principle of social segregation." [17] Such a statement

[17] *Courier-Journal*, June 21, 1942.

not only constituted an invitation to organized opposition, but struck at the very policy underlying the President's orders. For if defense plants must provide separate accommodations and respect the social code of the South, then the order will never be fully effective. Despite the fact that the FEPC has "not more than opened by a crack doors formerly barred to Negro workers," it is being quietly sabotaged in Washington. What has been accomplished, however, constitutes the clearest warrant for strengthening the FEPC, of providing it with effective remedies, giving it legislative sanction, and correlating its activities with some type of fair racial practice setup such as I have proposed.

Discriminatory practices are still powerfully entrenched in the trade-union movement, particularly in the American Federation of Labor. "Do you know," says Tom Ray of the Boilermakers Union in Portland, "when a white man sweats, salt comes on his skin to take the smell away; but when a nigger sweats he's got no salt." [18] A relatively simple way to correct trade-union discrimination would be to amend the Wagner Act so as to give the National Labor Relations Board jurisdiction to investigate discriminatory practices on the part of trade-unions. After investigation and hearing, the Board could order such practices discontinued and enforce its order by injunctive process and also by denying its protection to any trade-union which indulged in unfair racial practices.

Now is also the time to reconsider our naturalization and immigration policies. Every vestige of racism should be removed from these statutes. Our present policy, which makes non-white persons other than those of African descent ineligible to citizenship, should be corrected. It has worked a serious injustice and has been productive of needless national and international complications. No racial line should be drawn in determining eligibility to citizenship. Whatever the tests of eligibility should be — and I hope they are high — they should not be predicated on racial considerations. A first step would be to make all Orientals resident in the United States eligible for naturalization. No one act would do more, perhaps, to remove anti-American feeling

[18] *PM*, October 8, 1942.

in the Far East; nor would such a move jeopardize a single national interest. Similarly our immigration quotas should be corrected; here, too, all traces of racism should be removed. As Pearl Buck has said: "Another Chinese reservation is being made on the matter of our antiquated and obsolete immigration laws. . . . The Chinese appreciate our need to limit immigration, but they would like to be put on terms of equality with other peoples and come in on a quota. The number involved would be one or two hundred Chinese each year, and the value of changing the Chinese-exclusion law *now* would far outweigh, in the war effort, many tanks and planes. It would be a great move toward total victory." [19] The quota allowed Filipinos (fifty a year) is absurd. Not only should the Filipino quota be increased, but all nationalities should be placed on a basis of absolute equality. If we were to plan intelligently, it would be possible, for example, to bring in several thousand Filipinos a year, for training and work experience in American agriculture and industry. But immigration of this type should be placed on a selective basis and it should be handled purposefully and intelligently. In the past, the immigration service has functioned in a purely mechanical manner; in the future, its concern with immigrants should not cease once they have been admitted. In the last analysis, immigration problems constitute world problems and they must be handled by a world organization. A world-wide nationality and citizenship code, for example, is absolutely essential if the existing chaos is to be eliminated.

4. Towards a World Policy

One of our basic weaknesses in dealing with colored minorities has been our failure to recognize the basic similarity of problems which they present. We have never recognized, for example, a correlation between Indians and Negroes. Had we determined to make slaves of the Indians, it is altogether probable that we should have as many Indians today as we have American Negroes. But we decided to use Indians for other purposes; they could be used, for example, very conveniently to police Ne-

[19] *New Republic*, June 1, 1942.

gro slaves. William Christie MacLeod quotes one colonial writer to the effect that "in our quarrels with the Indians, however proper and necessary it may be to give them correction, it can never be our interest to extirpate them or to force them from their lands; their ground would soon be taken by runaway Negroes from our settlements, whose numbers daily increase, and quickly become more formidable enemies than the Indians can ever be, as they speak our language and would never be at loss for intelligence." Similar points of correlation may be noted throughout our history. The year 1876 seems to have marked a turning point in our dealings with all colored minorities, for about that time we decided to exclude the Chinese, place the Indians on reservations, and surrender the Negro to the South.

"The task of arousing interest in Indian affairs," writes Loring Benson Priest, "would have been considerably easier if the Negro and Indian problems had been connected in the public mind. While the former slaves were generally better qualified to share responsibilities with other Americans, both races faced the problem of adjusting themselves to white society. A common effort to prepare both minority elements for the obligations of civilized life might well have been undertaken. When Congress conferred citizenship on the Negroes in 1866, however, any mention of the Indians was omitted. The campaign for Indian advancement had to be conducted as if nothing had been accomplished for the Negro." [20] In another connection, Mr. Priest states: "Negro emancipation presented more than enough related problems to merit serious study by all interested in Indian advancement. Yet the two movements were so completely divorced in the minds of most contemporaries that the difficulties of adjusting Negroes to white society made little impression. United States citizens with few exceptions have believed that the problems of the American Indian and the Negro must be solved separately. The cause of Indian reform had gained nothing as a result of the successful crusade against slavery. Instead Indian workers were forced to cultivate an entirely new public opinion." Despite this fact, however, Mr. Priest believes that "the

[20] *Uncle Sam's Stepchildren*, 1942.

methods proposed for Indian advancement showed the unconscious influence of the experience with Negro emancipation had been strong."

When a parallel was noted, the differences seemed more pronounced than the possible similarities. "Negroes," wrote Francis E. Leupp, "are substantially one people in their later history, in language, in social condition, in customs, in mode of thought, in outlook." Whereas Indians, "in spite of their sense of racial separateness and their reluctance to part with it, have cultivated no homogeneity of interests. Every tribe has maintained its own laws, its own language, its own traditions and sentiments apart from the rest." [21] But to Mr. Leupp, a former Commissioner of Indian Affairs, these differences seemed to lie in racial traits rather than in a different historical experience. It has been only of recent years that, as Dr. Ralph Linton has observed, "an interest has developed in the general phenomena which result when groups of different cultures are brought together. The need for intelligent handling of all these situations," he writes, "is obvious and it is equally obvious that the first step toward successful planning must be to ascertain the general factors present in all contact situations and how they operate."

Each of these contact situations has something in common with every other. The second-generation problem — so striking in the case of the Chinese, Japanese, and Mexicans — is closely related to the problems of Negro youth. There is much to be gained, therefore, in attempting to correlate these various problems. Of course no one colored minority likes to think that its problems have any relation to those of another colored minority. The most articulate Negro publicists, for example, speak of Negroes as though they were the one colored minority in the United States. By insisting that these groups present race problems only in the sense that their "visibility" makes them readily recognizable, their problems can also be related to those of underprivileged non-colored groups. There is a marked strategic advantage, therefore, in regarding the problems of these colored minority groups as essentially problems of cultural adjustment.

[21] *The Indian and His Problem*, 1910.

If the research on these various groups were to be systematically correlated it might throw much light on matters of even larger moment. Dr. Julian Herman Lewis has pointed out that it has been only of recent years that scientists have become curious about the specialized medical and biologic problems of the Negro.[22] Only within comparatively recent years has the study of tuberculosis among Negroes been turned to scientific advantage by using the study of the disease among Negroes "as an approach to the understanding of some of the pertinent problems of the science." Tuberculosis among Negroes has "demonstrable differences and characteristics." While these are probably explained in terms of a different environment, the point is that the disease assumes different manifestations among Negroes and that specialized study of these differences may throw light on the nature of the disease itself. Tuberculosis is actually "a different disease in colored people." Negroes offer an excellent field for research into the disease since their living conditions are so variable. "In no other peoples," he writes, "is it possible to compare simultaneously such a wide diversity of factors," and such studies make possible the "evaluation of factors that may influence disease." Nor is tuberculosis the only case in point. In studying the prevalence of rickets among Negro children in the San Juan District of New York, it was found that "pigmentation that is protection where sunlight is intense is a hazard where sunshine is less available."

Other instances might readily be cited to establish the point that highly specialized studies of particular groups afford an insight into general problems. Some of the remarkable medical research recently undertaken in the Indian service might, for example, also be cited on this score.

Even in the social sciences and the field of public administration important gains have been effected through a specialized approach to the problems of particular groups. The National Youth Administration at one time established a Negro Department staffed for the most part by Negroes, and of all the relief agencies it came "the nearest to meeting adequately the relief

[22] *The Biology of the Negro,* 1942.

situation among Negro youth." [23] Stimulated largely by the example of Mr. Harold Ickes, most New Deal agencies came to
employ special advisers on Negro affairs. Mr. W. M. Kiplinger
has demonstrated how rapidly the tendency has developed.[24]
Among the agencies listed as now having Negro advisers on
Negro affairs are the following: War Department; War Production Board; Fair Employment Practice Committee; National
Youth Administration; Treasury Department; Social Security
Board; Civilian Conservation Corps; Works Progress Administration; Public Works Administration; Federal Works Agency;
Office of Civilian Defense; Federal Housing Agency; Department of Agriculture; Department of Commerce; Library of Congress; Office of Education; Public Health Service; Selective
Service; Office of Price Administration; United States Housing Authority; National Resources Planning Board; and Co-
ordinator of Inter-American Affairs. In a few cases, individuals
have been designated in these agencies to serve as advisers on
"race relations" or in respect to "minority groups"; but in the
majority of cases they are merely consultants on Negro affairs.[25]

In fact, early in 1942 a proposal was made to establish a Negro Affairs Bureau. This aroused instant opposition from the
NAACP on the ground that it would "make the Negroes mere
wards of the government." [26] While some of these advisers may
have been added for purely political purposes (as a form of Negro patronage) or for the purpose of being able to use a Negro
in dealing with Negroes (a public-relations device), nevertheless
most observers agree that Negroes have profited from the establishment of such special services. Some of the best studies of the
Negro problem have come about as a result of these special divi-
sions (following the experiment which I have already mentioned
in the Department of Labor in 1918). On the other hand, it
should be noted that much of this excellent research has had only
the most tenuous relation to the work of the particular agency

[23] *The Negro and Economic Reconstruction* by T. Arnold Hill, 1937, p. 62.
[24] *Washington Is Like That*, 1942, Ch. 15.
[25] Another list of federal agencies having specialized Negro consultants may
be found in Ira de A. Reid's *In a Minor Key*, 1940, p. 110.
[26] *Common Sense*, August 1942, p. 277.

in which it originated, as, for example, an admirable study of Negro employment during the depression which issued from the Department of the Interior. It would also seem that such special advisory services have been limited almost exclusively to Negroes. I know of no such service for Mexicans or Spanish Americans, although the need is obvious. In *Ill Fares the Land*, I called particular attention to the fact that the Department of Agriculture should at least get out a manual, in Spanish, advising Mexican workers of their rights under the Sugar Act of 1937. While Negro organizations have no objection to Negro services staffed by Negro personnel, they do object apparently to a forthright recognition by the government of a Negro problem. Actually minority services in the government could be far more effective if they were detached from particular agencies and functioned as an independent department concerned directly with minority problems. The subterfuge of having them merely attached to particular agencies as advisers on race matters certainly does not deceive the Southern delegation in Congress. "I think they are put there," says Mr. Starnes of Alabama, "to promote the idea that racial discrimination is being practised. . . . I think it is spotlighting something, and these people are special pleaders." [27]

While I would not be in favor of creating a Bureau of Negro Affairs per se, I can see some definite advantages to be gained by the establishment of an agency in the federal government directly concerned with minority problems. There is today, as Mr. T. J. Woofter, Jr., has observed, "substantial agreement as to what needs to be done for leadership, for health, for education, for law and order, for economic advancement, for social welfare." While he was speaking of Negroes, the same observation can be made of the other colored minorities. But how is special research to be undertaken and co-ordinated and how are action programs to be formulated, unless such activities find a direct focus at some point in the apparatus of government? In a recent report on Negro youth, Mr. Robert L. Sutherland makes a series of wholly admirable recommendations for social action. In mak-

[27] *Nation*, February 21, 1942, p. 214.

ing these recommendations, he suggests that "state governments" might do this and that "private foundations" might do that, but how much more effective it would be to assign the task of bringing these recommendations into effect to a federal agency directly concerned with the problem? The Southern states, which are the ones most immediately concerned, probably lack the resources as they certainly lack the will to adopt these or any similar set of recommendations. As to the foundations, we have it on the authority of Mr. John A. Davis that "the colored people of America are confronted by the gloomy prospect of the liquidation of the General Education Board and the Rosenwald Fund; which raises the question when will government — state and national, take over." [28] So far as the churches are concerned, the task of remedial action is quite beyond their resources and, as Mr. Davis observes, "there are no indications that the church is ready to lead off as it did in fighting the injustices of slavery." Hortense Powdermaker offers the wholly admirable suggestion that the basic principles of anthropology should be taught in the secondary schools as one means of combating race prejudices. But what agency in the federal government today can put this suggestion into effect? Mr. Edwin R. Embree, with a vast experience in such matters, suggests that "radical changes would come at once if the great body of people of good will in America *once saw in full,* alert, consciousness the wrongs we allow to exist" (italics mine). What agency today has the task of seeing to it that such information is made available?

If an agency of the federal government were merely invested with the full power of investigation (including the right to issue subpoenas and to hold public hearings and to report the facts), I think the public — including the Negroes — might be astonished at the results. For four years I had the privilege of directing the work of the Division of Immigration and Housing in the State of California. Created in 1913 to deal with the immigrant problem, this agency has merely the powers I have mentioned. Yet I have had occasion to be truly amazed by what can be accomplished simply by making the facts of a particular situation *offi-*

[28] *Survey Graphic,* November 1942, p. 501.

cially known.[29] What the Federal Council of Churches and the Rosenwald Foundation have to say about race relations is, after all, merely the opinion of two private unofficial organizations. What would be the effect, however, if an agency such as I have mentioned were to report each year in detail on lynchings in the United States? As the report of an official agency, such a report would reach every Senator and every Congressman; it would reach every public agency in the government; it could be effectively used by every individual and organization of good will in America in developing an intelligent public opinion; and, lastly, it would *present to the President* a set of facts which, coming from an official agency, he could hardly ignore. I mention lynching, but such an annual report would also deal with social conditions, with education, with public health, with the extent to which Negroes are disenfranchised, and many related matters. It would be a consistent method of keeping these problems under constant federal scrutiny and of thereby forcing them upon the public's attention. The reports of such an agency would be invaluable for a variety of purposes. For example, in testing the validity of restrictive racial clauses in grant deeds, no individual litigant, regardless of his resources, could possibly finance, much less obtain, the type of documentary evidence which should be summarized in a sociological brief to be presented along with the legal arguments to the Supreme Court.

Such an agency, however, should have broader powers than those indicated. It should be authorized to initiate, or at least to recommend the initiation of, specific action programs. The maternal death rate among Negroes is three times that among whites. Only 7.4 per cent of the native whites have had less than five years' schooling; but 41.3 per cent of the Negroes have had less than five years in school. The Negro death rate is 32 per cent higher than that of the rest of the population, the Negro's life expectancy is eleven years less than that of his white neighbor, and his toll of daily sickness is 43 per cent greater than for white Americans. Negro tuberculosis is 2.6 times that of whites

[29] See also Senate Concurrent Resolution No. 4, California Legislature, 1937, creating the Commission to Foster Better Race Relations.

in the South and 5.3 times that of whites in the North. The mortality rate from tuberculosis among Negroes is, on an average, from three to four times as high as for the white population. Theoretically there should be one hospital bed for every death from tuberculosis. But in 1934, with 21,099 Negro deaths from tuberculosis, there were only 3334 beds for colored tubercular patients. In 1935 it was estimated that some 7,138,455 Negroes, or 83 per cent of those in twelve Southern states, did not have access to a public library. Similar statistics might be endlessly multiplied and also correlated with similar figures about Indians and Mexicans.

Not one of these problems is insoluble. If the federal government, recognizing the special disabilities of American Indians, can provide them with schools, hospitals, medical service, and library facilities, it can certainly do so for the other groups similarly disadvantaged. If the Southern states are financially unable to provide adequate institutional services for Negroes, then the federal government can offer subsidies or grants-in-aid for this purpose. But these grants should be offered with a provision attached that there shall be absolutely no discrimination. If the Southern states refuse the grants under this condition, then the federal government should go ahead and provide the services for the Negroes. Why not detach the Indian Service from the Department of the Interior and consolidate it, along with the War Relocation Authority created to handle the Japanese evacuation program, in a larger agency of the type I have mentioned? If it be charged that such a suggestion is iniquitous paternalism, then create temporary authorities to accomplish particular objectives. If it be charged by Mr. Joe Starnes that this is tantamount to "spotlighting" certain situations, then let it be freely admitted that these same situations need spotlighting. If it be charged that such a proposal is undemocratic in that it is based upon a recognition of differences in social and economic condition, then have these differences been eliminated by the pretense that they do not exist? Would this objection be valid if the other measures proposed were also adopted?

The problem of colored minorities in the United States is

merely a reproduction on a miniature scale of a set of similar problems which will be faced by whatever federation of powers or international organization emerges from this war. Our Indian problem has its parallel throughout Central and South America. Our Negro problem has its parallel in the West Indies, in Central America, in Africa. Our small-scale problem with the natives of American Samoa and Guam has its stupendous counterpart in the whole problem of native peoples throughout the Pacific area. These problems are not "solved" merely by the declaration that "imperialism" must be banished from the postwar world. The problem of adjustment, of acculturation, of cultural conflict, remains. By taking the initiative here, we might be in a position to assert real world leadership in relation to these same problems after the war. On the other hand, by continuing an ostrich-like do-nothing policy at home, we are certainly inviting another Versailles.

* * *

Some years ago, it was my good fortune to meet Byron Darnton of the *New York Times*. We spent some time together traveling through the San Joaquin Valley in California where I was endeavoring to show him, at first hand, something about the migrant problem. Recently he was killed in an accident on the New Guinea front and was buried in the military cemetery at Port Moresby. He is in good company there, writes a colleague, for he was buried along with another American, a Negro soldier, an Australian sailor, and a native of the Papuan Infantry. That this would have pleased Darnton, Robert Sherrod of *Time* is certain, for "he had the firm conviction that all men would one day be brothers, or they would be slaves." This is the lesson which America must learn, for it is not only the color of America that has changed: the color of the world has changed.

Acknowledgments

I should like to acknowledge my great indebtedness to a number of individuals who have been of immeasurable assistance in the preparation of this manuscript. My thanks, then, to Mr. Hugh Calkins, Mr. Eshrev Shevky, Mr. Allen Harper, Dr. Joaquin Ortega, Dr. W. Lloyd Warner, Mr. William Hoy, Mr. Carlos Bulosan, Mr. Loren Miller, Mr. Edwin Bates, Miss Margaret Kalisch, Mr. Samuel Lee, Mr. Lim P. Lee, Mr. Albert J. Evers, Dr. Michel Pijoan, Mr. S. J. Oki, Dr. George Sanchez, and Mrs. Lorene Pearson. None of these individuals, needless to say, is in any manner responsible for any statements or opinions expressed in the text.